BREADCRUMBS

Discerning God's Leading
365 Day Christian Devotional

Tom Estabrook

Breadcrumbs

Discerning God's leading

365 Day Christian Devotional

Copyright © 2024 by Tom Estabrook

DEDICATION

This book is dedicated to my grandparents,

Paul T. & Clara O. Batchelder, two of the most sincere and godly people I have ever known. Their commitment and investment in family is paying dividends 45 years after their passing. It is an honor and privilege to be a product of their legacy.

CONTENTS

INTRODUCTION

BREADCRUMBS

Discerning God's leading

Everyone wants the big, bright, flashing neon sign that leads us into the will of God. How much easier life would be if we all got a "burning bush" experience. In my six decades of experience, if you get one neon sign or "burning bush" in your lifetime, consider yourself blessed. God works both overtly and covertly in our lives to lead us into His plans and purposes. God working overtly would be those no-doubt-about-it God moments where we know exactly what to do. What I have discovered over the years is that God leads through the still, small voices of thoughts, ideas, words spoken, a song, the Word of God, the voice of the Holy Spirit, and gentle nudges. I have labeled these encounters "following breadcrumbs." If you remember the story of Hansel and Gretel, the young Hansel left breadcrumbs to remember the way back home. God does the opposite; He gives breadcrumbs to lead us back to Himself and to help us find the path that He has laid out for us. How many big decisions were made after a lot of little, inconsequential choices and decisions that got you to the point of making the big decision? You did not recognize you were just following the breadcrumbs as God led you.

In the hectic, fast-paced lifestyle that is required to keep up with all the things we are bombarded with, it is easy to miss the breadcrumbs as they come to us. God never leaves us or abandons us to try and figure life out. He instructs us to ask, seek, and knock so that we might discover all that He has in store for us. To recognize God moments in our lives, we must slow down and get quiet. God is always speaking and answering our questions; we miss out because we have not trained ourselves to be aware of how God speaks to us. Listening for God is a skill that is developed over time. It takes time and practice to hone and perfect any skill.

"The two most important days in your life are the day you are born and the day you find out why" Mark Twain (1835-1910) American author.

Life is a journey of discovering who we are and why we are here. Our journey is filled with God moments that move us down the path towards His will. Let me be clear: God has revealed His will to us in His Word. As believers, we are to love Him supremely and love our neighbors. He calls us to go into all the world proclaiming the good news of the gospel, and it is His desire that His children grow to be like Christ, to name just a few things. However, in the day-to-day practical aspects of living, we can find ourselves at a loss as to what we are supposed to be doing. We can get stuck in the routines of life; we can find ourselves spinning our wheels and not moving toward Him or discovering why we were created. Breadcrumbs and God moments come to help us get unstuck and get us moving in our journey.

The problem with breadcrumbs and God moments is that they come wrapped in ordinary, everyday choices and decisions. "Life can only be understood backwards; but it must be lived forwards." Soren Kierkegaard (1813-1855) Danish theologian. As we look back over the course of our life, it is easier to see the hand of God moving and directing our steps. Life, however, is lived moving forward and dealing with mundane life decisions, so we are not always conscious of God in those moments. Breadcrumbs are effortlessly slipped in by God to assist us in our journey. It would be easy to assume that God is unconcerned with our journey and the choices we are making, but that would be faulty thinking. Psalms 139:16 makes it clear that before we were ever born, God saw us and had all the days of our life recorded. He is very much aware of your every choice and decision, and He cares deeply about everything you do. It is His greatest desire to bring you into the fullness of His plans and purposes for your life. You were created for a specific purpose, and you can only find peace, joy, and contentment when you are walking in obedience to His revealed will.

God sent the prophet Hosea to the children of Israel to tell them that they were being destroyed because of a lack of knowledge and their dismissal of the word of the law. God's concern about this is intense and it is recorded in Hosea 4:6 so that today we can understand how important it is to read God's word.

Today, the world around us is being destroyed because we have departed from the Word of God and violated His principles. Studies have shown that there is no discernible difference between how people outside of the church believe and live compared to those who profess to be Christians. As believers in Jesus Christ, we should have the inside track on what God is thinking and doing, but often that is not the case. Our lives should be an example to the world around us of the goodness and mercy of God. Unfortunately, we are being destroyed through a lack of kingdom knowledge.

Jesus told a story at the end of His Sermon on the Mount to stress to His followers how important it is to follow His words which you can find in Matthew 7:24-27. He describes two home builders. He says one was a wise home builder because he built his house on a rock – a solid foundation – and it didn't fall apart when strong wind and rains beat upon that house. But He said the other home builder was foolish and compared him to people who hear His words but don't apply them to their own lives. That builder built his house on the sand and it fell apart as soon as the rain and wind beat on it.

In this story, the wise and the foolish builders had some things in common. They both were subjected to the storms of life that eventually we all encounter. They both heard the words of Jesus. The main difference between the two builders was that one built his house on a solid foundation by putting the teachings of Jesus into practice, and the other builder rejected His words. Jesus said that this is like building your house on sand. One house will still be standing after the storms, and one will be destroyed. The buildings represent our lives; our lives are made up of the choices and decisions we make in a lifetime. Are we building and living our lives based on the principles of scripture, or are we being conformed to the world's standards of living? The only way to know for sure how strong your foundation is, is to see who or what is still standing after the storms have passed.

As a pastor of a small church in Northern California, I was concerned for our church. I wanted to challenge them to love and good works, but I was troubled by the lack of opportunities to feed my sheep. I recognized that the lives of believers, as well as non-believers, were being consumed with activities and social media. I was looking for a way to get the Word of God into them in a simple and practical format. Life is hard, but I also know that the answers to all that we need and are searching for will be found in God and His Word. I started writing a weekly blog that was put into our church bulletin and posted on our church website. I then began to post them on Facebook. Through the weeks, months, and years that followed, I would often sit at my computer and have nothing to write. I would pray for some nugget, truth, thought, or idea to please come to me. God always came through. What you hold in your hand is a compilation of those weekly messages. The main idea was to help my congregation draw closer to Jesus and to discover His will. We all need breadcrumbs and God moments to help get us down the road. My prayer is that as you read this daily devotion, the Holy Spirit will use these words to create a God moment and help draw you closer into the loving embrace of your Heavenly Father and His Son, Jesus Christ.

For His glory,
Pastor Tom

01
JANUARY

January 1
Greater Discovery Ahead

The New Year arrives ever full of potential yet long on mystery. What will this New Year bring? What joys and opportunities await? What disappointments, pain, and sorrow will this year hold? What is God teaching me this year?

God will give us exactly what we need to experience the richness and fullness of this new year, but He does this in concert with us engaging with Him. It requires our effort. He hides it in ways so that we must first seek Him and then He will guide us on a treasure hunt of discovery. Sometimes His treasure is on the other side of pain. Sometimes it is amidst triumph.

No matter what the New Year will bring, we can be confident of this very thing – God will be right there with us, cheering us on to greater discoveries both of ourselves and of Him. We must be intentional to live each day to its fullest not allowing yesterday's

disappointments rob us of the potential of all that God has for us.

Happy New Year.

January 2
A Fresh Start

The beginning of a New Year and the opportunity for a fresh start. How will we approach that change? We make our resolutions and do our best to change diet, exercise, attitudes, and to be nicer to those around us. Our best efforts to change last about as long as the excitement over our Christmas presents. The problem is we attempt to *will-power* our way to change.

Here is Godly advice:

"Blessed is the person who does not walk in the counsel of the wicked, Nor stand in the path of sinners, Nor sit in the seat of scoffers! But his delight is in the Law of the Lord, And on His Law he meditates day and night. He will be like a tree planted by streams of water, which yields its fruit in its season, And its leaf does not wither, And in whatever he does, he prospers" (Psalm 1:1-3 NASB).

The advice of the Psalmist is to give ourselves over to reading and meditating on the Word of God. It alone has the power to transform our lives and cause us to prosper in all we do. Let's try an experiment this New Year. Let's spend the year reading and meditating on the truths of the Bible and see if our lives are not remarkably different this year. It is a guarantee from God Himself. Happy New Year!

January 3
The Little Things

King Solomon writing in the Song of Songs states, "Take us the foxes, the little foxes, that spoil the vines: for our vines have tender grapes" (Song of Solomon 2:15 KJV).

To protect the vines when the grapes are first developing it is important to keep an eye out for the little foxes that can sneak past the defenses and do damage.

It is often the little things that sabotage our efforts to fulfill our potential. Samson lost his God-given superpower through compromising on God's promises. David sinned by not fulfilling his duty as king by staying home while his army went to battle.

We look out for the big issues in our lives but turn a blind eye to making little compromises that keep us stagnant.

It is doing the fundamentals consistently that lead to big victories. Every athlete has talent, but the successful athlete knows that success in competition comes from the hours spent consistently doing the routine disciplines that develop their potential.

As we begin a New Year, ask for God's help to be on the lookout for the little areas of compromise that hinder our growth and development. Let's be intentionally consistent in the things that will help us achieve our God given purpose and calling.

It is the little things that lead to big successes.

January 4
Live It Out. Raising the Bar

If we drop a frog into a pot of boiling water, he will immediately make every attempt to hop right out of there. But, if we drop a frog into a pot of cool water and slowly turn up the heat, the frog will eventually be lulled into complacency with the jacuzzi-like comfort and before he knows it, he's been cooked.

Have we been lulled into compromise? For those of us that name the name of Christ, have we been slowly cooked and don't even realize it? Have we become so accustomed to the culture around us that we aren't a living witness of the Kingdom of God?

The Bible calls us to a higher moral standard of living so that we can represent Christ to the world. I want to challenge believers to "Live It Out." To be bold and courageous in our faith. To examine our lives and see where we have lowered the bar. To allow the Holy Spirit of God to examine our hearts and convict us of the sin we do not even recognize in us. To step out and be bold in sharing our faith. To love and serve others. To join a community of faith. To sacrifice time and money to minister to those that are hurting.

This New Year can be another year or a year like no other.

January 5
New Opportunities

Everyone likes "New." New clothes, hairdo, furniture, car, and new beginnings. The problem is no one likes the bill that comes with "New." There is a price that must be paid for "new."

It cost God the enormous price of the sacrificial life of His only Son, Jesus, who paid the price to give believers New Life in Christ.

"Therefore if anyone is in Christ, this person is a new creation; the old things passed away; behold, new things have come" (2 Corinthians 5:17 NASB).

We celebrate a New Year but what makes it any better than last year? Just because the calendar changed does not make it any better…or does it? When I am in Christ, by way of my accepting the fact that Jesus died for me, it gives me the opportunity to start over at any time.

Since we have started a New Year, let us press delete on all the old harmful stuff and allow God to give us a fresh start. With God's help we can take whatever this year has to offer, and we can walk in relationship with the God of creation and live life to the fullest.

January 6
A New Beginning

It is the beginning of a New Year and a new decade. Think about how fast the last 10 years have flown by or even the last twenty. For those that are old enough, Y2K was important or at least it was supposed to be. Fear was gripping the world because of a computer glitch. The computerized world was going to come to a halt at the year 2000. Anyway, time is flying by. No matter what stage of life we are in, we have before us a chance at a "Do Over," a new beginning.

We may not be able to control some aspects of what happens to us but there is a lot we can control. We can let fear of the unknown lock us into a passive lifestyle or we can decide to live with gusto.

There are always excuses why we should not step out in faith, but there are a lot of reasons why we should. God has given us a great gift in Jesus Christ. The Bible tells us that through Christ we can do all things. We need to stop focusing on what is not happening or the lack of resources we have available to us and chose to do something about it. Life was meant to be lived not endured.

The year and decade are fresh upon us. What are we going to do with it? Happy New Year.

January 7
A Time for New Beginnings!

Life can leave us feeling weary. It can be a struggle to keep up with all its demands. It is tempting and way too easy to fall into the trap of living life as it comes. The next 358 days are going to happen no matter how much we want them to speed up or slow down. How are we going to use them?

We have forgotten the adage, "Find the thing that you love to do, and you will never work another day in your life." We can be consumed with the next thing on the list or just going through our routines and find another year has gone by.

Let's be proactive, and intentional about what we would like to see happen this year. Let's do something we have always wanted to do. Go somewhere new or take on a new challenge.

A friend of mine has always wanted to be a foster mom and last year she took the steps to become one. There is a world full of needs and we just might be the one to meet some of them.

Life is too short to just let it pass by. Our life counts. Let the New Year be a time of new beginnings. We ask God to awaken old dreams or even new desires and see what God does this year.

January 8
Return to God

Abraham Lincoln (1809-1861) the 16th US President of the United States, issued a Presidential Proclamation on March 30, 1863. He called for a National Day of Prayer and Fasting. In his proclamation he said this, "We have been the recipients of the choicest bounties of Heaven; we have been preserved these many years in peace and prosperity; we have grown in numbers, wealth, and power as no other nation has ever grown. But we have forgotten God."

If Lincoln was talking that way about our country then, what would he say about our country today? Not only have we forgotten God, but we have told Him to leave us alone. We have kicked God out of our schools and our government.

Lincoln then went on to invite the country to do this, "It behooves us, then, to humble ourselves before the offended Power, to confess our national sins, and to pray for clemency and forgiveness." Wise advice from a wise president.

As we kick off the new year, it is wise to begin with some prayer and fasting of our own. Let's join together with those around the country and take the next 21 days to seek God through Prayer and Fasting. It is time to return to the God from Whom all blessings flow. Let us humble ourselves and pray and seek God for His will to be done on earth as it is in Heaven. Amen

January 9
Get Involved

We usually do not appreciate something until it is diminished or gone. It might be health, friends, loved ones, influence, upward mobility, or a healthy church.

There may be good legitimate reasons why things change and possibly a few hard to swallow circumstances.

As we start the new year, let's appreciate our health, loved ones, and friends. Thank God for all His blessings in our lives. Let us not wait for them to be gone or diminished before we stop and appreciate what we have.

God instituted the family, government, and His church to be forces of influence in this world. If we are not part of a local church, we are missing out and need to get involved. His church needs us, and we need it.

Let's not wait until something is taken away making us wish for the good old days when we could go to church freely.

Happy New Year!

January 10
Freedom

John Wimber, (1934-1997) founder of the Vineyard Church Movement, is credited with saying, "God has no solution for things that we are not willing to call what He calls them."

We produce a lot of fancy names for issues in our life that God calls sin. We have come to tolerate fear, fornication, worry, division, hate, anger, and unforgiveness, to name just a few things that God calls sin. We can excuse it, justify it, and blame others for it, but it does not get rid of it.

Jesus came to bring freedom to those stuck in habits that are destructive to living life as He intended. The remedy for sin is found in the forgiveness only God can provide. Jesus died on the cross taking the punishment for our sins so that we do not have to. Repentance is the starting point in breaking the shame and guilt of our wrong choices. Repentance is agreeing with God's Word about behaviors that He calls sin, asking forgiveness, and collaborating with the Holy Spirit to change our behavior.

The door to freedom can be found if we continue to live in agreement with God's Word. "And ye shall know the truth, and the truth shall make you free" (John 8:32 KJV). "I have treasured Your word in my heart, So that I may not sin against You" (Psalm 119:11 NASB).

God is not trying to keep us from enjoying life. It is just the opposite; He wants us to get the most enjoyment and fulfillment from the life that He gave us. To do that we must live according to the owner's manual. When we do, there is freedom, when we do not, there is bondage and baggage. It is time to come to God to find forgiveness and freedom.

January 11
The Battle Belongs to the Lord

The children of Israel, as they wandered in the dessert, were miraculously given daily food by God. He gave them manna, a wafer-like food that appeared fresh each day, just for them. God supplied their need daily and fully. They didn't have to hunt or harvest or store it up. Despite God's loving, miraculous provision, they grew tired of eating the manna for breakfast, lunch, and dinner. They complained against God and wanted meat to eat. So, God caused quail to come into the camp, and the Israelites ate until it made them sick. They were stubborn and stiff-necked, and God gave them what they asked for to their own detriment.

Later in their history, they asked for a king, and God gave them a king even after He warned them of the damage a king would do to them. They wanted one anyway to their own harm.

America has looked to government to be a savior. God has given them what they have asked for. The answer for America will not be found in the Republican or Democrat parties. Government has a way of complicating things and being ineffective in the answer to humanity's problems. The answer to America's problems will be found in God bringing another Great Awakening. Man cannot fix man's problems and until we humble ourselves and return to God we will continue spinning on the hamster wheel. God reminded the Children of Israel in their time of need to repent from their evil practices and allow God to fight their battles. We are at a crossroad in America, and it is time to take responsibility for the ills of America and not expect answers to come from elected officials.

January 12
Cutting Edge

Solomon writing in the tenth chapter of Ecclesiastes, relates wisdom and effort to the condition of an ax. If an ax isn't kept sharpened, it becomes dull and it will take more effort to get the job done. If an ax is kept sharpened, it takes less effort and energy to get the job done – and with a better finished outcome.

Interestingly, we still think of wisdom or lack thereof as being sharp or dull. We describe something highly effective as cutting edge. Throughout scripture, God makes it clear that He is wise and wants us to be wise. When we approach matters with the sharpness of wisdom, we save ourselves and others a lot of unnecessary dull work. As believers in Jesus, God equips us with the wisdom of His word and the Holy Spirit indwelling us.

So, there is no excuse for being less than what He has called us to be. Jesus told us that we are salt and light in the world. We are to stand and do our best to stop the world from decaying around us and let the light of God's love bring hope and redemption to all that we can influence.

We must examine ourselves and see if we have lost our saltiness or if our light has been hidden. Abiding in God's word keeps us sharp. Are we a dull ax head? If we have allowed the ways of the world to influence us, and if we are living in a manner that is more consistent with the world's philosophy than scripture's, then we are not using wisdom and will not be as effective. It is time for believers to value God's wisdom and become innovative.

January 13
Change Happens

Change is inevitable. As much as we try to avoid change, it is just a matter of time before things change; everything from technology, the political landscape, to the changes in our bodies; change happens!

Change is not a terrible thing it just makes us uncomfortable because we are creatures of habit. We like routine even though we get bored with the same "Old, same Old."

If we are believers in Jesus then change should be expected, in fact, if change is not happening then something is wrong.

We can intentionally change in cooperation with God's leading. How? By all the various means of His grace: Reading His word every day, sitting under sound preaching, and plainly asking God to change us to be more like Christ. Change happens when we study our Bibles and when we commit ourselves, moment by moment to trust and obey the Lord. Change is evidence of progressive growth and development in becoming closer to, and more like, Jesus.

Being a Christian does not always make things easier, but it should make things better, including us. God is a God that changes not, which means we can count on Him to be what He declares Himself to be. But He is changing things in us and around us.

If we are not prepared for changes then we could miss opportunities that God is wanting to bring to us.

January 14
Jesus Only

Jesus invited those that were worn out and carrying heavy loads to come to Him and find rest. He said, "Take My yoke upon you and learn from Me, for I am gentle and humble in heart, and you will find rest for your souls" (Matt 11:29 NASB).

What an invitation. Let's not miss that. Jesus knows our condition, our needs, our weariness and wants us to come to Him so we can find rest – rest that resonates all the way into our souls. This is an unmatched invitation with unmatched impact. Nothing satisfies like Jesus.

People try different things to find rest and to recover from the demands of life; entertainment, substances to take the edge off, trips to the ocean or mountains, or religion, all to try to find a little peace and happiness. These are diversions that don't bring us the sustained rest and peace we seek.

Jesus offers another way. He offers the rest that only He can give. The rest that He offers starts with Him and is Him. We come to Him and spend time with Him. We pray, worship, meditate on His Word. These are spiritual disciplines, but they are also means of His grace – His means of working in us – that produce rest leading to spiritual vitality in us.

Let us come to Him and find the rest and peace we seek.

January 15
The Church Was God's idea.

People have many unkind things to say about organized religion and churches. Unfortunately, some of it is true.

Criticism may be a means of making excuses for not attending.

Anytime people are involved in an organization it's going to have flaws and there are going to be problems because people are flawed and have problems. Yet, somehow, people have unrealistic expectations that a church should never have conflicts, and that everyone should get along.

The reality is, people are broken, and broken people hurt people sometimes. That does not make it right, it is just the way it is. Instead of being critical of churches, let us realize that they are more like hospitals than courtrooms. The church exists to help people find hope and healing and not to be brought before judge, jury, and executioner.

The church is not perfect and has its share of blemishes, but it is still the vehicle God uses to proclaim His message. Instead of being critical, let's use our gifts and talents to make the church more effective in fulfilling its purpose.

January 16
Dead to Sin, Thanks to Christ!

"You contribute nothing to your salvation except the sin that made it necessary." Jonathan Edwards (1703-1758) American revivalist preacher.

Praise God, Christ does the saving and keeping.

Paul, writing to the church at Rome said, "So you too, consider yourselves to be dead to sin, but alive to God in Christ Jesus. Therefore, sin is not to reign in your mortal body so that you obey its lusts, and do not go on presenting the parts of your body to sin as instruments of unrighteousness; but present yourselves to God as those who are alive from the dead, and your body's parts as instruments of righteousness for God. For sin shall not be master over you, for you are not under the Law but under grace" (Romans 6:11-14 NASB).

Thank God for His saving grace! In Jesus Christ the power of doing life contrary to God has been broken, it no longer controls us. Paul is encouraging believers to no longer give their body or sight, hearing, words, hands, or feet to be used to engage in activities that are disobedient to God's commands, but to give ourselves to doing what pleases God. We are to surrender our whole being to the purposes of God. Just as we were a slave to our own lusts and desires, now we are to be a slave to doing what is right in God's eyes.

God help us to stop living for ourselves and seek to use our eyes, ears, mouth, hands, and feet in ways that bring glory to You.

January 17
Racing to Win

"Christ never was in a hurry. There was no rushing forward, no anticipating, no fretting over what might be. Each day's duties were done as each day brought them, and the rest was left with God." Mary Slessor (1848-1915) Scottish Missionary to Nigeria.

There is a lot to be said for longevity, perseverance, and patience. Waiting on God is a skill we develop as we learn to place our trust and faith in Him and wait for His leading.

We often live life like a sprint. Hurry and get there, get all we can as quickly as we can, and live each moment to the fullest. Frankly, that is too narrow a view. It is bad money management advice, bad physical management advice, bad marriage advice, and bad spiritual advice.

Life is a marathon. We tend to give up too quickly and look for the effortless way out. The best life has to offer comes with time. If we want the best that life can give us, it will take both time and perseverance. It will require us to work hard and ride out the storms that will seek to destroy us.

We should not be defined by our accomplishments but by the lives we touch along the way. Having a sprint mentality ignores the people around us and focuses on achieving the prize.

Marathon people know it takes others to finish the race. Let's take time and appreciate those around us. Let's wait on God for His leading. We will be glad that we did.

January 18
Knowing God

"When is a revival needed? When carelessness and unconcern keep the people asleep." Billy Sunday (1862-1935) American revivalist.

Somehow, just because we have an experience with God or we read His Word a bit we think we know all there is to know about God, and we become comfortable with what little we do know.

Why is it we do not pursue deeper knowledge and experiences with the God who came to us and said that He no longer calls us servants, but He calls us His friends in John 15:15? God desires to be known. He waits for us to put time and energy into knowing Him.

James tells us, "Come close to God and He will come close to you" (James 4:8a NASB). God has given us everything around us to point us to Him. The heavens declare the glory of God. Creation displays His character and nature. The Bible is a written love letter to His creation. If we look around us there are living testimonies of God's goodness and grace.

Let's not settle for what little knowledge we may have of God. God is the very essence of love, joy, peace, and hope. God is a deep mystery waiting to be revealed. The good news is that God hides in plain sight waiting to be discovered. Let's dig deep! He is inexhaustible.

January 19
Truth Leads to Liberty

Jesus said, "and you will know the truth, and the truth will set you free" (John 8:32 NASB).

Note the clear correlation between truth and freedom. When we understand and practice truth it will lead us to freedom. Freedom brings peace and the ability to receive and give love more freely.

Believing lies, false theories, and false philosophies will lead to bondage. Bondage creates anxiety and fear leading to tragic outcomes including demanding love and acceptance but being unable to give it.

We are in an era of rampant, subjective, so-called truth with no absolutes. False philosophies are declared as truth by leaders and authorities. Our once noble legal, governmental, and educational institutions desert our moral values while captivating and devastating our young and naïve. We are seeing the fruit of it played out. It is heartbreaking.

The answer is simple but not easy. Jesus declared, "I am the way, the truth, and the life" (John 14:6a NASB). Given the fear, anxiety, and turmoil of our day, put into practice the TRUTH as presented by Jesus. He invites us to cast all our care on Him, to enter His rest, to receive His love and truth, and to experience the fruit it produces in our lives. It will be immeasurably better than the information being presented every night in news and social media. The Truth leads to liberty.

January 20
We Were Created for a Purpose

The stories that move us deeply are about touchingly relatable characters who face monumental, sacrificial, terrifying challenges yet somehow, against all odds, triumph in such a way that we know they were made for that very purpose.

In the film, *Rocky,* the little-known boxer, Rocky overcame his self-doubt to fight champion, Apollo Creed. Luke Skywalker, Hans Solo, and Princess Leia found the strength to overcome the dark side and the evil empire in *Star Wars*. Peter, Edmund, Susan, and Lucy overcame their fear of the White Witch in *The Chronicles of Narnia*. David learned to rely on God to defeat Goliath.

God has planted within each of us a purpose that may be threatened by significant difficulties, hardships or obstacles. Our purpose may include raising our children and shepherding their hearts to the Lord in a culture that wants to turn them away from their parents and God and toward false gods. Our purpose may be to serve the Lord in our local church but family illness, financial setbacks, fractured marital relationships, or feelings of inadequacy make fulfilling our purpose feel as challenging as facing Goliath or Apollo Creed. Some may opt for the easiest life possible to avoid the potential obstacles of roles that just seem too hard.

"It's not by might nor by power, but by my Spirit" (Zechariah 4:6 KJV). With His Spirit to help us we can overcome every obstacle and achieve far more than we ever thought possible.

January 21
Life's Big Questions

"Nobody made a greater mistake than he who did nothing because he could only do a little." Edmund Burke (1729-1797) Anglo-Irish philosopher and statesman.

If God gave us life, what do we think is His expectation of us?

There is so much to life, relationships, kids, work, illness, vacations, pleasure, pain, learning, understanding, the beauty of creation, the stages of life, and eventually life is no more.

What really is life all about? Is this life in this world all there is? Is it all about entrance and exit?

The Bible states that living is but a mist, a vapor and then it is over! What constitutes a good life or a bad one? Will we be held accountable by God for the gift of life that He gave us and what we did with it?

The Bible has the answers to these questions and much more. Check out Micah 6:8 sometime soon.

Life can pass by in the blink of an eye. Let us not let it pass by ignorantly. God is big enough to reveal Himself to us if we are sincere in asking Him. Let us start asking!

January 22
Our Way or His Way

Life is full of adventure. We have no idea what a day will bring. We get up in the morning having a plan and things can quickly change in scope and intensity.

Some choose to ride the waves of life in a kind of "don't worry, be happy," vibe. Others do their best to keep a handle on things and try with all their might at dictating the journey. We sometimes call this being a control freak.

Both options can be successful but full of challenges.

A third option is to depend on Jesus. Jesus said, "These things I have spoken to you so that in Me you may have peace. In the world you have tribulation but take courage; I have overcome the world" (John 16:33 NASB).

Jesus took the world's worst and came out victorious. Instead of trying to navigate the seas of life on our own, if we will draw close to Jesus, He will show us the way. He would love to.

Here is the difficult part: admitting that we need help and being willing to surrender to His Lordship over our lives. We would much rather take our chances and see where the adventure takes us or use our own iron will to control things rather than surrender. Often at our own expense. Whatever adventure this life has to offer does not compare to the one that God has prepared for us. But, as always, it is our choice.

January 23
Be Daring; Live Life

What is our focus for the future? We can be consumed with the needs of our circumstances and miss the unexpected opportunities of today. We can be entrenched in our routines and worries and not see the potential in our future.

When we are young, we are waiting for opportunities. When we are older, we think we have missed them all. If we let it, life can strip us of our desire to try new things and take risks.

Let's challenge ourselves to do something crazy this year. Let's break out of the comfortable routines, and we might discover a side of ourselves that we forgot existed. Let's make the effort to build a better marriage, develop a deeper relationship with our kids and grandkids. Look for new and exciting opportunities.

Most worthwhile things take effort, so we debate the ratio of risk to reward. Is the risk worth the effort? What about just the little 3 letter word, T-R-Y? What if we just decide to try? A better marriage is worth a try. Lots of things are worth a try.

We can be so afraid of failure that we stop trying new things, or new attempts at old issues. Let's ask God to point out an area in our life He wants to help us take a try at bettering. We can trust Him to lead us. He loves doing that.

Let's live life as it was meant to be lived – with fullness and abundance in Christ.

January 24
The Power to Change

Why is it so hard to do what we know we need to do and so easy to do the things that we know we should not? The continual struggle seems almost impossible at times. We know we should stop eating, and start exercising, but eating is so much easier. We know we should not spend so much money and save more but spending is more fun. We know we should spend more time with our family and less time vegging, but vegging takes less effort. We know we should spend more time praying and reading God's word instead of doing just about anything else we can think of but there is less resistance when we are doing anything else.

The Bible says it this way, "The spirit is willing, but the flesh is weak" (Matthew 6:41 KJV). All the things we should be doing lead to a healthier, happier, more fulfilling, and stress-free life, but our desires want the easiest way possible.

Sheer self-discipline usually only gets us to about February. Only God can change our heart motives to set us free to be all that we can be. The Bible states, "So if the Son sets you free, you shall be free indeed" (8:36 KJV). If we come to Him during our struggle and ask for help, God will in time set us free and give us the power to do what we know we need to do.

He IS the Power to Change Us.

January 25
Worship Him

On Sundays, followers of the Lord gather at their local church for a worship service. Worship involves hearing the reading and preaching of the word of God, singing spiritual songs, clapping hands, opening our mind and heart to the God that created us to thank Him, praise Him, and seek Him. One of the things that believers must guard against is not letting a worship service become a time of empty ritual, or make the mistake that worship is a feeling that must come over us.

Worship is commanded. We gather together and consciously, obediently, reverentially, but imperfectly worship as an act of our will to honor the Lord Jesus Christ. We do this whether our favorite hymns are sung or not, whether our favorite person is in the pulpit or not, and frankly, whether we feel like it or not.

Worship is a choice. Our showing up to worship is no small thing in itself, but in addition, what we do once we are there matters greatly to the Lord and in a mysterious way that only God knows all about, our willingness to cooperate with the Holy Spirit in our heart's attitude of worship can be used by the Lord to influence the preaching and all aspects of the worship. It's not exactly like cheering on our favorite sports team, but in a somewhat similar sense, when we engage, when we are fully present, and our will cooperates with the Holy Spirit, He activates our worship. But as we know, He is a perfect gentleman who will never stay where He even senses His presence is not completely welcome. May we always fully welcome and worship the Living God.

January 26
The High Praise of God

"The high praises of God *shall be* in their mouths, And a two-edged sword in their hands, To execute vengeance on the nations, And punishment on the peoples, to bind their kings with chains, And their dignitaries with shackles of iron, To execute against them the judgment written. This is an honor for all His godly ones. Praise the Lord" (Psalm 149:6-9 NASB).

There are levels of praise and worship to God. We can worship to feel good. We can worship so that others are blessed. We can offer the high praises of God in worship so that God's heart is touched. The Bible tells us that when we worship to move God's heart, God will come and dwell among those that praise His name. We move into His manifested presence. His glory and power are demonstrated in transformed lives.

When we as believers move beyond our own needs and desires and enter heart felt praise, thanksgiving, adoration, and desiring above everything to love and know the one who gave everything for us, we will discover a deeper awareness of the very nature and character of God.

We find comfort in routine and ritual, however when it comes to worshiping God, creative expressions unlock our hearts from pride and stagnation. We were created to bring God pleasure. Only in God will we find everything our hearts desire and long for.

Let the high praises of God be in our mouths as we worship into deeper realms of knowledge and experience.

January 27
Be Still

"Cease striving and know that I am God" (Psalm 46:10 NASB).

What is our first thought when we read this verse? Are we picturing ourselves seated and watching in fascination for God do something, as if we are watching a movie? There is something beautiful in God's request for us to be still.

We are an anxious bunch. We are always trying to fix everything and everyone. We have 24-hour news, social media to keep us updated on everyone's business, and phones that we can take everywhere to receive calls, texts, and information.

Being still is about shutting down the noise, the craziness and information overload. Being still is shutting down my body to give it a rest. Being still so that we can know that God is God.

God invites us to know Him, to know Him as God, and to receive refreshing from the author of life. To receive God, we must be still and get quiet. God often comes in a still small voice to speak words of life and encouragement to us. Being still in His presence brings joy, peace, energy, and refreshing that can only come from God Himself.

"But they that wait upon the Lord shall renew their strength; they shall mount up with wings as eagles; they shall run, and not be weary; and they shall walk, and not faint" (Isaiah 40:31 KVJ).

Be still. A simple request that some find almost impossible to do. Let's try being still before the Lord for 15 minutes a day for 30 days and see if our whole being is better for it. Let's be still and know God.

January 28
He is a Good Father Who Offers Us Rest

Religion gives us requirements but no power to help us fulfill them. A relationship with God revolves around love. Godly love is focused on doing what is in the best interest of the other person. In Matthew 11:27-28 Jesus calls those that are tired and exhausted to come to Him and to learn from Him and they would find rest for their souls.

One of the most often repeated Psalms especially at funerals is "He makes me lie down in green pastures; He leads me beside quiet waters. He restores my soul" (Psalm 23:1-3a NASB).

All too often God is painted as a grueling task master with an endless list of do's and don'ts and if we should screw up then we can expect the wrath of God to fall on us but that is not the case at all.

God's heart is to give rest to those who would come to Him. God promises to lead those that need restoring to green pastures and still waters.

The problem is we think we can keep the pace of life, and it won't do damage to our souls. That is not the case. We were not designed to go 24/7, and the baggage we carry is destroying us.

There is an alternative, and that is to come home to God and let Him love on us. He is waiting!

January 29
God in Us, Before Us, and Through Us

God is looking for anyone that He can work in and through. There are a lot of people that want God to work through them but not necessarily in them.

How wonderful it would be if God used us to bring about a miracle of healing or deliverance or better yet, if God abundantly blessed us with finances so that we could help others financially.

The possibility of God working through us releases creative dreaming in us of ways in which God could use us to relieve the suffering of others. It is all good stuff until we realize that God wants to first work in us.

The problem is not that we do not trust God or have enough faith. The bigger problem is whether God can trust us. Have we allowed Him to work on our pride and character enough that God using us will not destroy us? God using us is a matter of alignment. Are we aligned with Him like Jesus was? Have we submitted to His will and His purposes, or are we still chasing our validation? Before God can use us, we have to be like Jesus, and then the impossible becomes possible.

January 30
Hope

There is a staggering range of emotions that occurs when a person goes from feeling hopeful to hopeless.

Hope is a powerful motivator that keeps a person moving forward, while feeling hopeless causes depression and can lead to a fatalistic attitude. It can stop a person in their tracks.

Paul writing to the church at Corinth said this, "now these three remain faith, hope, and love" (1Corinthians 13:13 KJV). Hope means a confident expectation of a future reality. When things are looking grim, and we are not sure what the future holds, hope allows us to live in confidence that God the Father and His Son will not abandon us. God will see us through.

Jeremiah the prophet writing under the inspiration of the Holy Spirit declared that God said He has plans to prosper and not harm us...plans to give us hope and a future. This is where faith plays a part in creating hope when things seem hopeless. It is putting our trust in God and His Word, allowing His promises to transform our attitude, and allow hope to rise in us.

January 31
Eternity

"They, then, who are destined to die, need not be careful to inquire what death they are to die, but into what place death will usher them." St. Augustine (354 – 430 AD) Theologian.

Sober words. We do our best to avoid conversations about the end of our lives and we also spend a good portion of our lives trying to avoid death. The reality is every day we are one day closer. Nobody knows for sure how much time we have here on earth.

The Bible tells us that we are eternal beings. St. Augustine reminds us that we are all destined to die. The question is not how we will die but where will we spend eternity. The Bible gives us two possibilities. We can either spend eternity with God or spend it apart from Him. The choice is ours.

In the world in which we live, it is not politically correct to ask such questions. The prominent thinking based on nothing other than man's resistance to God's truth is that either we will all make it to heaven or that when we die it is all over so there is nothing to worry about. Two lies with eternal consequence.

God's word says there is a judgment. "It is appointed once for man to die and after that the judgment" (Hebrews 9:27 KJV). It is too important a question to just guess at. Our eternal future rests on our decision. Where will our eternity be? Why not study God's word on this.

02
FEBRUARY

February 1
Trusting God

Do we put our trust in our ability to earn a living, or in God's ability to provide? Do we know what is at stake in our answer?

We have been taught that if a man does not work and provide for himself and his family he is not much of a man. We have heard statements like there's no such thing as a free lunch, and if you want something, you need to go out and earn it.

But what is at stake is a serious question of where we are putting our confidence. The Bible says that God is our provider. That God will supply all our needs according to His riches in glory in Christ Jesus. God asks us to first seek the Kingdom of God, and all these things (food, shelter, and clothes) will be added to us. When we put all our confidence in our ability to earn or provide what happens when we can no longer work, or if we become unemployed?

God desires for us to build our confidence in His ability to care for His children. This in no way suggests that we run out and quit our jobs and wait for God to provide. Work is in His nature, and He expects us to work as well. It all has to do with putting our trust in the Lord and His ability to sustain us no matter what our circumstances are. It starts right now, right where we are living. Begin by changing our heart attitude and look to Him to supply all our needs and desires. Desires? Does God really care about our desires? More than we could ever imagine.

February 2
Worship: A Proper Response to Who He is

Worship is not based on everything going well and having no problems. Worship begins to happen when we focus on the eternal, unchangeable attributes of almighty God: He is infinite – no beginning, and no end. He is unchanging – He is the same yesterday, today, and forever. He is self-sufficient – He has no needs. He is omnipotent – all powerful. He is omniscient – all knowing. He is omnipresent – everywhere at once, all the time. He is all wise – perfect unchanging wisdom. He is faithful –unchanging and true. He is good – kind, full of good will. He is just. He is merciful. He is gracious. He is love. He is holy. He is glorious. The angels around the throne of God get one glimpse of who He is and fall down worshiping crying, "Holy, Holy, Holy [is the] Lord God Almighty" (Revelation 4:8a KJV).

No matter what is happening in my life and circumstances, I can always worship who He is. I can lift my voice to the heavens declaring His name. The hard things that happen to me do not change who He is and do not give me reason not to worship Him. The hardest time to give praise and worship to God is when life is throwing everything at us. The Bible calls it a sacrifice of praise. It is not a sacrifice when everything is going well.

When I least feel like worshiping, that is when I need to worship. Worship and praise bring me into His Presence. That is where I will find all I need. Let praise and worship fill your mind and heart. Lift up your voice magnifying the greatness of our God.

February 3
New Wineskins

We would all like new experiences with God without having to change anything in our life. Change can be painful, uncertain, and uncomfortable. Which is why we resist the very change that can bring depth and richness in our relationship with the Lord.

Mark 2:22 teaches that the old ways of the pharisees was as rigidly inflexible as old wineskins. The new wine of the gospel grows and expands as new wine naturally does. Jesus said the gospel caused great discomfort in the pharisees as they felt the buildup of pressure like new wine in old wineskins.

Grace is so radical that it can make our pharisaical hearts uncomfortable. The pharisees clung to the comfort of their old religious habits preventing them from experiencing the new wine – the gospel.

God desires an ongoing intimate relationship with His children. What He started in the Garden of Eden He wants to continue with all those that receive the sacrifice of His Son leading to salvation. God invites us to know Him through the disciplines of reading His Word, talking to Him in prayer, and through humbling ourselves in worship.

Father, help us. We are creatures of habit and routine. We get comfortable in our style of relating to You. Help us to trust You in the deeply intimate, grace-filled relationship You want with us.

February 4
Ears to Hear and Eyes to See

When Jesus walked on our planet, He taught like no one else and performed miracles. He opened blind eyes and deaf ears, cast out demons, raised people from the dead, healed all manner of sickness, and multiplied food. The purpose of these signs and wonders was to verify the truth of who Jesus is: The Son of God and Savior of all who believe the gospel that salvation is by faith alone, in Jesus Christ, by grace alone.

How shall we then live? Some, trying to be good boys and girls, live in expectation of God blessing them as if they are owed it. Some follow the culture and in the name of tolerance embrace values and morals that do not line up with the Word of God.

Time is slipping away; we must develop our spiritual eyes and ears to see and hear what God is doing in this hour. It will take an all-out relentless pursuit of almighty God to be salt and light during difficult days. We will need the power of God like never before, but it does not come cheaply. It takes all our surrender and obedience. If we want to do the things that Jesus did, we must be in process to become like who Jesus is. We must be actively participating with God's program in our development.

Can we see and hear what the Spirit is doing? Do we recognize His voice? Do we know what is on God's heart for this hour? Are we heeding His call to obedience?

There is no time for putting it off. People get ready. Jesus is coming!

February 5
Living Life With Jesus

We can either live our life as if we are in charge or live our life in submission to Jesus. It does not work to do both. But we keep trying to do just that. We want control when everything is going well, and everyone likes us, but as soon as the rug gets pulled out from under us, we want God to fix it.

We try and live the Christian life as if we can fix ourselves. As if somehow, we can get the sin stain out of us without needing the Savior. We try harder, set goals, and even become religious. We go to church, read our Bibles but never confess our sin or let the Word of truth penetrate our hearts. We adopt the world's philosophies and think it is from the Bible, and then blame Him when our lives fall apart, and life does not go the way we want.

God invites us to come to Him; to be in a relationship with Him. He does not ask us to try harder. He asks us to be still, to wait on Him, to let Him come and fix us, to let His love penetrate our hearts and transform us from the inside out.

His way is so much better, but it requires us to trust Him. It is time to live life with Jesus. Only He can get the sin stain out of our lives.

February 6
Do We Love Him?

Peter, do you love me? Jesus asked.

You know I do. Peter responded.

Jesus then instructs Peter, *then feed my sheep.*

An interesting exchange in the gospel of John chapter 15. Remember, Peter had denied Christ and was feeling low at this point in their relationship. We tend to focus on the assignment Jesus is giving in this exchange, but Jesus's point was calling Peter back into a loving relationship. What grace. What love.

Everything God does is centered in love and based in relationship with Him. Man, how we can mess this up! If we love Him, we will keep His commandments, the scriptures tell us. But we can get upset with ourselves over our failures. Jesus knows. He forgives us when we acknowledge our sin. Jesus loves us and wants us to also show love and forgiveness to others.

When we stay centered in His love being yoked to Him is easy and what He asks of us will not be a burden. What grace Jesus showed to remind Peter that it's not about performance.

We will all make mistakes. He loves us. We need to be reminded that it's about the enormity of His love and staying connected through relationship with Him.

Let us hang with Jesus awhile and allow His love to capture our hearts once again. He's waiting!

February 7
The Divine Exchange

Jesus offers to us life to its fullest. Life as it was meant to be experienced. Not necessarily fame, riches, or power, but contentment, joy, peace, fulfillment, vitality, and purpose. He just asks one thing of us, that we surrender our life to Him. We surrender all that we are and all that we have, which means all our plans, expectations, desires, lifestyle, and attitudes.

There is just one problem. We have been taught not to put all our eggs in one basket. That we should diversify and keep our options open, and that we should not blindly trust anyone.

So instead of surrendering our life to Him. We give Him some things but not everything. We hold back part of our hearts and do not really trust that God can give us the best possible life.

Life lived on our terms, does not come close to living the life that God has for us. We forfeit His best life for us for our best attempts at living life. God gave us His best by giving us His Son. His Word tells us that since He did not spare His only Son for our sake, will He not freely give us all things?

He gives us the choice to lay down our life and receive from Him or hold on to our life and eventually lose out on the best life that He can give us. Choose wisely.

February 8
The Love Month

To love is easier said than done. It is easy to speak the words, but much harder to live out. Marriage vows have these words, "for better, or worse, for richer, or poorer, in sickness and in health." It's easy to love when it is all going well, but the real test of love is when it seems like everything is falling apart.

Love is more than a feeling. It is a commitment to continue to love when it is costing my time, my energy, and my desires. The Bible gives us the characteristics of love in I Corinthians chapter 13, a passage often read at weddings. It is poetic and romantic until we try to live it out.

Someone said, "Marriage is just two people refusing to give up on each other." Why is it that most marriages fail? There are many reasons but usually it can be traced back to one or both not sacrificing for the other.

February is known as the love month. In it we celebrate Valentine's Day. Perhaps instead of cards, candy, and flowers, try something creative and new. Think of a way to renew the connection and commitment to each other. Be inspired by God's love for us and follow His lead by sacrificing our wants, needs and desires by loving and serving the best interests of the ones we love.

We might be surprised by the response. It is not an event. It is a lifestyle. Let's love well!

February 9
The Precious Promises

"My son, pay attention to my words; Incline your ear to my sayings. They are not to escape from your sight; Keep them in the midst of your heart. For they are life to those who find them, And healing to all their body" (Proverbs 4:20-22 NASB).

"Therefore, I say to you, all things for which you pray and ask, believe that you have received them, and they will be *granted* to you" (Mark 11:24 NASB).

The promises of these two verses force me to deal with my unbelief. Do I really believe what these promises are telling me? It is quite possible that my believing is more like wishing. I wish I weren't sick, or I wish I had more money, instead of drilling down into the truth of these two verses.

The first truth tells me to keep God's word within my heart to stay focused on the truth of His promises. The second truth is not to just send up our wish list to God but instead focus on what I believe will happen when I ask God for something.

Do I really believe God answers my prayers when I ask?

God wants me to ask in confidence, trusting that my heart has come into alignment with His heart, and that I am asking for His will be done on earth as it is in Heaven. The promises are given so that I will train my heart by His Word and ask in faith.

February 10
Living for His Presence

David was king over all of Israel. God said of David, that he was a man that sought after God's heart. In the Psalms David wrote,

"One thing have I desired of the Lord, that will I seek after; that I may dwell in the house of the Lord all the days of my life, to behold the beauty of the Lord, and to enquire in his temple" (Psalm 27:4 KJV).

For David, the house of the Lord represented the presence of God. David's desire was to be in the presence of God on a continual basis and he set his heart to seek after it.

What was David able to see? To behold the beauty of the Lord is to meditate on all that God is. His holiness, His perfection, and the awe of His being.

As Christians, we can get distracted in our worship. David set His heart to worship God to a desired end; to be in His presence and to get a fresh revelation of God.

This Sunday, instead of letting the music move us, let us desire more of God. It is amazing what God will do when we seek after Him like David did.

February 11
Taking Territory

If our purpose in life does not need God to accomplish it, then we are living far below what is possible. When God put Adam and Eve in the garden He gave them this command, "To be fruitful and to multiply." He wanted them to take dominion over the planet and fill the earth. They were to expand the borders of the garden while maintaining their connection and relationship with God. They were to take territory.

We still live under that mandate. Our sin nature complicates the process but that is why Jesus came to uncomplicate it. With God's help we should be continually stretching the boundaries of our lives. In the book of Ephesians chapter one, Paul says that being united with Christ means we were given our inheritance from God in advance, and He makes everything work out according to His plan.

God has a plan for our lives and has given us everything we need to accomplish it. Are we living in the fullness of His divine plan for our life? What has God given us in the inheritance that we are not living out? An inheritance is something given to us when someone dies. All that Jesus is and does has been made available to us because He died and left it for us.

What is it? It is territory that we need to search out in His Word and then lay claim to. The Apostle Peter said, "Through these He has granted to us His precious and magnificent promises, so that by them you may become partakers of the divine nature" (2 Peter 1:4 NASB). Let's not settle for less than God's best for us. Let's start taking unclaimed territory.

February 12
Life to Its Fullest

What does it mean to live life to its fullest? Some would say that it that can only happen for the rich because it takes money and lots of it to live life to the hilt. Others might say, it comes through a successful, life-long career, or through seeing the world and the wonders of it, or possibly some would say that living to the fullest is found in meaningful relationships.

The problem with all these scenarios is that they are temporary. The joy they might bring does not sustain us.

Jesus said that He came so that we might have life and have it to the fullest. Living life to the fullest has nothing to do with money, careers, vacations, and not even relationships. What Jesus modeled and came to give us is so simple it can be missed.

Living life to the fullest is about giving and not about getting. Living life from the inside out. Giving love, time, and ourselves to serve others. God put into our DNA His nature and to live contrary to His nature is to bring confusion and dissatisfaction to our lives.

When we live to get all we can get at the expense of those around us, we slowly lose ourselves in the process. Only through giving ourselves away as Jesus did can we truly live life to the fullest.

Let's trust God and try it and see if over time we become a more contented and fulfilled person.

February 13
Why Pray When We Can Just Worry?

No matter what the circumstances may scream at us, we must keep our eyes fixed on the Lord who never slumbers, never sleeps, and is our ever-present help. Difficulties and hardships never knock God off His throne. Nothing ever takes Him by surprise. But, somehow, we forget to pray and just worry.

We may take a dive emotionally or spiritually and wonder what is going to happen, but God knows the end form the beginning. He knows how it is all going to turn out so all we need to do is declare our trust in Him. God's lovingkindness and mercy never fail.

We can try and fix everything ourselves but where has that gotten us in the past? So, we worry. It may come naturally, but worrying is worse than useless. It can cause physical problems, it never fixes things, and, actually, worry is faithless. Worrying is just meditating on the problem.

Here is the test. The next time we are worrying about a problem, let's give it to God and watch what He can do. Let's start meditating on how big God is and how He loves us and see what happens. Speak aloud, "God, I trust You," as many times as is necessary. Let's see the surprising difference it has on us and our circumstances.

February 14
Love, Love, Love, All You Need Is Love

Today we celebrate Valentine's Day. A day to celebrate love. Love is the most foundational emotional need of our lives. The absence of love can have a catastrophic impact on us emotionally, physically, and spiritually. The dynamic power of love can impact the world. Love can cover and heal a multitude of sins and hurts.

"There is a God-shaped vacuum in the heart of each man which cannot be satisfied by any created thing but only by God the Creator, made known through Jesus Christ" Blaise Pascal (1623-1662) French philosopher.

We try and fill the God shaped vacuum with romantic love, ambition, activity, and a host of other things that have no power to bring lasting fulfillment. Only when we come to the Savior can we be set free to experience the transformative power and wonder of His unequalled love. Describing it, the Apostle Paul said, "For I am convinced that neither death, nor life, nor angels, nor principalities, nor things present, nor things to come, nor powers, nor height, nor depth, nor any other created thing will be able to separate us from the love of God that is in Christ Jesus our Lord" (Romans 8:38-39 NASB).

Spend time with the One who loves us more than we could ever possibly comprehend and let the beauty of His love and grace wash away all the hurt, pain, and loneliness that often accompanies the experiences of seeking love in all the wrong places. "For God so loved the world, that He gave His only Son, so that everyone who believes in Him will not perish but have eternal life" (John 3:16 NASB).

February 15
Surrendered

God requires us to surrender our lives to Him for us to receive His best for us.

Jesus taught His followers that the Kingdom of God was like a buried treasure or an expensive pearl that once found, it's discoverer would go and sell all that he owned to obtain. At another time the Lord said, "So then, none of you can be My disciple who does not give up all his own possessions" (Luke 14:33 NASB).

Jesus offers anyone that will surrender all that they are and all that they possess to receive something of eternally greater value in exchange.

The psalmist put it this way: "Blessed is everyone who fears the Lord,Who walks in His ways. When you eat the fruit of the labor of your hands, you will be happy, and it will go well for you. Your wife will be like a fruitful vine. Within your house, your children like olive plants around your table. Behold, for so shall a man who fears the Lord be blessed. The Lord bless you from Zion, And may you see the prosperity of Jerusalem all the days of your life. Indeed, may you see your children's children. Peace be upon Israel" (Psalm 128:1-8 NASB).

We have a death grip on this life and God asks us to trust Him by releasing our lives into His hands so that He can release His blessing into ours.

February 16
Loving Well Every Day

"If I am a friend of Jesus, I must deliberately and carefully lay down my life for Him. It is a difficult thing to do and thank God that it is." Oswald Chambers (1874-1917) Scottish Evangelist to India.

In the Gospel of John, Jesus gives us this truth, "Greater love has no one than this, that a person will lay down his life for his friends" (John 15:13 NASB).

Selfishness runs rampant in humanity. We want to be served rather than to serve. We want our needs met before we think about taking care of anybody else's needs. Jesus's words are a lifestyle not a one-time event. It is much harder to lay down our life every single day. In 1 Corinthians 13, we see that genuine love is, among other things, patient, kind, doesn't behave rudely, doesn't seek its own interests, and endures all things.

Jesus demonstrated sacrificial love not just by dying for us but by demonstrating lowly, humble attitudes of the heart such as taking up the servant's towel and washing the disciple's feet.

There are many opportunities every day to lay down our lives for our spouse, families, and those around us. Just as Jesus modeled love for us, we need to be a living example of what true love looks like all throughout the year.

February 17
Setting Our Hearts to Worship

"Shout joyfully to the Lord, all the earth. Serve the Lord with jubilation; come before Him with rejoicing. Know that the Lord Himself is God; it is He who has made us, and not we ourselves; we are His people and the sheep of His pasture. Enter His gates with thanksgiving, and His courtyards with praise. Give thanks to Him, bless His name. For the Lord is good; His mercy is everlasting, and His faithfulness is to all generations" (Psalm 100 NASB).

The lyrics to this ancient song remind us that the entrance into the presence of God is through the door of worship and praise.

"Worship is giving God the best that He has given. Be careful what you do with the best you have. Whenever you get a blessing from God, give it back to Him as a love-gift. Take time to meditate before God and offer the blessing back to Him in a deliberate act of worship. If you hoard it for yourself, it will turn into spiritual dry rot, as the manna did when it was hoarded. Worship is more than something we do on Sunday morning at church. Worship is how we conduct our lives. Does our daily life reflect and bring glory to God?" Oswald Chambers (1874-1917) Scottish evangelist to India.

February 18
He Alone Is Worthy

Worship means reverent honor and regard paid to God. In this age of selfies, we have turned our reverent honor and regard on ourselves. We have become the focus of our worship. Worship is more than words or singing. It is an attitude of the heart that recognizes the omniscient, omnipotent, and omnipresent God.

God is all-knowing, all-powerful, and present everywhere at the same time. How do we even compare ourselves to God let alone think that we are deserving of our own worship? When we put God in His rightful place and give Him reverent honor and consider all He is and all He does we will inevitably fall back into our rightful place of exalting Him above ourselves.

In Revelation chapter 4, the apostle John describes worship in heaven. He hears them saying, "Worthy are You, our Lord and our God, to receive glory and honor and power; for You created all things, and because of Your will they existed, and were created" (Rev 4:11 NASB).

This day stop and give God glory and honor simply because He deserves it and because we need to have a proper perspective on who we are in relation to who He is.

February 19
Correction

Learning a new skill or attempting self-improvement in a certain area of our life can be an intimidating, discouraging venture. Whether the format is live instruction or digital, as we compare ourselves to others in the setting, it can feel like we are signing up to feel stupid. Many people won't even try, or quit after just a few attempts. The feelings of fear, failure, and frustration that go with the effort can keep a person from moving forward. Maybe there's a better way to think about it.

When we attempt to gain skills or knowledge in anything we will receive correction. Correction makes us feel judged as being stupid. We hate that. But the Bible says we are stupid only if we despise the correction. Check out Proverbs 12:1. Correction is just that, it is to correct us, to help us correct how we go about it so we can do it right. Let's change our perspective on correction as something meant for our good so we can stick with it and improve.

Correction and judgment are not the same thing. Correction is helpful. Judgment is condemning. Correction says, "You're almost there, try it again, but this time, like this." Judgment says, "You'll never get this. Give up."

God wants us to learn and grow. Learning may not be easy and can be challenging, but remaining the same is too high a price. Blessings and new vistas of opportunity await if we are willing to receive correction as something good for us.

February 20
Let It Go

Jesus said that whoever will lose their life for His sake will find it. How does one lose their life and still find it?

Life has a way of keeping the focus on ourselves. My wants, my desires, what will make me happy. And it never quite delivers what it is after. A life lived serving our cravings is no life at all. Losing our life is about taking the focus off self and pursuing a purpose and person bigger and more important than ourselves.

Jesus invites us into a relationship with Him which by its very nature will cause us to experience life at a whole new level. Everything will have a purpose to it. Every difficulty, every trial, every victory will bring us into new dimensions of His life and love.

Letting go of our ideals about what a life worth living should look like and trusting God to direct our steps to bring us into that very life is at the heart of losing our life for His sake.

It is a difficult decision to let go but it is one that must be made before we can find the life that God has destined us to experience. As the popular song says, "Let it Go."

February 21
Dunamis

Dunamis is a Greek word meaning power. It is the root word from which we get our word dynamite. Specifically, God's dynamite power that raised Jesus from the grave is the same power given to believers to work in us and through us. God knew we would not be able to live up to the standards of His Word so He has given us His Spirit to accomplish what we could not on our own. His Spirit resides within all those that have called upon the name of Jesus and have received Him as their Savior.

We no longer must work with all our might to break habits and try to live pleasing to the Lord. Jesus said, "without Me ye can do nothing" (John 15:5 KJV). It's not just about getting things done. It is about who we become along the way. If we want to do anything of lasting value, we need God's Dunamis power.

"For His divine power has granted to us everything pertaining to life and godliness, through the true knowledge of Him who called us by His own glory and excellence" (2 Peter 1:3 NASB).

God knew we could never accomplish His purposes in this life without His divine help. We can rest in His love and surrender to His plans knowing that He will bring it to pass. That's good news.

February 22
Make Today Count

It's the little things that matter. People tend to focus on big events, but life is full of an infinite number of small moments.

We move from holiday to holiday and plan special days to celebrate and forget about the day-to-day moments. Happiness can be found even in the mundane routines of life.

A simple gesture here, a smile there, and a compliment can go a long way in turning a frown upside down. We can miss out by looking past the ordinary. Time flies by and the things we take for granted can soon be gone forever.

The Bible says that there is a time for everything, a time to be born and a time to die. The good book also tells us to give thanks and to think on good things. There is plenty of negative stuff all around to take the joy out of life. Maybe it's time to stop, look and listen for the special moments God has blessed each one of us with.

Let's do our best to make each day unique and special. We just never know what will come our way when we least expect it. Make today count!

February 23
Stinkin' Thinkin'

Confession is a powerful thing. The Bible tells us, "For as he thinks within himself, so he is" (Prov 23:7 NASB). It also tells us to, "Watch over your heart with all diligence; for from it flow the springs of life" (Prov 4:23 NASB). What we believe about ourselves, about life, about God, and about others all flow out of the heart. What we think on reflects what we believe. What we think on comes out of our mouth in confession.

If we want to know how we really feel about things, pay attention to what we are saying and what we are thinking on. If we have "Stinkin' Thinkin,'" there is a good possibility that it's tied to a deep-seated belief.

How do we change what we believe, think, and confess? It starts with the only source that has power to change us – God through His Word. "Blessed is the person who does not walk in the counsel of the wicked, nor stand in the path of sinners, Nor sit in the seat of scoffers! But his delight is in the Law of the Lord, and on His Law he meditates day and night. He will be like a tree planted by streams of water, which yields its fruit in its season, and its leaf does not wither; and in whatever he does, he prospers" (Psalm 1:1-3 NASB).

When we take in the truth of God's Word and as we confess the truth it changes what we believe, which changes the way we think, which changes what comes out of our mouth. Both actions move us from "Stinkin' Thinkin'" to a healthier mental mindset. Which helps us prosper in all that we do.

February 24
Dependence: A Forgotten Characteristic

In the age of self-sufficiency, asking for help in any area of our life is perceived as weakness. We do not want to appear needy or incapable of taking care of ourselves. We bravely live through unspoken trauma and struggle to keep our heads above water all because we are too proud to seek or ask for assistance.

"Better is a neighbour that is near than a brother far off" (Proverbs 27:10 KJV). We all need a friend that is close by, that we can confide in and share our struggles with. It takes courage and strength to admit that life is sometimes more than we can manage. Jesus invites us to come to Him when we are tired and worn out and He will give us rest. There are several examples in the Bible of people reaching out and asking God for help and He gave it to them. The shortest prayer in the Bible is, Lord help me.

We can go it alone and try to get by in life, or we can learn to be dependent on God. Pride precedes a fall; it is better to be humble and dependent than wait too long and crash. There is a saying that is not biblical but quoted as if it is, "God only helps those that help themselves." Jesus said, "Blessed are the poor in spirit, for theirs is the kingdom of God" (Matt 5:3 KJV). Jesus was teaching an attitude of dependence as if we are poor. It does not matter how much money we have in the bank, we can still have a dependent attitude. Self-sufficiency only gets us the best that we can do. Dependence on God gets us His best for us.

February 25
More Than I Can Ask or Think

"Now unto Him that is able to do exceeding abundantly above all that we ask or think, according to the power that worketh in us" (Ephesians 3:20 KJV).

The Bible tells us that God can do way beyond whatever I could ask or think. I can think big thoughts as I imagine you can, too.

But how does that manifest in my daily life? Jesus said that we need to come to Him when we are tired and overworked and He will give us rest. See Matthew 11:28-30. For God to do more than I can ask or think, I must first come to Him. The scriptures teach us that faith starts with believing that God exists and that He rewards those who diligently seek Him. See Hebrews 11:6. The Prophet Jeremiah tells us to call out to Him, and He will answer and show us great and mighty things of which we do not know.

God can do amazing things in our lives when we consistently and passionately pursue Him. It puts us in a position for God to do more through us than we ever could imagine. If we do not believe that He cares or that He will answer our prayers, then we will not pursue Him. God gives the invitation, it is up to us to do our part of spending time with Him for Him to do His part.

February 26
Our Faith Journey

When we say yes to God, we begin a journey of faith that requires us to trust Him even when nothing makes sense, and it feels like He has abandoned us to figure it out alone. That is why faith is required.

We always have a choice in who or what we are going to trust. Will we trust the arm of flesh or lean into the promises that God has given us in His Word?

Every day is filled with opportunities to answer that question one way or the other. If we choose God, we must develop trust muscles to weather the storms that will eventually come, and the uncertainty of having our needs met.

God never disappoints and He's never late, but it still requires faith not to abandon the process. As we navigate life's obstacle course it takes courage and a constant dependence on God to negotiate every decision. If we partner with God and allow Him to lead us, we will find a life full of adventure and fulfillment. Without faith it is impossible to please God, we must believe that He is and that He rewards those that diligently seek Him.

Our faith journey is a lifetime process of growing in faith to trust in all circumstances. It is not easy and never boring. Let the journey continue.

February 27
Words to Live By

"To err is human; to forgive, divine." Alexander Pope (1688-1744) English poet.

"Science, my lad, is made up of mistakes, but they are mistakes which it is useful to make, because they lead little by little to the truth." Jules Verne (1828-1905) Science Fiction Author.

We are going to say something, do something or behave badly at some point in our life. The power of forgiveness keeps our heart free from anger and bitterness. Unforgiveness eats away at our ability to enjoy life.

We all err, it's part of the human package. If we have offended someone, we go and make it right by asking forgiveness and then changing our behavior, so we don't offend again. If someone has offended us, we forgive them. In Matthew chapter 6, Jesus teaches His disciples to pray and ask for God's forgiveness of our debts of sin and for His help to extend forgiveness to others for their debt of sin against us.

Heavenly Father, forgive me for all my wrongs against You and I forgive all those who have wronged me.

If we start our day already forgiving others, we will be less likely to be offended by others. Words to live by.

February 28
Unconditional Love

Genuine unconditional love is attractive. It draws us in and lets us be ourselves. No pretenses, no masks, and no hiding. It has a way of removing all shame and forces us to stand taller.

Genuine unconditional love makes a person want to be their best, to strive to be the person that love sees them to be. We all know our own shortcomings, failures, and mistakes. We live with them and are reminded of them almost every day. The power of love can transform and set us free from the scars and hurts of our past.

The Bible states that God is love. It is His very nature. God demonstrated His love for us by sending His Son. Jesus declared that if we have seen Him, we have seen the Father. When we study the life of Jesus in the Bible, we find that He was full of compassion and love for others. We can trust Him to be the same with us.

He loves us unconditionally and is waiting for us to open our hearts to receive His love. Little by little God's love transforms us into people that love unconditionally also.

03
MARCH

March 1
"If My People, Who Are Called by My Name"

The battle is raging and it's time to take a stand. A former Pastor is declaring that the church is irrelevant when it uses 2000-year-old letters as its defense for morality. People are flocking to a movie that romanticizes sexual bondage in the name of love.

People, where are we headed and what kind of world are we setting up for future generations? We as a country are accepting evil as good and good as evil. We have become so desensitized to deviant behavior that we no longer object when it is flaunted right in front of us.

Not many years ago we were told that we must be tolerant and accepting of those around us that might be different from us, virtually no matter what. But recently that has escalated to pretty much requiring that every viewpoint be tolerated except Christianity.

That doesn't change our responsibility to stand for righteousness and to cry out to God for revival. God tells us exactly what to do: "If my people, which are called by my name, shall humble themselves, and pray, and seek my face, and turn from their wicked ways; then will I hear from heaven, and will forgive their sin, and will heal their land" (2 Chronicles 7:14 KJV).

We need to turn from our wicked ways and repent, and then ask God to heal our land. It's time to PRAY and keep praying until change happens or He returns. Those that have ears to hear let them hear what the Spirit is saying!

March 2
God Dependent

Transitioning from self-dependent to God dependent is no easy thing. We are taught from an early age to be responsible and to work hard. So, we set out in life trying to make a go of it. We stumble and fall, pick ourselves up again and keep going. We learn how to navigate life through trial and error, all the while trying our best not to mess it up too badly. We live under pressure to make wise choices for ourselves, our families and our future. This pressure robs us of the joy and happiness we constantly seek after.

God has a better way! He invites us to seek first His rule and His way. An invitation to become God dependent, trusting in Him to lead and guide us to the right opportunities. As we become more and more God dependent we are relieved of the pressure of having to figure it out.

We still have a responsibility to follow the path and work hard and to continually seek His purposes for our lives. As we become more God dependent, we find more joy and happiness rising from within as the fruit of the Spirit develop within us.

Are we trusting in our ability to earn, or in God's ability to provide? How God dependent are we?

March 3
Getting the Handle on Prayer

Keeping our motives on track when we pray is a lot easier said than done. If we are not careful prayer can become just a giant wish list of needs and wants.

The heart of prayer is about alignment and connection. We can live scattered lives of dependence on many things, and the tyranny of the urgent can pull us away from higher priorities. Prayer helps us to get re-aligned with God. When our cars are out of alignment, the result is unnecessary wear and tear on our vehicles. When we are not properly in line with God we experience added stress and wear and tear on our spirit, soul, and bodies.

We all need times to connect with our heavenly Father. To allow His presence to bring restoration to us. Connection with the Lord involves waiting in awareness of our dependence on Him: "they that wait upon the Lord shall renew their strength; they shall mount up with wings as eagles; they shall run, and not be weary; and they shall walk, and not faint" (Isaiah 40:31 KJV).

Waiting on God in prayer also brings peace, comfort, joy, and clarity. Clarity helps us to focus on what's important and let go of the things, that aren't. Then we can ask God for what we need. It's amazing when we have time to reflect and don't feel pressure, how our needs and wants change. Let's take time to be with Him before we lift up our prayer list and experience what prayer is really all about.

March 4
Heaven Is a Wonderful Place

"Heaven is a wonderful place, filled with glory and Grace, I want to be where my Savior is because heaven is a wonderful place, boom, boom, boom." A cute children's church song.

Do we live with an expectation of our eternal home? Romans 12 tells us not to be conformed to this world's way of living but instead to be transformed by the renewal of our minds to know what God's will is and what is good and acceptable and perfect.

Going to heaven should be an extension of how we live in this world. It will be an incredible upgrade but if we are living to bring heaven to earth then it shouldn't be too much of a change.

Heaven will be about living encapsulated in the presence of God and fulfilling our eternal purpose. On earth we can have experiences with the Holy Spirit that prepare us for forever. We can passionately pursue His presence here and now.

Is the lens through which we live our life shaped by the philosophies of this world or by the Word of God?

Are we living our lives to bring heaven to earth and experience more of God or just hanging on till we get to heaven?

Does the reality of heaven shape our choices and decisions? Just something to ponder.

March 5
Love Is a Choice

Do you realize that someone has chosen to love you?

It is easy to unconsciously believe that love is a feeling. People go around waiting for that feeling of love to hit them and send them into romantic blissfulness, like the mythical Cupid's arrow. The truth is feelings are fickle. They change. We can feel a love for something or someone today and lose that feeling tomorrow and even wonder what in the world we ever saw in it in the first place.

Christ-like love is more than just a feeling, it's a choice, a decision to love and keep loving.

God demonstrated that kind of love. Jesus, in the gospel of John, declares that we didn't choose Him, but He chose us. God chose to love us despite our failings, no matter where we are, or what is going on, He loves us unconditionally. It's hard to grasp that kind of love.

God has chosen and committed Himself to love us. When we feel down or alone, look up and know that we are loved.

March 6
What is Faith?

The word faith and trust are closely linked. "Now faith is the substance of things hoped for, the evidence of things not seen" (Hebrews 11:1 KJV).

Saying a person is faithful means they are trustworthy. When we make a deal, we say we dealt in good faith meaning each person was honest. When we loan money, we say we are taking them on faith that they will repay. When someone withholds truth in a venture, we say they dealt in bad faith.

When I enter my living room and sit in my chair, I am certain that it will hold me. I have no reason to question it. I know my chair. I'm experienced with my chair. I trust my chair. You can trust my chair to hold you, too. Some people can put more faith in a chair than they can muster to believe in Jesus as their Savior. When you read that Jesus said, "Let not your heart be troubled: ye believe in God, believe also in me" (John 14:1 KJV) trust Him in faith. Believe Him. Receive Him.

March 7
Freedom

Jesus has a lot to say about freedom.

Freedom means the ability to make choices and decisions without any internal or external constraints. Being free gives us the power to choose to do the right thing even when the right thing is difficult.

Jesus teaches us that true disciples will remain faithful to His teachings and that knowing the truth will set us free from slavery to sin. Paul teaches us in the book of Galatians that Christ has truly set us free and warns us not to get tied up in slavery to sin or the law. Through the power of the cross, Jesus has broken the power of sin in our lives and has released us into freedom.

If this is true, why do so many people walk in bondage to sin? If a slave has been set free but does not change his mind set, he will continually see himself as a slave even though he is free. We must grow in our understanding of freedom to walk in it. Growth is a partnership with the truth of God's word challenging us to put off the sinful practices of our flesh and learning how to be obedient to the truth.

As we walk in obedience to the truth, we will experience more freedom in our lives. Growth does not happen unless we are intentional.

Know the truth and the truth will make you free!

March 8
The Word of God

"If you have a Bible that's falling apart, you'll have a life that's not." Adrian Rogers (1931-2005) American preacher.

Jesus said, "Man shall not live by bread alone but by every word that proceeds from the mouth of God" (Matt 4:4 KJV).

Guinness World Records estimates that as of 2021, over five billion copies of the Bible have been sold, making it the best-selling book of all time.

Some years ago, I was going through a difficult period in my life, and someone shared a verse of scripture to encourage me. I was so discouraged that when I read the verse my immediate thought was "this is just words on a page." My very next thought was "you are right – until you put faith in those words on the page."

The Bible could be just a collection of archaic stories, rules, and cute religious sayings to you. However, if you apply a little faith, you just might find a God that is the answer to all you need.

The Bible has been a source of strength and encouragement to many whose life was falling apart. Spend some time reading it and see what it does for you.

March 9
In the Heat of the Battle

Every day is a struggle. A struggle to do the right things. A struggle not to be selfish. A struggle to believe the best of ourselves and others. A struggle to keep our words from hurting other people. It can feel like a battle.

Some live for the moment and don't really care about the consequences of their choices and decisions. However, I believe most people really want to be the best and do the right things.

The battle is real and can be exhausting. The Bible has an incredible promise that says, "And let us not be weary in well doing: for in due season we shall reap, if we faint not" (Galatians 6:9 KJV).

In the midst of the battle, if we keep going, there is a reward. God promises to be with us, sustain us and give us the spoils of victory for persevering.

If you find yourself struggling to stay on the right path, be patient. A new day is about to dawn, and the victory will be ours.

March 10
Eternal Beings

Parenting isn't for cowards. It's an awesome task when you think about the fact that you are raising an eternal being. We will all spend eternity either with God or apart from Him.

God gave us the ability to partner with Him in the creation of life, and the responsibility to raise children in a way that would point them in the direction of spending eternity with Him. We only know what was modeled for us and often we either repeat the mistakes of our parents or over correct and pass down a new set of problems to our kids.

Parenting isn't easy but we would do well to keep seeking knowledge and wisdom to do the best job possible. There are no guarantees, but if we shoot for raising not just good kids, but responsible adults, we will have done well.

Remember, kids need time with you – not stuff. Being there to listen to them and hear what's going on inside of them goes a long way in helping to achieve the desired results. We would do well not to confuse our children's need for parents with our desire for respect and admiration. We can be fooled into thinking our kids are following us when maybe it is because we give in to their wants and desires. If we haven't built a solid loving relationship with them, they will go their own way as soon as they can.

Eternity apart from God is the last thing I would want for my children. What will your legacy be?

March 11
Help Needed!

When God needs to get something done, He often looks for a man. In the Bible, He continually called and commissioned men into Kingdom service. Unfortunately, today most men have declined to get involved. In many churches, woman do the majority of the heavy lifting. Thank God for Godly women!

There is nothing more noble and heroic than for men to sacrifice for the good of their country, community, church, and family. The role of men in our society has come under attack for being controlling, aggressive, manipulative, or non-existent. It is time for a new breed of men to rise and take their rightful place in society.

This new breed of men is called, "The Godly Man." A Godly man lives his life seeking to serve his God. A Godly man loves, sacrifices, and serves those around him. A Godly man seeks to emulate the greatest man who ever lived, Jesus Christ.

If we want to see God restore a proper definition of masculinity, we need men to be better examples of what it is to be a man. No more hiding in plain sight, no more living selfishly, and no more dodging responsibility. Our families, churches and communities need men. God is calling.

March 12
Faith That Moves Mountains

"And He said to them, 'Because of your meager faith; for truly I say to you, if you have faith the size of a mustard seed, you will say to this mountain, 'Move from here to there,' and it will move; and nothing will be impossible for you" (Matthew 17:20 NASB).

This is amazing. It doesn't take great faith to pray and see figurative mountains moved in our lives and situations. So why don't we see great things happening in our lives?

The problem is we have belief but not much faith. We believe God can, but we don't have faith that He will. "Faith is to believe what you do not yet see; the reward for this faith is to see what you believe." St. Augustine (354 – 430 AD) Theologian.

Faith is taking hold of the promises that God gave us in His Word and not letting go of them until you see God move. If He made the promise, we can rest assured He will back His word. We need more Christians to be hungry to see God's Kingdom on earth as it is in Heaven.

It's just possible that God is waiting on us to start exercising our faith muscle instead of complaining about what God isn't doing. What promise of God are you putting faith to? I would love to see some mountains flying around. How about you?

March 13
Who He Really Is

We tend to define God based on our own perceptions and observations. When things don't line up with what we believe, we just move on and ignore the discrepancy.

When we allow people to be the definition of who God is, we are already in trouble. People make mistakes, they sin, and sometimes they are horrible representations of who God is. We have all heard stories of abusive parents that were Christians or elders in the church that failed in one way or the other. Who do we blame? God!

People walk away from God all the time because of something someone did. Some look at the problems around the world and blame God as if He created them. People look at the worst aspects of mankind and use it as an excuse to stay away from God.

God is best defined through the life and actions of Jesus. He came to help not condemn. He demonstrated unconditional love to all. He healed, delivered, relieved suffering, and forgave sinners.

God defines who God is and God is good and loving all the time.

Let us try and look past our own misconceptions of who God is and be challenged to find out who He really is!

March 14
Being Authentic

It has been said that first impressions are telling. I imagine that is true to some extent. But are those first impressions accurate? To really know if our first impressions about a person are accurate, we need to see that person in different environments over time.

It is easy to be a chameleon, adapting to whatever environment we find ourselves. One of the problems with being a chameleon is that we end up losing who we really are because we spend too much time being what we think we need to be to be accepted.

To be authentic, a person must be the same on the inside (attitudes and motivation), as their behavior and actions. The Bible tells us, not to be conformed or pressed into a mold but be transformed by the renewing of our mind. You can see the whole verse in Romans 12:2.

Conformity is looking the part without being the part. We can play nice but be full of rage and anger under the surface. Social media has created a picture-perfect world. People present their best self without having to be their best. Being authentic takes arduous work and honest assessment of ourselves.

As our world spins out of control, we need individuals to be authentic, especially Christians. As believers we must allow the Holy Spirit to help us be an authentic person. Being authentic and a person of integrity produces a healthier and happier life.

March 15
Humility

The secret to relationships is humility. Humility is not thinking less of yourself, it's not thinking of yourself at all. Humility is removing yourself from the relationship so that you can focus on the needs of others. Relationships can be destroyed through self-ishness and self-centeredness. People are driven away when we focus on our own needs and neglect theirs.

The key to getting our needs met is to follow the example of Jesus. Jesus demonstrated humility for us when He lowered Himself to come in the likeness of man and submit to death on the cross for all of mankind. He was God and could have thrown His weight around and wiped everyone out, but because of love, He humbled Himself and gave Himself up for others.

Whenever we forsake humility in our relationships, we are undermining the very thing we desire; to be loved and accepted. When we humbly focus our attention on others and seek to really know who they are as a person we give ourselves the opportunity to have a rich and full relational life.

March 16
Insatiable Hunger

We live in the land of plenty. We have everything we could possibly want at the tip of our fingers. One click, and it can be delivered by tomorrow. In our affluence we have satiated our hunger for more satisfying aspects of life. We substitute our desire for intimate relationships with surface social media interactions. Instead of eating healthy meals we eat unhealthy prepackaged microwaveable meals. We snack and nibble our way-out of our hunger pains and wonder why nothing ever satisfies.

We have grown accustomed to sacrificing the best for what seems good. We have lost our deep desire for life and God. We have sacrificed a relationship with God on the altar of religion. In the gospel of Matthew, we have the words of Jesus instructing us in the beatitudes. "Blessed are those who hunger and thirst for righteousness, for they will be satisfied" (Matthew 5:6 NASB).

Those that have a deep insatiable hunger and thirst for the King of righteousness and to see His righteousness fulfilled in our lives and world, shall have that hunger satisfied. To understand the passion of this verse we must understand the depth of hunger. Most of us do not know what it is to be desperate for food or water and so we do not comprehend the lengths we must go to for righteousness. We are easily satisfied with occasionally attending church, reading our Bible, or praying.

We need to get our insatiable hunger for God back!

March 17
Love Is Impossible Without God's Grace

Genuine love is the answer to most of the world's problems. It's that simple and that difficult. The best place to start is in our own hearts recognizing our utter inability to genuinely love others apart from total dependence on God's grace.

In Matthew, chapter 5, in the Sermon on the Mount, Jesus delivers a magnificent description of how God ideally wants His creation to treat one another. It's not normal. It's beautiful. It's glorious. It's challenging. It's impossible in our flesh. I encourage you to read this chapter and experience the awe of God's divine character and will. Be inspired.

In Matthew 5:43, Jesus touches on a part of the Old Testament law that teaches us to love our friend and then He mentions the unwritten companion misquote of that day that we are to hate our enemies. He deals with that head on and turns it all around saying we must love our enemies. What He says we should do is nothing like what our human nature wants to do. In fact, we cannot do what He asks relying only on our human nature. We need to rely on the abundant grace of God.

With God's grace and power, loving the unlovable is what God does through us. Yes, He can use us in this. He gives His best—the sun to warm and the rain to nourish—to everyone, the good and bad, the nice and the nasty. If all we do is love the lovable, do we expect a bonus? Anybody can do that. The bar has been set high to love others even as God has loved us in our worst moments and His grace empowers us to obey.

March 18
Time Stops For No One

Time keeps ticking onward, moving us into the future, forcing us to confront the unknown of our days. Most people hope for a better tomorrow not realizing that how we use our time today helps prepare for the future. Events and circumstances move us along in our day and we spend most of our time just reacting instead of being intentional. Time may pass but that doesn't mean that we have grown or developed.

Goals may be accomplished, and success achieved but has our time mattered? Did we discover the beauty of life all around us? Do we really know our spouse or are we just living together? Have the demands of life or just laziness caused us to drift apart?

Do we know our children or grandchildren? Are we so busy telling them what to do that we have no idea what they like to do?

How good a friend are we? Are we givers or takers in relationships? Do we bring life, love and laughter or do we suck the life out of people? Are we critical of others or an encourager? Does my relationship with God take priority in my life or does it even matter? Time is passing and soon it will be over. All of our success and achievements will matter little when we stand before God if there is no one standing with us. Do the people we love and that matter the most to us know it? The clock is ticking. Let's be intentional.

March 19
Heed the Warning

My people are destroyed for lack of knowledge. Since you have rejected knowledge, I also will reject you from being My priest.

Since you have forgotten the Law of your God, I also will forget your children" (Hosea 4:6 NASB).

God, through the prophet Hosea, issued a grave warning to His people in the Old Testament. Because they had abandoned God and His Word, God had no choice but to turn them over to their own desires and decisions.

God's blessings are still tied to obedience to His Word. If we walk away from His Word, then we forfeit God's blessings. The Bible also tells us that there is a way of living that seems right to mankind, but the end results lead to death.

We think we know the best way to live but it only leads to an empty and unfulfilled life. God issues this warning to bring us back to His Word and His ways so that He can bless us.

We are sliding down a slippery slope in America. We have left our spiritual roots and are walking away from God. It is time like never before to return to God and His Word. Our nation, communities and families are hanging in the balance.

March 20
Authenticity Is Still the Real Deal.

Anyone can sound good, but proof is always in the pudding. We can hide behind our social media accounts and be anything and anyone we want to be. But the reality is, we are who we are and given enough time our true character and motives expose us.

To be a genuine person of character takes hard work and a strong moral code. It has become way too easy to hide in our houses and become critics of everyone else but ourselves. It's necessary to take a good hard look in the mirror and ask ourselves if people see the real me or am I just putting on a show for approval.

Jesus Christ came to set us free but that can only happen if we are honest about ourselves. If we have to spend time telling everyone how good we are then we're probably not as good as we perceive ourselves to be.

The world doesn't need more Christians pretending to be holy and righteous. The world needs authentic, genuine Christians humbly loving and serving humanity. Humility begins before God and allowing Him to confront our hidden sins and transform us.

The acid test is this, who are you when nobody is looking and what comes out of you when life hits you hard? Just something to think about.

March 21
Who Do Men Say That I Am?

God. Such a big subject with so many ideas, opinions and philosophies concerning who He is.

He was asking His disciples, "Who do people say that the Son of Man is" (Matthew 16:13 NASB)? The disciples gave the Lord a variety of answers. Then He said to them, "But who do you yourselves say that I am" (Matthew 16:15 NASB)?

Jesus wanted to know who His disciples said He is. Jesus wants to know who we say He is. This is the biggest question of our lives.

Jesus has stood the test of time. Had He been crazy or a liar, He would have faded out like all the rest. Jesus is God in the flesh. If we want to know who God is, all we must do is study the life of Jesus. Jesus said, "The one who has seen Me has seen the Father" (John 14:9c NASB).

If our opinions and ideas don't line up with who Jesus is, then we must change our opinions and ideas.

God loves us and doesn't want us guessing as to who He is or what His motives are, so He came to show us. Once again, who do you say Jesus is? It really does matter.

March 22
Lovers

When we see and hear the word "lovers," we most often think of marriage intimacy. The term "lovers" is a more than that. Being lovers is supposed to be about being so wrapped up in the other person that you know what they are going to say before they say it. To know what their expression means and to be able to read their body language. It is a deep knowing of the other person so much so that there is communication without words. It is two people walking in unison in life and purpose.

When we think of God and our relationship with Him. we do not often use the term lovers because in our mixed up crazy, backwards world we think of marriage intimacy. God calls us His beloved and desires a deep intimate relationship. Again, we must change the definition of "lovers" in our head for this to make any sense. God wants to be known. Anyone desiring to know God must try to learn His ways, His movements on our heart, and discover His voice.

Religion kills intimacy because it becomes all about lists and duties. God never intended for our relationship to be formulaic and about must do's. From the beginning, God desired a people that would choose to love Him and walk with Him in a loving relationship sharing our hearts, hurts, dreams and desires. I used the term lovers to try and get across the depth of relationship God desires with each of us. Passion is the fuel of discovery. May you begin your journey of discovery. He loves you!

March 23
Genius

Albert Einstein comes to mind when we think of what it means to be a genius. Yet at a young age, his teacher sent him home with a sealed note to his mother saying he was not mentally capable of doing his schoolwork and could not return. His wise, loving mother kept the note to herself and educated him at home. He just went about things differently, as a genius will do.

We do that with ourselves and others. We judge ourselves by what we can't do or are not good at and let those facts define our lives. We were all created with unique talents and abilities to bring fulfillment and passion to our lives. Unfortunately, life has a way of taking us down roads we never intended and holds us captive to routines that rarely bring out who we were meant to be. For a few, it may seem like life worked out okay, but many are trapped in a life that brings little success or fulfillment.

Only God can help us recover the life that He intended for us. When we allow God to strip away the impression we have of ourselves based on the opinions of others or our own self-incriminating judgements, we just might begin to find out who we really are.

Easter is about bad news on Friday but great news on Sunday. God has a way of resurrecting lost dreams, identity, and purpose. This Easter discover God's amazing resurrection power for your own life and discover the genius in you.

March 24
Growth Must Be Intentional

As His church, we must be passionately, intentionally pursuing God through prayer, worship, reading and meditating on His Word, fellowship with believers, and being still in His presence. This is how we grow. These are disciplines of grace in becoming more Christ-like. At the same time, we trust God to help us break habits and remove or help us overcome obstacles that keep us from developing the disciplines that bring godly change and personal growth in our lives. We replace detrimental habits with godly, grace-filled routines. We ask the Holy Spirit to search our hearts and show us our hidden sins, bad attitudes, and wrong thinking. We acknowledge them and repent – we go the other way or come into agreement with God on a situation. Our repentance brings freedom to love others unconditionally and pursue being more like Jesus as we depend utterly on Jesus.

Growing in our relationship with Him puts us in a position to receive His love, give love to others, and be obedient to whatever He asks us to do. We are the body of Christ, and we must be committed to being connected to each other so that we can have a greater impact on each other, helping each other reach our fullest potential.

Change is inevitable but growth must be pursued.

March 25
No Fear

Fear is the devil's playground. The Bible tells us that the devil goes about as a roaring lion, seeking whom he may devour. The roar of a lion brings fear and terror to any who hear it, especially, if you are his next meal.

The enemy does his best to incite fear in the hearts of anyone he can. Fear paralyzes one into inaction and keeps us second guessing all our decisions. Fear keeps us up at night, afraid of what might happen next. The enemy uses circumstances to bring fear and once the door of fear is cracked open he comes flooding in with every kind of negative thought and dread.

The Bible encourages us with this truth, "There is no fear in love, but perfect love drives out fear, because fear involves punishment, and the one who fears is not perfected in love" (I John 4:18 NASB).

When fear starts to rise in us, we can turn to the one who is love and focus on Him. Difficult times are part of life, but fear is emotional energy that is usually wasted on what might happen. The love of God is real and tangible, and His promises bring hope.

During these coming days let's not let fear take over and drive us to decisions that are not rational. Let's be centered in the love of God and let His peace lead us.

March 26
Embracing Different

When is the last time you thought differently. We can get into ruts in our thinking. We think about the same old things over and over. Our lives are the sum total of our thoughts. Thoughts lead to decisions which lead to behaviors that lead to life patterns.

When is the last time you heard something, read something, watched something, said something or something was revealed in your devotional time with God that turned your world upside down? We spend too much time in mind numbing activities that cause us to continue the status quo. God blessed us with a mind for us to use to continually grow in our understanding of life and Godliness.

Too many minds have stagnated and slipped into a coma continuing to live Groundhog Day type of lives (living the same day over and over.) I can look back over my life and remember "aha!" moments that changed the way I saw and did life. It's time for another "aha!" experience. To encounter a new truth as revealed by God in any way of His choosing. To have a paradigm shift. To be stretched in our thinking.

There is too much to life to keep seeing it from the same old perspectives. What about you?

March 27
Let Go and Let Love Win

Control is an illusion. We think we have control over our lives and then some random, unplanned event destroys our world. We seek to control relationships so that we can get maximum love and support and minimal pain, only to discover no one likes to be controlled. We end up getting the one thing we feared, rejection.

We seek control of our physical bodies with diet and exercise only to find some insidious disease invade us and wreak havoc. We can have a death grip on life only to discover life is like catching oil; it slips from our grip.

At the end of the day, it's best to hold life loosely and roll with the hills and valleys that inevitably come. Control is self-centered and usually leaves a trail of brokenness, hurt and pain in our wake. We can learn from our Creator. He created us and then gave us free will to choose to accept His love or reject Him. He has all power and could dominate us with His will, but He doesn't. He lets us reap the rewards or consequences of our choices and actions.

So, let go of the illusion and set yourself and others free to discover the beauty of unconditional love.

March 28
The Church That Jesus Builds

Jesus said, "And I say also unto thee, that thou art Peter, and upon this rock I will build my church; and the gates of hell shall not prevail against it" (Matthew 16:18 KJV). The church of Jesus Christ has been under attack ever since Jesus uttered these words.

Unfortunately, the church is considered more and more irrelevant to modern culture, especially in America. "Many churches of all persuasions are hiring research agencies to poll neighborhoods, asking what kind of church they prefer. Then the local churches design themselves to fit the desires of the people. True faith in God that demands selflessness is being replaced by trendy religion that serves the selfish." Billy Graham (1918-2018) American evangelist. I wonder if that is what Jesus meant when He said, "I will build my church."

Mr. Graham also said, "God has given us two hands - one to receive with and the other to give with. We are not cisterns made for hoarding: we are channels made for sharing." God's church must turn outward to hurting humanity and bring living water to the lost and dying. "Give me one hundred preachers who fear nothing but sin and desire nothing but God, and I care not whether they be clergymen or laymen, they alone will shake the gates of hell and set up the kingdom of Heaven upon earth." John Wesley (1703-1791) English Evangelist.

That's the church Jesus desires to build. It's time to make it so!

March 29
Set Apart?

In America do we practice Biblical Christianity or cultural Christianity?

Biblical Christianity is a radical departure from societal and cultural norms. The Bible calls us to live set apart from the culture, to live differently than our neighbors. Biblical morality calls us to a higher standard of behavior.

Cultural Christianity is different. It teaches that we can believe what we want so long as we keep it to ourselves, and that Christians are to be tolerant of what others believe and practice. Those that believe or live differently than Biblical Christianity can declare their opinions from the rooftops. But proclaiming Biblical truths can get you vilified with impunity for the acuser.

Biblical Christianity isn't tolerant. We are to love at all times, even those with whom we disagree. But that doesn't mean that we keep quiet when they contradict scripture. Cultural Christianity blends into the culture and doesn't distinguish itself from other beliefs. Biblical Christianity tells us that we are a light set on a hill to draw others to Jesus Christ.

Are we blending in or shining bright? It's time to examine ourselves and determine if we have compromised the truth of scripture and have allowed the culture to determine how we live. God calls us to be set apart. Are we?

March 30
Love

"What does love look like? It has the hands to help others. It has the feet to hasten to the poor and needy. It has eyes to see misery and want. It has the ears to hear the sighs and sorrows of men. That is what love looks like." Saint Augustine (354-430 AD) Theologian.

Everyone is looking for it but so few know how to give it. Love is a human need that must be both received and given. The essence of love is to focus on the other person and what is in their best interest. Selfishness destroys love because it seeks its own desires and pleasure.

We must be retrained by the Holy Spirit in our ability to love others and give everything we are for the betterment of those around us. Love means sacrifice and letting go of what we want. Love is letting go. Control, guilt, and manipulation are tools we use to get people to do what we want them to do instead letting them make their own choices. Such tactics are not love.

The Bible has a lot to say about love. The whole chapter of 1 Corinthians 13 describes what love is to look like. Jesus said that the world would know that we are His disciples by the way we love one another.

How do you think the church measures up to that standard? We must be connected to and dependent upon God who is the source of Love to be transformed in our ability to give love that is not tainted by selfishness.

March 31
Keeping Our Eyes on the Lord

Our modern lives are complicated. One of the casualties is focus. Experts in fields of personal success and health emphasize the importance of maintaining focus to attain a desired outcome. Part of the need is pure physiology. We can't appropriately learn or discern if we are not focused.

It was the same in Jesus's earthly lifetime. The disciples were out in the middle of the sea of Galilee fighting the waves and getting nowhere.

Suddenly they saw Jesus come walking on the water to check on them. Amazed, Peter jumped up and called out to the Lord asking if he could walk on the water with Jesus. Peter stepped out and started walking. Poor guy did not last long before he took his eyes off the Lord, and looking around at the sea he became overwhelmed and began to sink. Jesus caught him and pulled him up and into the boat.

Isn't it wonderful that even today, when we lose our focus and take our eyes off the Lord, He reaches out and puts us back into the boat? What a Savior. Keeping our eyes on Jesus through all sorts of waves of life keeps our focus right where it belongs.

04
APRIL

April 1
The Cross of Easter

The cross is called "the emblem of suffering and shame" in the beloved hymn, "The Old Rugged Cross," written in 1912 by George Bennard (1873-1958) American hymn composer.

Today we celebrate the resurrection of Jesus Christ. However, there would be no resurrection if He hadn't willingly gone to the cross for your sins and mine. Jesus took the punishment we deserve to redeem us back to God. He suffered for our shame.

We can attempt to convince ourselves that we are okay and don't need a savior but down deep in our souls we know we are not as good as we try to tell ourselves. We all have sinned or fallen short of our own expectations and not lived up to our own standards of right and wrong. What makes us think we could measure up to God's standard and come out unscathed?

It's quite simple really. God so loved the world that Jesus willingly surrendered His earthly life to be our substitute in taking God's punishment for our mistakes and wrongdoings. As a result we get pardoned and receive God's forgiveness so that we can begin to live an eternal life here and now in communion with God. It's a free gift. We don't have to do anything to earn it, all we must do is receive it by believing in the one who died for us, and confess with our mouth that Jesus is Lord. When we, by faith, receive Jesus, we are told that we get the same power that raised Jesus from the dead to help us to live a holy and Godly life. Good News indeed. Happy Easter!

April 2
The "One Anothers" of a Significant Life

Marriage, babies, funerals. The cycle of life. Our time on earth is but a fleeting mist as the Bible points out in James 4:14. Yet, we get so caught up in our lives as if our life is the only thing that matters. What makes a life significant? It's not the amount of money we make. It's not how smart we are.

What makes a life significant is how well we love one another.

God knows how naturally selfish we are, so He instructs us in His word how important it is to Him and how beneficial it is to us that we treat each other as He wills. There are over fifty "one another" commands throughout the New Testament all of which are grounded in love because just doing them without love would have little impact and, in a few cases, could have negative impact. Here is a sample of what we are to practice unto one another: We are to overarchingly love, forgive, pray for, encourage, teach, admonish, be at peace with, show hospitality toward, have fellowship with, live harmoniously with, bear with, bear with the burdens of, agree with, welcome, greet, honor, comfort, care for, build up, exhort, instruct, sing with, stir up to good works, serve, do good toward, and be humble toward. Let's live significantly.

Love well and pass it on.

April 3
Transformation

The Bible tells us not to allow the world to bring us into conformity with its ways, philosophies, and values. Rather, we are to allow the Spirit of God to transform our thinking so that we align ourselves with God's ways, purposes values. Our word transform is from the Greek word metamorphosis which means a change of the form or nature of a thing or person into a completely different one, by natural or supernatural means.

Transformation for the Christian is a supernatural experience through revelation that comes by way of God's word and God's Spirit within us.

We do not have the power to change our nature through willpower, self-help books, or good old fashioned hard work. We might be able to conform our behavior to reach a goal or reach a certain desired outcome, but we cannot change our inward desires to satisfy our cravings.

As we spend time with God and His Word, a supernatural phenomenon transpires, and we find ourselves with different desires, habits, and attitudes. We often get discouraged by the lack of change in our lives and fail to see the connection between our efforts and trusting God to do the work in us. If we try doing it our way, God will let us. It is usually out of frustration that we try God's way. Transformation is possible even in the most troublesome patterns and habits. Call out to God and let Him do what He does best. Miracles are waiting to happen.

April 4
Blame Game

"If you could kick the person in the pants responsible for most of your trouble, you wouldn't sit for a month." Theodore Roosevelt (1858-1919) The 26th US President.

It's so much easier to blame others than to take responsibility.

Last week we celebrated the resurrection of Jesus. Can you imagine, after being raised from the dead, Jesus going around complaining and blaming everyone for the mistreatment He received? He could have come out of the grave angry and ready to do some damage. Isn't that a person's typical response? We even blame or hurt others for the mistakes we have committed.

If we are going to be successful in life, we need to take responsibility for the way life is going for us and look for ways to make things better. Jesus offers us a way out of our circumstances, but He very rarely does it for us. We must partner with Him and give Him opportunity to show us where we need to change. That's right, change. We are usually the culprit of our own unhappiness. It may take months and years for change to happen, but change will never happen if we don't start. And it will never happen by blaming and hurting others.

Follow the example that Jesus left us. Don't let death have the final say. With God nothing is impossible.

April 5
The Unexpected

Dead usually means D-E-A-D. No more life. The final curtain. A permanent "hasta la vista." Unless of course you believe in the zombie apocalypse. We do not!

The wild ride the apostles had been on came to a screeching halt when Jesus was put to death. Three and a half years earlier, Jesus had started gathering disciples, choosing twelve to come and be closely with Him. They had seen the dead raised to life, many people healed, and the demon possessed set free. Jesus had at one time fed over 5,000 with two fish and five loaves of bread; who does that? Once, they were all in a boat when a storm broke out. They were taking on water and Jesus was asleep in the back of the boat. Jesus woke up and rebuked the wind and the sea and it all calmed down. Jesus taught like no other and had authority never seen before. And now He was gone. Murdered by the religious leaders because of their jealousy. The disciples took his body and laid it in a tomb. Then the unexpected happened. Three days later He was alive and visiting His disciples. The disciples had a front row seat into the greatest man who had ever walked the face of this earth and yet they were completely shocked at what had taken place.

Life has a way of killing our hopes and dreams. If you give God a chance, He just might do the unexpected in your life as well. All it takes is a little faith!

April 6
God's Thoughts

"For my thoughts are not your thoughts, neither are your ways my ways, saith the Lord. For as the heavens are higher than the earth, so are my ways higher than your ways, and my thoughts than your thoughts" (Isaiah 55:8-9 KJV).

Isaiah tells us that God's thoughts and ways are not like ours. However, that does not mean that the Lord's thoughts and ways can't be known to a great degree. God has given us His Word and Spirit to assist us in discerning His thoughts and ways.

The Berean Church in the New Testament is praised for their dedication to search scripture for its wisdom. "These were more noble than those in Thessalonica, in that they received the word with all readiness of mind, and searched the scriptures daily, whether those things were so" (Acts 17:11 KJV).

Proverbs tells us to mine for the gold of God's wisdom in the Bible: "Make your ear attentive to wisdom; Incline your heart to understanding. For if you cry out for insight And raise your voice for understanding; If you seek her as silver And search for her as for hidden treasures; Then you will understand the fear of the Lord, And discover the knowledge of God. For the Lord gives wisdom; From His mouth come knowledge and understanding" (Proverbs 2:2-6 NASB).

He's given us everything we need. He's waiting for us to search it out. Are you?

April 7
Relief Versus Restoration

"Do what you can, with what you have, where you are." Theodore Roosevelt (1858-1919) The 26th president of the US.

There are points in our lives when our routines experience unwelcome, even frightening change. The Covid pandemic was one of those times on a national and international scale. Many of us did what we could with what we had where we were.

At such times, we must learn to make and accept a new normal even though we want our old normal back, and even though we may not have been all that happy with the old normal.

We need to learn how to find restoration, not just relief. Relief is temporary. It gets us by, but not for the long-term, or maybe not even in a healthy way. Restoration takes time. It takes stillness. It takes finding your unique off switch.

Take a moment to read the 23rd chapter of Psalms in your Bible. It gives us a picture of our Lord as our shepherd taking care of us. It paints a picturesque scene of God with us, leading us to places of rest and renewing our strength. It's there waiting for us.

If you haven't worked into your schedule some quiet time with God, there is no time like the present to get started.

Change happens slowly over time. Relief is an escape, not an answer. Restoration takes time but will be worth the effort.

April 8
He Is Risen

At Easter we celebrate the greatest event in human history. Easter is about the resurrection of our Lord and Savior Jesus Christ. He defeated Satan, sin, and death. His body was beaten and broken and then He suffered a horrible, agonizing death.

He suffered public humiliation and died on a cross taking our punishment for our crimes against a Holy God. He did all that so that we could be free from the tyranny of our sinful nature and to restore hope for the human condition. Then, He rose from the dead three days later. He overcame sin and death for us.

His death and resurrection opened the door for all to experience the life that God intended when He created us so that the brokenness of this world would no longer dominate our existence. And so that we could live a life above the frailty and difficulty that characterizes so much of our daily lives including the hurts, pains, strongholds, the addictions we can't seem to break, the injustices that happen to us, sickness, disease, the failures, and the disappointments that can all be swallowed up in His death.

God makes available to us the same resurrection power to give us a new beginning, to bring life where there is death. All of this is possible by doing one simple thing. Believing it! Believing is more than mental acknowledgment; it's staking your life on it.

April 9
Living Large

It's time to break free from anchors of self-dependence that keep us from arriving at exciting God dependent destinations. The Lord's teaching on the ways of His kingdom introduces new thoughts on how to live. The way of the kingdom is so foreign to our way of doing life, that our first reaction is to disregard His teachings, thereby, keeping us anchored in shallow waters.

In the gospel of Matthew, Jesus starts out by saying our lives will be blessed or full of joy. Joy comes to the person that chooses to adhere to the attitudes that the Lord is introducing. The first correction in our attitudes about life is to reject our need for self-sufficiency and self-reliance. Jesus tells us that joy will be produced in us when we give up our need for control and put our dependence in God.

The instruction to be "poor in spirit" is an attitude that brings us face to face with our pride and independence. Jesus knows that to be successful in the Kingdom of God we must become completely dependent on God for everything. It doesn't matter how much money you have accumulated; dependence is an attitude not a condition. Jesus states that when we learn to be dependent on God, all of Heaven's resources are made available to us, and that's when we really begin to live. Self-reliance is an anchor that keeps us from discovering all that God has for us.

April 10
Live Unto the Lord alone

One of my favorite sayings is:

We would worry far less about what other people think of us if we realized how seldom they do.

We can spend a great deal of time worrying about other people's opinions of us or trying to get their approval. We can't let fear disable us into paralysis. We should live for the approval of One. God has given us life and purpose. He thinks of us constantly:

"Many, Lord my God, are the wonders which You have done, and Your thoughts toward us, there is no one to compare with You. If I would declare and speak of them, they would be too numerous to count" (Psalm 40:5 NASB).

God knows everything about you and still loves you. He has been thinking about you since before the world began. He knew exactly who you would be and every decision you would make. We cannot let our past dictate our future. God sure does not. It is up to you to think like God thinks concerning you. Do not worry about what others say or think about you. Spend some time in prayer asking God for His thoughts about you. You might be surprised at what He might say. Live unto the Lord alone.

April 11
"Jesus Lives"

When all hope seems lost, Jesus Lives.

When life is going crazy and doesn't make sense, Jesus Lives.

When we've fallen and can't seem to find our way back, Jesus Lives.

When we find ourselves going through the motions of doing life, Jesus Lives.

When we are lost with no sense of direction, Jesus Lives.

Last week we celebrated Easter and the resurrection of Jesus Christ. What that means for you and me is that nothing could hold him down. Jesus told His disciples that in this world we would have difficulties and hardships, but we could be happy because Jesus has overcome the world. The world threw it's meanest, toughest, and cruelest hate and anger at Him and thought it had won. Three days later Jesus Lives.

No matter where we find ourselves, we can cry out to Jesus and know that He will answer. How do we know He will answer? Because He Lives. Don't let despair, hopelessness, anger, bitterness, boredom, fear, loneliness, or confusion reign.

Let Jesus in, and He will walk you through the valley of the shadow of death into everlasting life. Good news my friend, Jesus Lives.

April 12
Call Out to Jesus

Life doesn't always go as planned. Unexpected changes and events can cause disruptions in our daily routines.

How we deal with these changes can determine our quality of life. The Bible tells us that God is a very present help in the time of trouble. When things seem to be falling apart, we can count on God to be there with us and be our source of help.

We complain when we must go through hardship and difficulty wondering that if God really cared He would have stopped it from happening. Life is difficult and God only gets involved where He is invited, even then we don't always see the why from our perspective and get mad at God.

God promises that if we call out to Him, He will hear from Heaven. Things don't always change immediately but what can change is our attitude as we go through it. God can give us a peace that whatever we are going through is not the end of the story. Whatever circumstances you may find yourself in today, look up and call out to Him. You might be surprised at the results.

April 13
Walking the Walk

"Let your light so shine before men, that they may see your good works, and glorify your Father which is in heaven" (Matthew 5:16 KJV).

We have a job to do, and we are supposed to do it at such a high standard that it blows people away and they remark that it must be God. How do we let our light shine? And what is the light that should be shining? Is the light something good within ourselves that we share with the world around us?

The human capacity to do good is something within all of us. The problem is we live in a body of flesh and have a nature that is dominated by pride and self-centeredness. The light that should radiate through us is the character and nature of Jesus. It shines when we see the needs around us and don't look the other way. It shines when I'm dog tired but when my kids or grandkids need help, and I don't shut them down. We have choices every day to let the light of Jesus shine through us as we interact with the people around us. Do your actions and words prove you are a follower of Jesus?

April 14
Fear Not

No greater words were ever spoken. They are repeated over one hundred times in the Bible. God's word encourages us not to let fear dictate our lives or our responses to any circumstances that crash in upon us.

"Fear thou not; for I am with thee, be not dismayed; for I am thy God: I will strengthen thee; yea, I will help thee; yea, I will uphold thee with the right hand of my righteousness" (Isaiah 41:10 KJV). We have God's promise to be with us in those seasons that would cause us to fear or be discouraged. He reminds us, who we belong to, and He promises to give us strength to walk through the difficulty. He reassures us with His help and supports us with His mighty and victorious right hand.

What an incredible promise, as we navigate the turbulent waters of our lives. We are accustomed to focus on our problems and complain how unfair life can be at times. God reminds us to change the way we think and focus on His ability and not allow fear to rob us of our victory. Fear is disabling and can lead to hopelessness which causes a fatalistic outlook.

When we take the Word of God and meditate on His promises, faith and hope begin to wash over us. As our minds clear, we can see and think differently. Today let us declare with faith, that fear will not take hold, for we serve a God that does not abandon us but gives us strength in all circumstances to be victorious. Fear Not!

April 15
There Is Power, Power, Wonder Working Power

What do you do when you don't know what to do? Jesus Christ is more than a name that is used when one is frustrated at someone or something. There is power in the name of Jesus. One of the ten commandments is not to use the name of the Lord in vain or make His name common. Is it possible that we have so trivialized His name that it no longer holds power for us? Oh, do not mistake what I'm saying. God has not lost His power to do what He said He would do. It's that we have made His name so insignificant, that we have lost faith in calling upon His name.

God promised that when we call out to Him, He would hear from heaven and would respond. Jesus told us that we could use His name to carry out His purpose on earth. When you don't know what to do; begin to call on the name of Jesus, begin to ask and to seek. "Call unto me, and I will answer thee, and show thee great and mighty things, which thou knowest not" (Jeremiah 33:3 KJV).

When we use His name, we have His attention, and He desires to interact with us. Let us restore the reverence for His name and come to Him expecting Him to answer. There is power in His name.

April 16
Do Not Settle for Being "Good Enough."

It is easy to become complacent with being "good enough." Life can be challenging and sometimes the effort to be above average is too big of a price to pay, so we settle for "good enough." To be successful at any endeavor requires maximum effort. To have a successful marriage, to raise your children to be well adjusted, productive adults requires time, energy, and a whole lot of patience. It is easy to put in half the effort and be "good enough."

To grow spiritually requires a sacrifice of time, energy, and discipline. It is much easier to look around and compare ourselves to other Christians and think we are "good enough." We will not be held to a "good enough" standard by our Creator. He will measure us based on how well we used the gifts, talents, and abilities He gifted us with.

Jesus tells a story about a rich man who called his servants and distributed to them a sum of money to invest and at some point, He would call them to account for how they used His money. Jesus was talking to us. We can make all kinds of excuses about why we did not give it our best efforts and why we settled for being "good enough." Life is too short, and our relationships are too precious to give them a "good enough" attitude. Let us work to bring our best effort into all that we do and let our lives be a praise to God for all the blessings that He has given us.

Do not settle for "good enough!"

April 17
I'm Third

When I was but a boy I read an autobiography about Gale Sayers. Gale Sayers (1943-2020) was a Hall of Fame football player. The title of the book was "I am Third." Gale Sayer's priorities were God first, others second, and I am third. Reading that book began the process in me of realizing that it's not all about me. It's not something that's easy to live out but if God is going to use me, I must make sure that I am third.

April 18
Because of Jesus We Can Face Tomorrow

Hope is having an optimistic expectation of a better tomorrow. Whatever challenges we may be facing today we can have hope of something better in the future. What is the basis of our hope? Is there something we can count on to ensure a better tomorrow?

Because Jesus rose from the grave, because death could not hold Him, He is alive and with us facing everything in life with us. We have hope that, because Jesus triumphed over all that hell and this world could throw at Him, and because He promises to be with us, then we can be victorious in Him as well.

Jesus promised us that no matter what tribulation we may go through, we can be of good cheer because He has overcome the world. Jesus keeps His promises.

Our hope is not in government, political activism, money, power, education, or status. Our hope is in Jesus Christ. Putting our faith in the one who died for us can give us courage to face all of life's struggles.

An opportunity for new life to begin may be revealed when thigs seem to be fading or dying. Don't faint in the day of adversity but look up for your redemption is drawing closer. He Lives so that we can too!

April 19
Believing Versus Knowing

Believing means that you have accepted something as being true. Knowing means that you have knowledge through experience that something is true. I believe that my car can go 120 mph because the speedometer has a marking at 120 mph. I know that my car goes 120 mph because I have experienced it going 120 mph.

We can believe God is loving, kind, compassionate, gracious, and merciful because His Word tells us that He is those things whether or not we are aware of having ever personally experienced them. God desires to have a personal relationship with His children and through that relationship we can knowingly experience all those attributes of God.

Economic turndowns, lawlessness, political upheaval, and turmoil can have us questioning our future and worrying whether things will return to normal. It is good to believe in God and that He holds the future. But let's come to know it personally. Let's be careful not to allow our believing to turn into mere wishful thinking and wishful hoping. Believing is good but God wants us to know and trust Him based on our experiences with Him.

The Bible tells us that He is the same yesterday, today and tomorrow. He was faithful in the past and He will be faithful in the future. Turn your believing into knowing and wait with anticipation at all the good things that God will do through this season of our lives.

April 20
Let Love Transform Us

Life sends many messages to us about who we are and who we are not. It starts in grade school and is reinforced throughout our life. If we have been deemed worthy of adulation and praise by our peers or those in authority, then life takes an upward path. If we have been deemed unworthy to receive the accolades for our efforts, then life takes a path of survival.

We can spend a lot of time trying either to prove everyone wrong or prove them right. We compensate by looking to things to give our life meaning and worth. The Bible tells us that the Father's love is unconditional. By His love He heals our damaged self-worth and personal identity. Value and identity come from knowing we were created in the image of God and that He determined our worth by dying for us. We are transformed when we allow His love to penetrate our heart. We are then faced with the dilemma of having to choose between what we have believed all our lives or the truth of His overwhelming audacious love.

We don't have to prove ourselves when we know that we have been truly accepted with no strings attached and knowing that truth redeems our life from the destructive powers of this world, restoring us to live our lives to the fullest of our potential.

April 21
Life Overflowing

Jesus said that He came so that we might have life – not just be alive – but have a life overflowing. The American dream and a life overflowing are not one and the same. Material possessions and leisure are signs of success in obtaining the American Dream. Jesus modeled life overflowing in selfless, loving acts of service to others and in godly contentment.

Jesus stands at the door of our heart and knocks because He wants to come in and work from the inside out. He wants to heal hurts, and change motives and attitudes that affect our overflowing life. He changes us from the inside so that circumstances and difficulties don't destroy our joy, happiness, peace, love, contentment, and passion for living.

The American dream has become about getting. Jesus is about really living. Which are you chasing after?

April 22
Keeping the Main Thing the Main Thing

We live in a time when multi-tasking and packed schedules are the norm. Juggling duties and responsibilities isn't just an optional skill anymore; it is a requirement. Life is pulling us in different directions with all its demands taking a toll on us mentally and physically. Is this the life that God designed for us?

A long time ago, when things were not going so well, and I was frantically trying to find answers, I had a very clear impression. It was a statement that went through my mind. The statement was this, "I cannot bless anything that takes you away from Me." I knew that it was a God thought.

In our harried and hurried life, we are missing out on the blessings that God has for us because we are too busy for Him. In Psalm 27 David cried out that the one thing he wanted more than anything else was to dwell in the house of the Lord forever.

David knew God is the main thing. Where does God sit on our priority list? Is He the first thing to go when life has us spinning so many plates that we can't keep up? How would life be different if we made the main thing the main thing and moved God to the top of our priorities? What things would we need to cut out of our lives to keep Him number one? Something to think about.

April 23
Only God

Only God! Who can change a life, turn hopelessness into possibilities, and take broken families and restore love and unity? Only God!

Today we celebrate the ultimate Good News. He who once was dead is now alive. He sits at the right hand of the Father ruling and reigning as the Son of God.

What does that mean for you and me? It means death is no longer scary, life has purpose and meaning, and no matter how bad things may look, God is bigger.

Jesus's followers were scattered and confused at the turn of events they never saw coming even though He forewarned them many times. Their whole world came crashing down in front of them. They didn't realize it was the beginning of what God had in store for all of them.

Sometimes we are given devastating news, or things fall apart, no matter how hard we try. The Good News is that the end might just be a new beginning. The key is to look up and trust that the same power that raised Jesus from the dead is available to take our broken lives and dreams and breathe new life into them. Only God!

April 24
Amazing Grace – The Message of the Cross and the Forgiveness of Our Sins.

"Amazing grace! How sweet the sound. That saved a wretch like me. I once was lost, but now am found, was blind but now I see. 'Twas grace that taught my heart to fear, and grace my fears relieved. How precious did that grace appear. The hour I first believed! The Lord hath promised good to me. His word my hope secures. He will my shield and portion be. As long as life endures. When we've been there ten thousand years, bright shining as the sun, we've no less days to sing God's praise than when we first begun." Written in 1772 by John Newton. Amazing Grace is considered the most popular hymn of all time.

The message of the cross and the forgiveness of our sins, is all because of the amazing grace of God. The Resurrection of Jesus is the power to restore our broken lives and give us a reason to keep going. Because of grace we are found and promised good. We can have confidence in a Savior who has conquered death, hell, and the grave to see us through the most difficult seasons of our lives. When God gives us His grace to see past ourselves, we can see the beautiful story of His love and redemption. It takes a little faith on our part to receive and accept the gift of His forgiveness. This Easter will you pause and look at the greatest act of love in all of humanity with fresh faith-filled eyes and receive His redeeming act of mercy and grace? Ask Him to forgive you and to fill your life with His love. It is as simple as that.

April 25
A Dose of God's Medicine

Recently I was at my granddaughter's 7th birthday party. As I sat back and watched the kids run around, laugh and play I was reminded of the words of Jesus, "Truly I say to you, unless you change and become like children, you will not enter the kingdom of heaven" (Matthew 18:3 NASB).

Religion has a way of draining joy and laughter from those that seek to keep their behavior from breaking any of God's rules. There is a proverb that states that "a cheerful heart is good medicine." Has our view of God become so warped that we don't think that God laughs or smiles? The Bible tells us to rejoice and to count it all joy, to be thankful, and to celebrate.

If God wanted us to have sour dispositions, I think Jesus would have instructed us to quit acting like children. It makes God happy when we are laughing and enjoying life. Let's take time this Sabbath to take a dose of God's medicine and laugh – out loud even. God has a sense of humor, just look at some of His creation and I'm not talking about your neighbors.

April 26
Be Not Conformed

The pressure not to stand out can be crippling. Most people do not want to be a cookie cutter copy of everyone else and yet end up looking like everyone else. Even our attempts to be wild and crazy end up looking like everyone else's attempt to be wild and crazy. It can be clothes, hair, or tattoos, but it looks like everyone else.

God made us all special and unique in our looks, personality, talents, and abilities but we spend most of our lives trying to blend into the crowd. Instead of using our voice to speak truth about our opinions and beliefs, we hold back for fear of rejection or ridicule. Instead of being friendly and outgoing, wanting to meet and learn the history of people in our sphere of life, we shrink back into isolation and build walls of comfort and protection. Instead of taking risks and trying new adventures we stay in the same old predictable patterns.

We have been shaped and molded by our painful experiences in life. They have taught us to conform to people's expectations and in the process, we have lost our created uniqueness. We were formed with a purpose in mind. Do not allow the world to press us into its version of us. Let's discover who God created us to be and break out of the patterns of living that keep us from experiencing life to the fullest. The pathway of discovery starts and ends with our Creator. Letting ourselves be known is a risk that must be taken if we are going to find contentment and fulfillment in this life. Let's begin the journey now.

April 27
Three Ingredients

In the love chapter of the Bible, I Corinthians 13, we find the three essential ingredients desired by all of humanity: faith, hope, and love. The greatest of these is love. When we are faithless, hopeless, and feeling unloved, life is unbearable, depressing, and not worth living.

Having faith means we have put our trust and belief in someone greater than ourselves. Hope is knowing that there is a better tomorrow coming and we can endure whatever hardship we are facing. Love describes our God who is loving, kind, and compassionate. To be loved and to love makes life worth living.

When the winds of adversity are blowing, and it seems like our lives are about to be shipwrecked, we can either listen to ourselves or preach to ourselves. We are just listening to ourselves when we allow fear and anxiety to rob us of faith, hope, and love. But we preach to ourselves when we focus on Jesus, the one in Whom we have believed. We allow hope to arise in us because we know Who holds the future. We meditate on the truth that we are loved by the one who created all things. We preach faith, hope, and love to ourselves through our Lord Jesus.

When we preach to ourselves, the peace of God that passes understanding begins to flood our minds. Then our emotions begin to align with our thoughts. Soon we find strength to keep going. We can meditate on the circumstances or allow faith, hope and love to bring us nourishment for our souls.

April 28
The Resurrection

Easter and the Resurrection of Christ give us proof that with God nothing is over until it's over and even then, it's not over.

Paul in his letter to the church at Corinth writes, "But as it is written, eye hath not seen, nor ear heard, neither have entered into the heart of man, the things which God hath prepared for them that love Him" (1 Corinthians 2:9 KJV).

God demonstrated His ability to take the most final human condition and reverse it.

We are incapable of comprehending what a good God could do for us with His imagination and power. Let's love Him and find out.

April 29
The Value of Wisdom

Knowledge can be free, but wisdom comes with a price. The price is effort and a desire to please God, and in all honesty, may involve trials. Knowledge is information. Wisdom is acquiring the skill to do the right thing at the right time in the right way with the right motive.

We have access to information all around us. We can Internet search anything and get knowledge. We can learn from the success and mistakes in our life situations. But actual wisdom isn't always gained in that process. People can keep making the same dumb mistakes and never learn from them and never gain wisdom. Keep reading to see that it doesn't have to be that way.

All through scripture we see that God places a premium on wisdom. There is no question that He wants us to be wise and walk with the wise. If we want to be successful in life, it's important to keep learning new things. But it's imperative to gain wisdom. Wisdom keeps us from making the mistake in the first place and sets us up to do the right thing in all circumstances.

We have God's promise to give us wisdom by asking Him for it: "But if any of you lacks wisdom, let him ask of God, who gives to all generously and without reproach, and it will be given to him" (James 1:5 NASB). God will answer that prayer no matter how many times we ask, and He will not get annoyed with us for asking. He will see us through the working out of our gaining that wisdom which may involve enduring trials. He will not abandon us and the wisdom we gain is worth its cost.

April 30
Resurrection Sunday

What has died in your life? An opportunity or a youthful dream? A once promising life or a marriage? Life has a way of stripping us of hope and it can knock us to our knees. The disciples of Jesus had the wind knocked out of them when they saw everything they believed and hoped in being crucified.

Jesus tried to get them to understand what was going to happen, but they never could grasp the reality of it until it was slapping them in the face. Jesus had brought more life to them over the last three and half years than they had experienced up to that point in their adult lives. He spoke truth and did miracles. There was something in the way He interacted with them that caused them to see life from new perspectives.

All of that was lost as they watched Him being carried away to be crucified. In their despair they deserted Him and were left to try to figure out the rest of their lives.

Here's the rest of the story. What seemed dead on Friday came roaring back to life on the news of His resurrection on Sunday. Jesus was ALIVE. They ran to the tomb and discovered it empty. Jesus revealed Himself to the disciples, even to the one that doubted. Here is the Good News, my friend: we can bring the dead areas of our lives to Jesus, so that He can resurrect them. Just as the disciples had to believe it, so must we. Give Him the opportunity to bring resurrection power to your situations. Happy Easter.

05
MAY

May 1
Living Water

"Now on the last day, the great day of the feast, Jesus stood and cried out, saying, 'If anyone is thirsty, let him come to Me and drink. The one who believes in Me, as the Scripture said, 'From his innermost being will flow rivers of living water.' But this He said in reference to the Spirit, whom those who believed in Him were to receive; for the Spirit was not yet given, because Jesus was not yet glorified" (John 7:37-39 NASB).

We all need living water that will quench the deep thirst of our souls. It can only be found in Jesus Christ who will give us rivers of it.

We must come to Him thirsting and wanting Him to fill us. Does it seem impossible that such a simple desire and request can lead to deep fulfillment and satisfaction? We will never know unless we simply ask Him. Draw near to Him and spend time pursuing Jesus through worship, reading His Word, and the fellowship of other believers. We come to Jesus in faith trusting that what He offers to us, He will give us.

If you find yourself spiritually parched and thirsting allow the One that gives living water by the rivers-full to fill you and make you whole.,

May 2
Reputation and Character

"I hope I shall possess firmness and virtue enough to maintain what I consider the most enviable of all titles, the character of an honest man." George Washington (1732-1799) Our Nation's first President.

Our reputation is what others think of us. Our character is who we really are. Congruity is when both are one and the same. Our nation's Founding President, George Washington, valued and actively pursued the development of his character. That has never been an easy thing, but in our culture today, we are swimming against the tide if we do the same. Today's culture values wealth, possessions, and happiness more than character.

"But godliness with contentment is great gain" (1 Timothy 6:6 KJV). Wealth, possessions, and happiness are good things. How they are obtained is key. They can be the byproduct of doing right things. But they can also be pursued as the main thing. When that happens, happiness and contentment are fleeting. Many of us are characters but not necessarily men of character. To make a difference in this world, we must be intentional about being honorable and compassionate towards others. To quote the Greek philosopher Socrates, "The greatest way to live with honor in this world is to be what we pretend to be." Socrates (469 BC-399 BC).

Do those that live with us respect us the most? Does our reputation and our character line up? Let's pursue godliness.

May 3
Truth

We live in a protective bubble of our own making, shielding ourselves from reality, only seeing what fits into our narrative.

Many of us hold to an assumption that life is supposed to be easy, fulfilling, and go our way. I know this because if we didn't think this, we wouldn't be so upset when things don't go our way. Despite all we know about life, we irrationally expect smooth sailing and react as if there is something terribly wrong when it isn't.

We see life as either unfair or as privileged. We think there are those who get everything they want and those who struggle to get even a little.

"No legacy is so rich as honesty." William Shakespeare (1564-1616) English author. Today may be a good day to have our bubble popped by a good dose of truth. And here it is: Our best plans, ultimately, are only OUR best plans. Let's submit ourselves to God and accept our circumstances as having first gone through His completely loving and trustworthy hands. He knows what He's doing.

We don't have to take a vow of poverty, but we can joyfully trust Him, come what may. Let's look to the future with confidence in Him, and not our circumstances.

May 4
Only What's Done for Christ Will Last

My grandmother often used to say this line, "Only one life will soon be past; only what's done for Christ will last." It is from an old hymn written by C. T. Studd, a British Missionary (1860-1931) considered to be one of England's most outstanding Cricket players of all time.

C.T. lived his life sacrificially. He had it all and gave it all away. He came from a wealthy family but gave away all his inheritance to missions and subsisted as a faith missionary. He longed to see Christ transform lives.

"Some wish to live within the sound of a chapel bell; I wish to run a rescue mission within a yard of Hell," he once said.

We only get one shot at life. Will our life be spent on ourselves, or will we use our life to invest in others? What impact are we making, and who are we influencing? The Lord impacts us so that we can impact others.

How do we want to be remembered?

May 5
The Seriousness of the Hour

While many are adjusting to the changes that have come to most of the country, there is a battle being waged for the future of our nation.

God blessed the founders of our country with the wisdom to form a republic that has lasted for over two hundred years. There are forces seeking to undermine the very freedoms we hold so precious, which have set us apart from all other nations. The ideological battles we see playing out on the news or between political parties are symptomatic of the greater battle being waged.

Paul wrote to the church in Ephesus, instructing them, "For our struggle is not against flesh and blood, but against the rulers, against the powers, against the world forces of this darkness, against the spiritual forces of wickedness in the heavenly places" (Ephesians 6:12 NASB).

The way to fight a spiritual battle is not through intellect but on our knees, praying and asking God to deliver us. Jesus instructed His disciples to watch and pray, to be alert in our praying. To be aware of what is going on around us. The seriousness of the hour dictates that we do not focus anxiously on the new normal but focus confidently on the foundations of our faith.

God has given us more time at our disposal; let us not waste it through the distraction of change. We must fight to ensure the nation we were been blessed to grow up in is the same one we pass on to future generations, only by God's grace and power.

May 6
What Is Truth?

Jesus told Pilate that He had come to testify to the truth. Pilate cynically asked in response, "What is truth?"

That's the question being asked in our day. What is truth? Some ask in sincerity, and some with derision. We have made truth relative and tolerant. So few stand for anything that people end up following anyone who sounds like they have a little conviction in what they are saying.

I find it interesting that while the Bible hasn't changed in 2000 years, neither have the responses to it. There are those who believe it, those who say they believe it but don't practice it, and those who try to discredit it and say that it is irrelevant.

Jesus said He is the way, the truth, and the life. Pretty bold stuff! He came to tell us the truth and show us how to live in the truth. The amazing thing about truth is that it doesn't change, and we either conform to it or suffer the consequences.

I may not believe in gravity, but it won't take long for me to be harmed if I act as if it doesn't exist. Jesus said, "And the one who falls on this stone will be broken to pieces; and on whomever it falls, it will crush him" (Matthew 21:44 NASB). We can either let truth change us, or it will crush us by ignoring it. We can either follow Jesus or ignore Him and be crushed by Him when He returns in power.

It's time to stop playing with truth and start following Jesus!

May 7
Life's Struggles Are Real. So Are God's Rewards

"Whatever you do, do your work heartily, as for the Lord and not for people, knowing that it is from the Lord that you will receive the reward of the inheritance. It is the Lord Christ whom you serve" (Col 3:23-24 NASB).

When we are serving the Lord and find ourselves between a proverbial "rock and a hard place," we can either quit or mine for gold. We must be willing to go through the struggle to find the gold God has for us. Serving Jesus means serving others, and it comes at a cost. But it also includes amazing rewards.

Just to be clear, we don't work to do good deeds to earn our way into heaven. We can't. Salvation is a gift. But in addition to God planning a beautiful eternity with the Lord for those who receive Him as Savior, He has other rewards for us. None of us can begin to imagine just how amazing the rewards He plans for us will be.

To live the life God planned for us requires dedication and perseverance. Don't lose hope or give up on God's best for your life, which is dedicated to Christ, no matter what struggle you find yourself in. "Let's not become discouraged in doing good, for in due time we will reap, if we do not become weary" (Galatians 6:9 NASB).

May 8
Doing All Things Through Christ

We were created to do the impossible.

We try to live a life of comfort and ease, but God wants us to live on the edge. Most Christians can quote the scripture, "I can do all things through Christ who strengthens me," (Phil 4:13 KJV) but only attempt what is humanly possible.

Where are the Davids who are willing to take on the Goliaths of today? Is it possible we don't see any great exploits because we are the ones who are unwilling to trust God for the extraordinary?

I heard someone say, "I'd rather shoot for the stars and hit the top of the fence than to shoot for the top of the fence and never get off the ground."

Let's start shooting for the stars and get out of our comfort zone.

May 9
Live Passionately. Dream Big

"Each time we face our fear, we gain strength, courage, and confidence in the doing." Theodore Roosevelt (1858-1919) 26th US President.

The life God has for us can't be attained through passive seeking; it takes a diligent heart. Many live thinking that somehow God owes it to us to lavish resources upon our every need; that we should be able to wake up and have everything we need at our disposal. That is lazy, immature thinking.

God has given us an imagination to dream and to seek after whatever is in our hearts. Unfortunately, most stop trying because fear has paralyzed them into inactivity. Worse yet, there are those who have settled for whatever life has dealt them and have stopped pursuing their dreams.

A successful life will not be handed to anyone. It takes hard work and determination to rise above mediocrity to succeed in any endeavor.

Fear is a powerful force. It can protect us from harm. It can prevent us from pushing ourselves forward. Fear is overcome by faith and love when we grasp the magnitude of God's unconditional love for us and how He longs to help us overcome every fear that holds us captive.

Let's ask God to free us to pursue and live our dreams. Let the dreaming begin!

May 10
Trust

In what do you put your trust? When things are falling apart, and you don't know what to do, what is your go-to? Some might escape and bury their head in the sand, hoping that it will soon be over. Some run to their parents – or their children to bail them out. Some look to their own ability to work their way out of it. Some turn to credit cards or government assistance. There are many sources that we can turn to and put our trust.

Sometimes we may even have dodged the bullet and gotten through it, but did we emerge better from it?

The Psalmist declares, "In Thee, O Lord, do I put my trust. Let me never be put to shame; Deliver me in Your righteousness" (Psalm 71:1-2a KJV). In other words, God, I'm putting my trust in you. Don't fail me. God looks for those who will put their trust in Him. God promises that when we look to Him and put our trust in His ability to rescue us, He will come through. He also declares that when we trust Him, He can turn our mistakes and hardships into something good in our lives. All the rotten, difficult, bad decisions, stupid things I've done, and the mean, cruel things done to me, God promises to make them beneficial for me. He's not saying all those things are good; He's just promising to make good out of them. Only God, only when we invite Him in, and only when we put our trust in Him.

I believe it's worth a shot to give it a try.

May 11
Happy Mother's Day

It is frustrating that a simple acknowledgement and greeting could possibly come under fire. Those of us who seek to keep the time-honored traditions and morals of long ago practically must go into hiding for fear of being singled out and labeled. Life has certainly been turned upside down, and what was once considered evil is now paraded as good, while what was once considered good and decent is considered evil and bad. "Woe unto them that call evil good, and good evil" (Isaiah 5:20a KJV).

The sacred marital union has been cheapened.

The uniqueness of male and female, that was once held in high regard, is now being beaten to death so that the beauty of masculinity and femininity is lost.

I, for one, am tired of it. In the beginning, God created males and females with unique characteristics and abilities. The differences are to be celebrated and honored.

Ladies, we appreciate your beauty and celebrate you. Moms, we thank you for the role you provide for our children and families.

Today, we honor our moms for all the demanding work they do to make our lives overwhelmingly better. Thank you for giving your best so that we can be our best.

Happy Mother's Day!

May 12
Honoring Our Mothers

"No man is poor who has a Godly mother." — Abraham Lincoln (1809-1865) The 16th President of the United States.

Today, we honor our moms. Where would any of us be without the love and prayers of our moms and grandmothers? There is no one that will fight for the health and welfare of her children like a mother.

"Strength and dignity are her clothing, And she smiles at the future. She opens her mouth in wisdom, And the teaching of kindness is on her tongue. She watches over the activities of her household, And does not eat the bread of idleness. Her children rise up and bless her" (Proverbs 31:25-28 NASB).

"A mother is the truest friend we have, when trials heavy and sudden fall upon us; when adversity takes the place of prosperity; when friends desert us; when trouble thickens around us, still will she cling to us, and endeavor by her kind precepts and counsels to dissipate the clouds of darkness, and cause peace to return to our hearts." Washington Irving (1783-1859) American author and historian.

"As one whom his mother comforts, so I will comfort you" (Isaiah 66:13 NASB).

Happy Mother's Day! You were always right, and we should have listened.

May 13
Mothers

Moms, you are a special gift from God. You have been uniquely created to meet the deepest needs within the hearts of your children and families. You are a divine revelation into the heart of God. Your grace, compassion, and nurturing instincts leave a stamp on our hearts that guide us through the storms of life. No matter what life throws at us, the sound of your voice lets us know that all will be well. Your unconditional love and acceptance give us a foundation on which to build our lives, and when we stumble, you are always there to encourage and impart your wisdom to get us back on our feet and on our way. Your prayers keep us steady and eventually lead us back to the loving arms of our heavenly father.

Only God knows the amount of trouble your prayers kept us from getting into and probably protected us from far worse outcomes.

Today, we thank and honor you for all the sleepless nights, endless meals, sacrifices, unending rides, and for all the attitudes and ungratefulness we exhibited when you gave us nothing but your best.

Happy Mother's Day to all the moms. God bless you and give you strength to endure the grandkids. Hopefully, they will be better than their parents.

May 14
Being Over Doing

Talk is cheap. Love and faith must be demonstrated.

With God, our demonstration takes a different turn. God does not want His children running around like a chicken with its head cut off. God prefers our BEING with Him over doing for Him.

Life keeps us going from sunup to sundown, and we throw a little religious observance on top of it because we feel guilty for not giving God more time. God doesn't want time; He wants you. He wants to be our total focus. Let's step back, slow down, and be with God.

I want to throw out a challenge to spend one hour with God every day. He could have asked for a tithe of our time (that would be 2.4 hours a day) but knows we are still trying to handle giving a tenth of our money.

It's not about performance; it's about presence. Be in His Presence. He's waiting.

Join me, one hour a day, being instead of doing.

May 15
No Weapon Formed

God spoke through the prophet, Isaiah to give a promise to those who put their trust in the Lord.

"No weapon that is formed against thee shall prosper; and every tongue that shall rise against thee in judgment thou shalt condemn. This is the heritage of the servants of the Lord, and their righteousness is of me, saith the Lord" (Isaiah 54:17).

It is a wonderful promise from God giving us comfort in times of difficulty and hardship. It does not matter if the attack is from individuals or from the enemy of our souls. God declares that whatever the weapon of choice is, words or weapons of destruction, it shall not be effective in destroying God's plans and purposes over His creation.

We may find ourselves going through the valley of the shadow of death, but we can be confident in the Lord that He will sustain us through it. The fulfillment of this promise is not based on our sustained goodness but on the righteousness of God that covers us. God supplies the basis for His protection over us.

To win the battle, we do not have to rely on our own strength or creative ability. All we need to do is trust Him and be confident in His goodness.

It's time to look up and give God the glory and honor He deserves.

May 16
The Difference Mothers Make

I don't know what kind of mom you had growing up, but moms can sure make a difference in our lives. Unfortunately, some do for all the wrong reasons, and I'm truly sorry if that is your situation.

God uniquely equipped females to nurture and love their babies. Moms never give up believing the best about us, even when we make so many mistakes, and we give up on ourselves. Don't just go through the motions and throw her a little attention today. Take the time to honestly honor your mom and express love and appreciation for her.

Stop and ask yourself these questions. What makes your mom special to you? What did she do for you that only you and her know about? How appreciative are you of the fact that she whooped your behind when you needed it? Would you be the person you are today if she hadn't always been there for you? No parent is perfect, but moms come closer than anyone to laying down their lives for their kids. Do you even realize the sacrifices she made for you?

The truth is there are a lot of people who would like one more opportunity to express their love for their moms. P. S. husbands honor the mother of your children because if you don't, your children will follow your example. Happy Mother's Day!

May 17
Wives and Mothers

God blessed humanity when He saved the best for last in the sequence of creation. When God was creating the heavens and the earth and filling each day with light and life, He was building up to His finest moment. He created man, giving him qualities from God's own nature that man would need to fulfill his calling and purpose. Then He created the woman, truly His finest work.

He gave her qualities that were different from the man's, not better and not inferior, just different. They were to complement each other and not compete against one another. They both were to reflect God in their unique expressions of humanity.

Today we celebrate the uniqueness of the woman. We honor an aspect of her role as a woman called motherhood. Rudyard Kipling (1865-1936) English journalist and author of *The Jungle Book* said, "God could not be everywhere, and therefore he made mothers." (Not theologically correct, but a nice sentiment.)

Moms play an important role in representing God to their children. They show the tenderness and compassion of God like no other. They have that intuitive sense of knowing their children's needs and wants before the child can articulate what they need. Most importantly, they demonstrate the power of unconditional love. Moms, today we salute and honor you for all the love and sacrifices you give to your families. May your day be filled with love and special moments.

Happy Mother's Day!

May 18
When Heaven Invades Earth

When teaching His disciples to pray, Jesus taught them to bring heaven to earth. In other words, what is in heaven can be on earth. There is no strife, hunger, poverty, sickness, or emotional turmoil in heaven. In heaven, there is peace, joy, love, wholeness, every need supplied, and fulfillment.

When we are experiencing trying times in our lives, we are to pray, "Thy kingdom come, Thy will be done in earth as it is in Heaven" (Matthew 6:10 KJV). In stressful times, we can be so fixed on our circumstances that we can doubt that God even cares about what we are going through. We have a hard time looking up for help because our feet are cemented in this life as if that is all there is.

"Desire gives fervor to prayer. The soul cannot be listless when some great desire fixes and inflames it...Strong desires make strong prayers...The neglect of prayer is the fearful token of dead spiritual desires...There can be no true praying without desire." E.M. Bounds (1835-1913) American author and attorney.

Our desire for more of God should drive us to seek His kingdom and bring it into our situations. Keep praying until heaven invades Earth. He waits for us!

May 19
Rest for Our Souls

"Come unto me, all ye that labour and are heavy laden, and I will give you rest. Take my yoke upon you and learn of me; for I am meek and lowly in heart: and ye shall find rest unto your souls" (Matthew 11:28-30).

Jesus gave us a promise that if we would come to Him, He would give us rest. That if we would yoke up to Him and let Him teach us then we would find rest. The only way to allow Him to carry our load (yoking up to Him) and let Him teach us how to live is to spend quality quiet time with Him.

Let's not forget that apart from Him, we can do nothing. Let's not lapse into acting as if we can do better without Him. Let's not give Him what little we have left. When we do, the evidence shows in our lives. We become hurried, harried and exhausted. We know that isn't what God had in mind for us. He promised rest for our weary souls.

Rest is to describe our existence. For one hour each day, let's set ourselves apart to unload, unwind, and yolk up to the One who has promised to give us rest and fullness of life.

May 20
Showing Appreciation to Our Mothers

Today, we celebrate and honor Mothers. Moms have an incredible capacity to love and nurture their families. Moms are usually the first one up and the last one to bed. They make sure that there is enough food for the family before they eat a meal and if there isn't enough, they will make the excuse, "I'm not really hungry anyway."

Moms sacrifice their time, energy, and resources to make sure the family is taken care of. Mom's may seem like superheroes, but they are only human, and sometimes the pressure of life can cause us to see their imperfections. Love on them anyway.

This Mother's Day, take the time to appreciate and thank your mom for all she does. Most moms I know appreciate the once-a-year acknowledgement very much, but what really fills them up is to be appreciated and honored all year long. What that looks like can vary, but it doesn't need to be elaborate – it just needs to be genuine and consistent. Remembering to thank our mom, show her our appreciation for anything she does with a smile or a hug, and letting mom see the joy we feel over her efforts can carry a mom for a long time.

Today is a good day to start. Remember, many moms feel inadequate for the job. Only you can change that with your words of encouragement.

May 21
Longing

Deep in the heart of man, God has placed a desire for something more. It's an itch that only God can scratch, but not in our lifetime.

It's a desire that, at times, can be satiated by the things of this world but eventually, those things no longer satisfy.

Money can't touch it and material possessions mean little. Even the best of relationships can't bring total fulfillment. However, relationships, especially good, fulfilling relationships, come the closest to satisfying that deep God-placed desire.

The Bible in Ecclesiastes 3:11 tells us that God has put eternity in our hearts. God has placed a desire in us that can't be fulfilled in this life. He has placed an itch in us that can only be scratched by being with Him in eternity.

That desire forces us, at times, to question why we are here and what our purpose is. What we do with those questions determines whether or not the itch gets scratched, or the desire finds its fulfillment. Only God, through Jesus Christ, can fulfill the desire that He placed in us.

If you haven't yet found the answer to those questions, I want to encourage you to start asking before eternity comes knocking at your door.

May 22
Eye Has not Seen

"But just as it is written: "Things which eye has not seen and ear has not heard, And which have not entered the human heart, All that God has prepared for those who love Him" (1 Corinthians 2:9 NASB).

Preachers often use this reference to point to heaven and the incredible things God has in store for us. Paul goes on to describe that through the Holy Spirit we have access to unlimited knowledge.

When we become Christians, we receive the Holy Spirit to dwell within us. That same Holy Spirit searches the deep things of God and wants to reveal them to us. The Trinity wants to make known the hidden mysteries of creation and the things God has prepared for those who love Him. When we are walking in our relationship with God, the Holy Spirit is willing and able to reveal the Father's plans and purposes to His children.

We must ask in faith, trusting that those thoughts bouncing around in our mind are more than just creative imagination. He is the God of all knowledge. He did create it. He should know. Ask Him!

May 23
Everything We Need for Life and Godliness

"For His divine power has granted to us everything pertaining to life and godliness, through the true knowledge of Him who called us by His own glory and excellence" (2 Peter 1:3 NASB). The Lord gives us everything we need for life and godliness.

"And with great power gave the apostles witness of the resurrection of the Lord Jesus: and great grace was upon them all" (Acts 4:33 KJV). The apostles were assigned the task of spreading the good news concerning Jesus Christ. The news that He died and rose from the dead. God did not leave them to figure it out or abandon them to do it on their own.

Notice that they gave witness with great power, and great grace was upon them all. The word grace is both the unmerited favor of God and the supernatural ability to accomplish all that is set before us in obedience to God's will.

When we do not feel like we can carry on and finish the task, or when life throws more at us than we think we can handle, remember God's grace is sufficient to get us through. All we must do is ask for His great grace by faith. He gives it to us because He loves us, not because we deserve it.

Receive His enabling power even now. Just ask!

May 24
Individual Beauty

We are all created in the image of God. When we take time to look at the beauty of others, we see a God of infinite creativity.

It is too bad that so much emphasis is placed on outward physical attractiveness per a certain body type, athletic ability, or acceptable, non-offensive personality traits. When we use these social standards to judge worthiness, we miss the true beauty of every individual.

The Psalmist writes, "I will praise thee; for I am fearfully and wonderfully made: marvelous are thy works; and that my soul knoweth right well" (Psalm 139:14 KJV).

It is a beautiful picture of God overseeing every individual and His involvement in the process. We are all uniquely complex.

It is too bad that we are uncomfortable around those that are different from us. We miss opportunities to admire God's handiwork and see a side of God that we might not otherwise have known.

Next time you look in the mirror, recognize the beautifully unique person that you are and give thanks to the God who made you that way.

May 25
Being Still

"Be still, and know that I am God" (Psalm 46:10 KJV). This is not a call to inactivity but an invitation to partnership. By partnership, I mean live in relationship with Jesus. We desire to be obedient to all that He requires as we read and study the Word of God, and we will do anything that He might prompt us to do through the Holy Spirit.

Typically, when we are prompted by Jesus, we try to fulfill the assignment in our own ability and strength. For example, if God were to ask us to build a boat, we jump into action to do the best job our talent and ability allows us. That is not partnering. Partnering with Him is slower. It means allowing Him to work through us. We start by praying, "What kind of boat? God if You want me to build a boat You are going to have to supply the materials and the financing." We don't start until we know it is time to start. We try to do too much on our own without allowing God to put all the pieces together. Partnering with Jesus is waiting on Him. God expects us to do our part, to listen and obey, to take responsibility for the life that He has blessed us with. Then God wants us to sit back and trust Him; to rest in His ability to do exceedingly abundantly beyond what we could ever imagine. God has given us examples in His word of the things that He can do through vessels that partner with Him. David slew Goliath, Joseph led a nation, Moses delivered a people, Daniel tamed the lions, and the disciples turned their world upside down. What can God do through us if we partner with Him? Let's be still as long as it takes to allow God to WOW us.

May 26
Love God. Love Our Neighbor

Isn't it interesting how we can be so focused on outward behavior when God states that He looks at one's heart? We spend so much time trying to clean up the outside and look presentable to those around us when the whole time we are not fooling God at all.

God looks at why we do what we do and not always at what we do. The truth is we are so focused on what others think of us that we conform accordingly. We don't even know how to examine our own heart or motives, and yet, that is the starting point with God.

The focus has become so centered on behavior that criticism and being judgmental have become coveted attributes.

How about we take some advice from Jesus and get the beam out of our own eye before we get the speck out of someone else's eye? Let's start at home, examine our own hearts, and root out attitudes that aren't pleasing to God.

The goal is to love freely and accept unconditionally. Until we get there, we really can't complain about anyone else.

Love God. Love our neighbor. That's where freedom and healing begin.

May 27
Stay Faithful to the End

Someone has said that Christianity is a "long obedience in the same direction." Being a believer in Jesus is about the long haul. But He goes with us and helps us. He comforts and guides us.

Life is going to have its ups and downs. The test is, are you still a believer when it's all said and done? Jesus Christ set a high bar of spirituality and morality that most don't want to adhere to.

Real Christianity isn't for wimps. It challenges us in the very thoughts and intents of our hearts, and it requires obedience in everything we do and say. We fail and need God's gracious forgiveness, but we keep pressing onward toward God's high calling for our lives. The Bible tells us that we have never seen or heard the things that God has prepared for those who love Him. Check out 1 Corinthians 2:9.

Jesus will help us to stay obedient and faithful to the end. The rewards He has for us will far surpass the temporary pleasures of this world.

Stay strong in the Lord, my friend, and live faithfully to God. It will be worth it all in the end.

May 28
Choosing Life or Death

There is an old saying that goes something like this: "Some people can be so heavenly-minded that they are no earthly good."

They have become so focused on God or religion that they have no ability to be useful here on earth.

Unfortunately, the opposite is true, "people have become so earthly-minded that they are no heavenly good." People have become so ingrained in this life that they are no longer concerned with God and what He would want of us.

The Bible tells us to be of the world but not in the world. While in this life, we all are subject to the laws of humanity but there are higher laws that we are to live by. God asks us to trust Him, love, and be obedient to what He asks of us.

Moses, in repeating the laws that God had passed down to the children of Israel, said it this way. I put before you life and death, life if you obey God's laws, and death if you don't. God gives us the choice to either have our heads and hearts buried in the world or to live our lives focused on Kingdom purposes. It's our choice to choose life or death.

It might be time to be so heavenly-minded that we become useful here on earth.

May 29
My Sheep Know My Voice

Everything God has His people do begins with a thought, idea, or dream. God gives us a thought, idea, or dream and then prepares us to be successful, just as He did with Joseph. Or He first prepares us and then gives us the thought, idea, or dream as He did with Moses. He promises that we will know His voice.

God has specific work for us to do, which was designed by Him just for each of us individually before time began. "For we are his workmanship, created in Christ Jesus unto good works, which God hath before ordained that we should walk in them. (Ephesians 2:10 KJV).

We are God's masterpiece! God created us with the perfect gift mix to make a difference in the lives of those He puts in our lives.

Those thoughts, ideas, or dreams that have been stirring us but that we might ignore need to be offered up inquisitively to the Lord, asking Him, is this Your will for me to do? Speak Lord. Your servant listens. He will make it clear. There is a need out there that God has been equipping each of us to be the answer to. We may initially dismiss God's call because we don't feel qualified, or we think we are too busy, or don't know what to do or how to do it. Fear not. John 10:14-16 tells us we sheep know His voice. He will make His voice known to each of us. We just need to listen expectantly, knowing He has work for us to do.

God is waiting to partner with us to kill some giants. Let's change the world. It all starts with a thought, an idea, or a dream.

May 30
God, Please Bless America

"Righteousness exalteth a nation: but sin is a reproach to any people" (Proverbs 14:34 KJV).

When we can't agree on what's right and wrong, it makes it hard to promote righteousness and condemn sin. We have lost our moral compass as a nation and are allowing behaviors that will eventually sink the ship. We can only bail water so fast.

There was a time when kindness and common decency were expected and practiced by the majority. There was a basic sense of correct behavior that we all could agree on and practice. Not anymore.

If we try to stand for any character-based behavior, we get put down for stifling a child's sense of expression. Heaven forbid that we should label a child male or female. Do we really think that we are still deserving of God's blessing when we fail to honor Him or His rightness?

What made America great was established by the Founding Fathers. They sought God and sought to live in accordance with God's word. God blessed America.

When we move away from God, we forfeit His blessing. The moving trucks are packed and are moving as fast as they can away from God and His blessing. It's time to come back to God, practice righteousness and once again be blessed by Him.

May 31
Be Filled With the Spirit

Paul, encouraging the church, said this, "And be not drunk with wine, wherein is excess; but be filled with the Spirit" (Eph 5:18 KJV).

Paul was encouraging the followers of Christ not to come under the control or lose control through wine but to be continually filled with and influenced by the Holy Spirit.

Living under the influence of the Holy Spirit takes focused attention. We become aware of the little choices that we make every day and consider what the Spirit would have us do. We will miss the still, small voice of the Spirit nudging us to a different response if we react emotionally, out of stubbornness, or habit.

Paul again speaks to the church, "For the kingdom of God is not meat and drink; but righteousness, and peace, and joy in the Holy Ghost" (Romans 14:7 KJV). Life in the kingdom of God is designed to be about more than eating and drinking. When we are being filled with the Spirit, it will produce in us right living, and our lives will be characterized by peace and joy. It takes a quick examination to determine if those are the foundational hallmarks of our lives. If they are not, then we might need to evaluate our priorities and focus.

God has given us everything we need, both in this life and the life to come. We must be the ones to activate it. Be filled with the Spirit of God!

06
JUNE

June 1
God's Gift of Potential

Our lives are bursting with Godgiven potential.

A wasted life may be defined as never fulfilling the purpose for which we were created.

Potential means "capable of being or becoming, a latent excellence or ability that may or may not be developed." Potential is a God-given possibility for us to develop.

Athletes are pushed by coaches to get the most out of their bodies. Students are pushed by teachers to get the most out of their brains. Professionals are pushed by bosses to get the most out of their occupations and careers.

Yet, who pushes us to fulfill our potential? Who pushes us not to settle for less? It is the Lord in a mysterious relationship between our will and His sovereignty. The final test will be how close we come to realizing the fullness of what God intended when He created us.

June 2
The Power of Passion

Passion is a strong, barely controllable emotion. Passion will drive us to conquer enormous mountains in our lives. Some have lost their passion for life and simply survive.

"It is only when the whole heart is gripped with the passion of prayer that the life-giving fire descends, for none but the earnest man gets access to the ear of God." E.M. Bounds (1835-1913) American author and attorney.

There are many things that can steal our passion and reduce us to the status quo. What gets your blood pumping? What drives you to go beyond your own limitations? If we reconnect with our passions, it will give us energy and excitement to pursue life to its fullest. Don't settle for a passionless life. Dream big. Trust God and light the fire of passion to get you moving.

June 3
Waiting on the Lord

The Bible encourages us to wait upon the Lord to renew our strength. The book of Isaiah informs us that "those that wait upon the shall mount up with wings as eagles, they shall run and not be weary and walk and not faint" (Isaiah 40:31 KJV). Waiting and patience are not in our DNA. We want what we want, and we want it now.

So why does God instruct us to wait and be patient? Waiting produces something in us that can't be produced any other way. We confuse activity with productivity and then wonder why we don't get more accomplished.

Waiting on God allows Him to be more involved in our lives. When we wait and listen, He will help us to prioritize what is important and what isn't. He will cause us to rest more and slow down. When we invite Him in and are patient, waiting for God to work in our situations, our faith grows stronger because we see Him fixing things we thought were impossible.

Waiting causes us to be healthier, happier, and less stressed. It doesn't seem possible, but being patient actually works.

Take God at His Word and start waiting on Him. You will be surprised at the results.

June 4
Pray for Good to Overcome Evil

We live in a world of unimaginable beauty and unimaginable evil. How can anyone in their right mind use their vehicle to plow into defenseless people? But this happened in New York City and on the London Bridge.

We can find great joy in a newborn baby, peace in a beautiful sunset, serenity by the ocean, wonder in dense forests, and exhilaration at a massive waterfall.

Unfortunately, we can turn on the news, the internet, or any social media source and find sadistic evil paraded before our eyes. It seems all rules of decency have been abandoned.

We need to spend more time valuing and appreciating beauty and less time being captivated by evil. God has given us the tools to fight against evil. Praying for good to overcome evil, for righteousness to be exalted, and for us to take a stand against anything or anyone that would seek to destroy the lives of others.

"All that is necessary for the triumph of evil is for good men to do nothing." -- Edmund Burke, Anglo-Irish statesman (1729-1797)

If good men do nothing we will have less and less beauty to behold. It's time to fight.

June 5
Accomplishments

"There are basically two types of people. People who accomplish things, and people who claim to have accomplished things. The first group is less crowded" Mark Twain (1835-1910) American author.

To be successful in life requires overcoming obstacles that stand in the way of our success. They can be our own self-doubts, finances, addiction, opportunity, apathy, and even laziness. There are many opinions on how to overcome obstacles, but when it gets right down to it, hard work and faith in God are usually the best combination.

God expects us to do what we can and then trust Him to do what we can't. For this to work, it requires us to get to work and set aside time to spend with God. It is easy to quit when obstacles present themselves, but obstacles are opportunities to grow smarter intellectually and stronger in our faith. We won't know how big God is if we never ask Him for help, and we will never accomplish anything if we don't think we can.

Instead of talking about success, let's move into the first category by not making excuses, rolling up our sleeves, and getting it done.

June 6
The Search for Truth

Blaise Pascal (1623-1662) French philosopher, mathematician, scientist, inventor, and theologian, said, "Truth is so obscure in these times, and falsehood so established, that, unless we love the truth, we cannot know it." It would seem he was writing about the times in which we now live. It has become most difficult to know the difference between truth and fiction.

Jesus was being interrogated by Pilate, who asked Him if He was the king of the Jews. Jesus answered and said, "Thou sayest that I am a king. To this end was I born, and for this cause came I into the world, that I should bear witness unto the truth. Everyone that is of the truth heareth my voice" (John 18:37 KJV). Pilate responded with the same question being asked today, "What is truth?"

Truth is not hidden. It can be known if we are willing to investigate and push past established falsehoods.

We were created by a God who is still active in the lives of His creation. Jesus gave us truth. Jesus said of Himself that He is truth. Do we really want to know the truth, or are we satisfied with keeping our heads in the sand and letting the truth be buried with us? It is time to rise up and stand for Biblical Truth.

June 7
Hang on and Look Up

These are certainly days that no one could have predicted. A disease is causing fear to cultivate in our nation while social injustice is bringing out the worst in humanity. Social isolation is wreaking havoc on mental and emotional mindsets, and the shutdown of our economy is forcing many to seek alternative means to support their families.

Peter, writing to the churches of his day during intense persecution had this to say, "Blessed be the God and Father of our Lord Jesus Christ, which according to his abundant mercy hath begotten us again unto a lively hope by the resurrection of Jesus Christ from the dead, To an inheritance incorruptible, and undefiled, and that fadeth not away, reserved in heaven for you,

who are kept by the power of God through faith unto salvation ready to be revealed in the last time. That the trial of your faith, being much more precious than of gold that perisheth, though it be tried with fire, might be found unto praise and honour and glory at the appearing of Jesus Christ" (1 Peter 1:3-7 KJV).

While we may endure many hardships and difficulties in this life, there is the promise of an incredibly beautiful and fulfilling future when this life is over. If we remain faithful while enduring the trials, we will have joy beyond anything we can experience in this life. No matter how hard this life can be, it does not compare to the promises of eternity. Hang on and look up, for God has prepared a place for us where there is no sorrow or tears.

June 8
Let Hope Arise

"Brothers and sisters, I do not regard myself as having taken hold of it yet; but one thing I do: forgetting what lies behind and reaching forward to what lies ahead, I press on toward the goal for the prize of the upward call of God in Christ Jesus" (Philippians 3:13-14 NASB).

Paul never rested on his accomplishments or how much knowledge he had obtained but continued to push forward for more of God. God is the prize for which we are running this race.

It's not for material or financial gain. It's not for the accolades or awards. The prize is the knowledge of God that comes from experiencing life with Him.

Paul tells us to leave the past in the past, both the good and the bad. Many are stuck in the pain or the success of the past. Today is a new day with new opportunities to experience God and learn more about who He is and what He can do with yielded vessels focused on Him.

Let hope arise in us that through God's amazing love, healing can come, and through our worship, His presence will bring us to new and exciting revelations of Him.

June 9
Finding Happiness

"Delight thyself also in the Lord: and He shall give thee the desires of thine heart" (Psalm 37:4 KJV).

Happiness, as a goal, is an elusive target. When we seek the high of happiness, it never lasts and requires more and more to achieve the same high. God created the emotion of happiness for us to experience but not live on it. Life, with all its crazy ups and downs, can never sustain a state of continual happiness. The more we seek after it, the harder it is to find.

We go after the quick fix instead of realizing where happiness can be found. "He has no design upon us but to make us happy. Who should be cheerful if not the people of God?" Thomas Watts (1819-1892) English writer and theologian. God has always wanted our happiness. True happiness, is therefore, found only in God.

"For whosoever will save his life shall lose it: and whosoever will lose his life for my sake shall find it" (Matthew 16:25 KJV).

In a world obsessed with happiness, it fails to go to the one source where happiness can be found. God and His Word call us to be content with what we have and to lay down our lives for His purposes. The prescription is the opposite of what we think will bring happiness, and that is why so few have it.

Happiness starts with changing the way we think about life and how to get it.

June 10
The Call to Impact

"If Jesus Christ is God and died for me, then no sacrifice can be too great for me to make for Him." C. T. Studd (1860-1931) British Missionary.

We can be passionate about a lot of things, but where does Jesus rank on our list? If Christians aren't excited about the God they serve, who else will be.

C.T. was a man of great passion for the Lord. "I am getting desperately afraid of going to heaven for I have had the vision of the shame I shall suffer as I get my first glimpse of the Lord Jesus; His majesty, power, and marvelous love for me, who treated Him so meanly and shabbily on earth and acted as though I did Him a favour in serving Him! No wonder God shall have to wipe away the tears off all faces, for we shall be broken-hearted when we see the depth of His love and the shallowness of ours."

God has given us abilities to use in ways that impact others. We are living in a time when God needs passionate people who love Him, are willing to be stretched in new areas of their lives and impact people for His kingdom. Will you?

June 11
Take Stock. Make Changes

Remember back to the night of high school graduation? Remember that awesome awareness of crossing a huge milestone toward independent adulthood? It was a time of great excitement and joy. We felt optimism about the future. We believed we could conquer anything thrown at us. We were excited to take the responsibility for the next steps in our journey.

Very quickly, we started to discover the limits of our control. Things didn't go as planned. Things took longer and were more challenging or costly than expected. We learned to take stock and re-evaluate, and with course corrections, we kept going.

As the years go on, a new generation graduates. We observe the unbridled optimism of youth, and we can't help but roll our eyes and say to ourselves, "just wait a few years, and you see what life is really like."

Whatever stage of life we are in, it's not a bad idea to grab some of that youthful enthusiasm, take stock of our lives, and make changes.

God may want to reawaken lost dreams to bring about the life we always desired.

June 12
Fighting on Our Knees for America

At the time of this writing, the primary election season has come to an end with two potential candidates for President. When we look at the ills of our country, it's clear that it is going to take more than a President to fix them. There are no easy answers or solutions to the problems we face, but I do know this: if we go back and look at the process our Founding Fathers used in establishing this nation, we might find the answers to why we are in this mess and how to fix it.

Revisionists have written God out of our history books and just tell the stories of how we came to be. If you dig deep enough and read authors who don't have an ideology that removes God from our history, you will find our Founding Fathers on their knees calling out to God for help. It took divine intervention to establish this country, and it's going to take divine intervention to fix it.

One of the problems we face as a country is that we have become selfish and self-centered and only care about our own best interests at the expense of others. The church has fallen asleep and forsaken our divine responsibility to fight on our knees for the health of our country. It's time to awaken the sleeping church, humble ourselves, fast and pray for the sake of future generations.

Will you join me in calling out to God for His divine intervention? He's willing if we ask.

June 13
Living for Truth

We can be so consumed with standing for truth that we forget to live for truth.

Jesus was truth personified and yet did not beat it over the heads of those who came to Him needing help. Jesus spent most of His time with the broken and hurting. He could have called out all their sin and mistakes, but instead He demonstrated love and compassion. The few times He did call out sin, He did it in such a way that the person was drawn to Him and opened themselves to His healing.

It is difficult to want to stand for truth and not become a sledge-hammer pointing out everyone's failures and faults. Jesus had every right to act superior to humanity in every way but chose to humble Himself and to be patient and compassionate toward people. We could learn from Jesus.

Walking in and standing for truth does not equate to moral superiority. Living for truth means we understand what it means to be a sinner in need of a savior. Living for truth means graciously demonstrating to others the love and compassion that we have received. Let us live for truth by showing others who Jesus really is.

June 14
In God We Trust

Today, we honor and celebrate "Old Glory," The flag that represents the United States of America. That flag represents all that America stands for. It was established on June 14, 1777, and in 1916, President Woodrow Wilson issued a proclamation that officially established June 14 as Flag Day; on August 3, 1949, National Flag Day was established by an Act of Congress.

Our country's flag and our national motto "In God We Trust," and the statement, "One Nation under God," in our pledge of allegiance are uniquely American and have been a source of national pride for a long time. But not nearly as much today. We have lost our moral anchor, and the ship *America* is adrift at sea.

Our Founding Fathers knew that the only way for our fledgling nation to survive was for its people to be religious. They knew and understood that religious people have higher standards and morals because religious people answer to a higher power. The phrases "Love your neighbor" and "Do unto others as you would have them do unto you" and many others were common values instilled in Americans from childhood. These phrases come from God's Holy Word. However, for the last 50 plus years, God and His Word have been kicked out of mainstream thought and instruction, and we see the devastating results all around us.

As we celebrate "Flag Day," let us remember all that it represents and seek to re-establish her former Glory. In God We Trust!

June 15
Leaving a Legacy

Men, Dads, Grandfathers, and Great Grandfathers, we leave an impression upon whomever we come into contact. God gave men the ability to impact others by their very presence. Men and dads, we leave a legacy on those we helped to create and those around us.

A legacy is something handed down from the past, such as from an ancestor or predecessor. We have been impacted by those who have gone before us, our fathers. What has been passed to us can either be a positive legacy or a negative one. The question is what we are passing down to our families and to those around us.

What messages are we sending, not just by our words but by our actions? By what we value. We have the greatest opportunity to mold and shape future generations by our actions today.

What message would you like to impart to the next generation that will impact future generations? Trust me, a message will be passed down. You can create the message.

You can speak it now. What will it be?

Happy Father's Day

June 16
Happy Father's Day, Dad

It's not easy being a dad. It's easy becoming a father, but much harder to be a dad. Being a dad requires a large investment of time. Kids spell love T-I-M-E.

Men are pulled in so many directions that the temptation to phone in their responsibility as parents is a daily problem. It makes us appreciate even more those who don't give in to that temptation.

Studies have proven that the role of dad in a child's life is critical to their development and self-esteem.

Today, we honor those who sacrificed and loved their families well. Billy Graham (1918-2018) American evangelist, said, "A good father is one of the most unsung, unpraised, unnoticed, and yet one of the most valuable assets in our society." The role of a father can impact future generations.

Someone once said, "What you teach your children, you also teach their children." When raising our family, it is hard to measure how well we are doing. Margaret Truman 1924-2008, the only child of our 33rd president, said, "It's only when you grow up and step back from him—or leave him for your own home—it's only then that you can measure his greatness and fully appreciate it."

So, this Father's Day take a few minutes to say thank you to your father. Men – realize how valuable you are as a dad. Happy Father's Day!

June 17
Father's Day Blessings

The Bible records in Matthew 3:17 and Mark 1:11 that His Father spoke from heaven over His Son these remarkable words: "this is my beloved Son, in Whom I am well pleased." I don't know if Jesus needed the words of affirmation from his Father, but I can't think of a single person that doesn't need to hear it from their father.

George McDonald (1804-1925) Scottish evangelist, said this, "In my own childhood and boyhood my father was the refuge from all the ills of life, even sharp pain itself."

Being a good father is hard work. Truth be told, fathers make far more mistakes than they get right. Some say 90% of being a good dad is showing up. "God chooses ordinary men for fatherhood to accomplish His extraordinary plan." G.K. Chesterton (1874-1936) American author.

This Father's Day let your kids know how much you love them and appreciate the father you were blessed to have. Have a Happy Father's Day

June 18
Honoring Dad

"All we have of freedom, all we use or know, this our fathers bought for us, long and long ago." Rudyard Kipling (1865-1936) English journalist and author of *The Jungle Book*.

Today, we honor and celebrate Dads. Dads, you do a great job leading your families and being an example to your kids.

I know dads are not perfect, and some have made some real blunders. Like this one, for instance: the father of Isaac Watts became so annoyed with his son constantly going around the house rhyming that he made him stop under threat of getting a switch to his backside. In response, the irrepressible young Isaac Watts replied:

*"O father, do some mercy take,
and I will no more verses make"*

What's a father to do? Thankfully, Father Watts relented, and as a result, through his son, Isaac, we have some of our most cherished hymns, such as "When I Survey the Wonderous Cross" and "Joy to the World."

Dads remember this piece of advice: "A father is neither an anchor to hold us back nor a sail to take us there, but a guiding light whose love shows us the way."-- Author unknown.

Dad's, keep on giving, keep on believing, keep on loving, and continue to be the guiding light for all who call you dad.

June 19
Life and Legacy

This past week, my father-in-law graduated to heaven. At his funeral, there were many who testified to the life and legacy that he left behind. He was a spiritual giant, and he was still impacting others up until the time of his death.

He was 39 days short of reaching the century mark. While his body was frail, his mind was still sharp, and he continued to read to stay current with the world around him.

His was a life lived with purpose and meaning.

Today is a day to honor our father's and those father figures that have impacted our lives. Don't miss the opportunity to express your appreciation for them because you never know how long they will be with you.

Dads, don't lose sight of the fact that you are impacting those around you, and it is always good to stop and ask yourself, what kind of legacy am I leaving? Start building a legacy that you would be proud of when they stand and speak about the kind of man you were.

June 20
Changing the World

"Everyone thinks of changing the world, but no one thinks of changing himself." Leo Tolstoy (1828-1910) Russian author of War and Peace, among others.

We live in a world of changing values and morals. We see the problems and chaos being played out in front of us. Everyone feels the uncertainty of the future and wonders if it will ever get back to normal.

Most people recognize that change is needed for others but do not think change is necessary for them. I learned a valuable lesson when my children were growing up. I was complaining to my heavenly Father about my children when I received a clear impression that if I wanted my children to change their behavior, it needed to start with me changing mine. At first, I did not see the correlation between my behavior and attitudes and theirs (I am a slow learner sometimes). Over time, I discovered the truth of God's instruction.

Change is hard for everyone, and no one likes to think they are part of the problem. Where have we become tolerant of our own sins and bad attitudes? Change needs to start with us.

Be the change you want to see in the world.

June 21
The Power of Dads

"One father is more than a hundred schoolmasters." George Herbert (1593-1633) English poet and orator.

"A father should remember that one day his son will follow his example, not his advice." Charles Kettering (1876-1958) American innovator and inventor in the automobile industry.

We are living with an epidemic of fatherless households. Sadly, there are absent father households even when the dad is living in the house. Being isolated and detached while living in a house full of people causes emotional and psychological damage to our children.

Someone once said, "Dads are a son's first hero, a daughter's first love." As dads, we can either dismantle and destroy this concept or build and develop it.

Dads aren't perfect. Dads make mistakes. But we are given an incredible responsibility to instill in the next generation the values and tools to be successful professionally and spiritually.

There are many dads doing a great job. Today, we honor and celebrate you. Happy Father's Day!

June 22
Fullness of Joy Is Worth It

Happiness is a wonderful thing. But at what cost? What is sacrificed at the altar of happiness?

Pursuing happiness has become a full-time religion. We live for the weekends and dread the work week. Morals and values are compromised so that we can feel good… temporarily.

One aspect of the fruit of the Spirit is joy. It is an emotion created by God and one that He wants to produce in us. Hear this: God wants us to be happy and full of joy. Godly joy is not dependent on circumstances or success. When we actively pursue something apart from God, it can very easily become an idol or addiction. The problem with searching outside of God is that it can only satisfy temporarily, and then we need another fix.

We give God a few moments, and then if we don't get a rush of emotion, we give up and move on to the next thing. What we have lost in our instant gratification society is the will power to stick with it until we get it.

Pursuing God means that we go after Him until we find Him. If we seek, we will find; if we knock, it will be opened, and if we ask, it will be given. Let's try it His way. Fullness of Joy is worth it. The fulfillment, contentment, happiness, joy, love, and peace can only be realized and consistently lived out in a relationship with God.

June 23
The Power of Hymns

When I was a young lad, my parents would load us all up into the family station wagon, and off to church we would go. The service began with singing from a hymnal accompanied only by a piano and a lady standing in front using arm motions, keeping time with the hymn. It's a lasting impression.

Hymns are a way to sing the great truths of the Bible. They were written by ordinary men and women, sometimes under extraordinary circumstances. Some of the hymns were born out of extreme hardship and were written while holding onto a beautiful truth or promise from God and His Word.

Horatio G. Spafford (1828-1888) was an attorney in Chicago. In 1871 He lost his investments in the Great Chicago Fire. A short time later, he lost his son to scarlet fever. A few years later his wife and four daughters were on a ship bound for Europe when it was struck by another ship. All four of his daughters perished. "Saved alone. What shall I do?" said the telegram from his wife. He quickly boarded another ship to join her. As his ship was passing the area where his daughters' ship had sunk, he went to his cabin and wrote the comforting, faith-filled hymn, "It is well with my soul."

"When peace like a river attendeth my way, When sorrows like sea billows roll; Whatever my lot, Thou hast taught me to say, it is well, it is well with my soul."

The next time you find yourself in need of encouragement, you might pick up an old hymnal and be reminded of the truth contained in those old songs.

June 24
The Essential Stuff

"The remarkable thing about God is that when you fear God, you fear nothing else, whereas if you do not fear God, you fear everything else." Oswald Chambers (1874-1917) Scottish Evangelist to India.

Jesus was going to dinner at the home of his friends, Lazarus and his two sisters, Mary and Martha. Martha was busy in the kitchen preparing a meal for them all to enjoy and she felt the pressure to get it all done. Mary was sitting at the feet of Jesus, intently listening to all that He had to say. Annoyed, Martha came and interrupted to get Mary to help her in the kitchen. Jesus told Martha that she was worried and consumed with many things, but Mary had chosen the essential part.

Fear can keep us running in all kinds of directions and miss what is essential. Fear wears disguises, making it hard to identify when we are in its grip. But fear is also a feeling that is helpful in being able to stop and realize that knot in our stomach or that tension in our neck is a warning that we are operating in fear. When we pay attention, we can stop in our tracks and surrender that fear, asking the Lord to help us not be overwhelmed.

What are the essential things? God, family, and others. Let's love, worship and honor God, nurture and love our family, and treat people as who they really are – God's creation made in His image.

June 25
Prayer

"We tend to use prayer as a last resort, but God wants it to be our first line of defense. We pray when there's nothing else we can do, but God wants us to pray before we do anything at all." Oswald Chambers (1874-1917) Scottish Evangelist to India.

God allows delays in answering prayer to build our character, patience, and perseverance. When our prayers aren't answered right away, it forces us to make a choice. Are we going to be patient and trust Him, or are we going to run to religion?

Religion looks like a relationship but has no power to change anything. Religion is a bunch of activity: doing for God instead of God doing through us, doing spiritual disciplines out of duty rather than delight, and trying to fix all the problems before God can intervene.

Religion has a form of holiness that is not genuine. Prayer is a transfer of ownership, my will to His will, allowing the Holy One to transform us into His image.

We want answers immediately, pronto, quickly, and ASAP. God disciplines or disciples the ones He loves. The way God disciples is through delay. When God answers prayer, we know it because there is no way to manufacture His answer. That is why He is God and why patience is a virtue. Keep asking, and don't rush the answer. It's always worth the wait.

June 26
Godly Example

Showing is better than telling. A Godly example is the best legacy we can pass down to our children. A Godly example is a life lived in a strong faith in God demonstrated by consistency in church attendance, trust in God, moral uprightness, love, and forgiveness lived out in front of the family.

The Bible tells us to instruct, model, and train up the succeeding generations in the ways of God. That means teaching them how to pray, how to study and apply God's word to everyday life situations, and how to live a life of integrity, honor, and commitment.

I have been blessed to have a Godly heritage and am doing my best to pass that along to my children and grandchildren. My grandparents set a Godly example of how to live a Christian life and left a legacy to live up to and carry on.

Today is a good day to look at what kind of legacy you are giving to your children. What character traits will the succeeding generations say that you passed down to them? Faith or Fear? Trust or Independence? Passion or Passivity? Commitment or Laziness? Virtues or Vices? Wealth or Poverty? Ego or Humility? It's never too late to make changes.

June 27
The One Anothers of Life

"So, as those who have been chosen of God, holy and beloved, put on a heart of compassion, kindness, humility, gentleness, and patience; bearing with one another, and forgiving each other, whoever has a complaint against anyone; just as the Lord forgave you, so must you do also. In addition to all these things put on love, which is the perfect bond of unity. Let the peace of Christ, to which you were indeed called in one body, rule in your hearts; and be thankful. Let the word of Christ richly dwell within you, with all wisdom teaching and admonishing one another with psalms, hymns, and spiritual songs, singing with thankfulness in your hearts to God. Whatever you do in word or deed, do everything in the name of the Lord Jesus, giving thanks through Him to God the Father" (Colossians 3:12-17 NASB).

Our relationships, "the one anothers" of life, are very important to the Lord. The scriptures above detail this well.

People are messy and require a lot of patience, love, and forgiveness. Jesus demonstrated extreme patience with us, and we must do the same for others. When life has dumped on us, and we have closed our hearts, we can go to the heart mender. His grace and love restore our broken and bruised hearts. In Him, we find the peace that sustains us during sudden and unexpected storms. Trust Him by surrendering your heart to Him and let Him mend and heal what only He can.

June 28
A Crime of Passion

In some acts of violence, the evidence will lead the investigators to describe the motive behind it as a "crime of passion." The perpetrator became so emotionally charged that they lost their sense of right and wrong, crossing the line of law and order with devastating consequences.

There are everyday crimes of passion that inflict deep wounds on those we are supposed to love and cherish: harsh, anger-filled words, hitting, impatience, negativity, disrespect, criticism, complaints, comparisons, jealousy, unbridled hatred, screaming, yelling, slamming doors, temper tantrums, haughtiness, flagrant disrespect, lashing out. It's a sad, scary list.

If we are anywhere close to exhibiting any of the above, we make a big mistake if we try to minimize or excuse ourselves. We need to run to Jesus for His forgiveness, mercy, and a changed heart and behavior. Our families deserve better.

The cure for the human heart can only be found in the transforming resurrection power of Jesus Christ. Only Jesus can heal and deliver us. Pray: Father, we give You our hearts and emotions to be bathed in Your love. We surrender our will to Your Lordship.

June 29
Jesus Wants Us Full of His Joy

As the Father hath loved me, so have I loved you: continue ye in my love. If ye keep my commandments, ye shall abide in my love; even as I have kept my Father's commandments, and abide in His love. These things have I spoken unto you, that my joy might remain in you, and that your joy might be full" (John 15:9-11 KJV).

The love expressed by our Lord compels us to draw near to Him. Jesus wants us to be full of His joy and not to lose it. His desire for us is that we learn how to live joyfully. Lovingly, He points us to the purpose and safety of His wise commandments. And He doesn't leave us alone in our efforts to obey Him – He gives us His endless grace, mercy, and forgiveness. What a Savior.

If we view the commandments of God as an arbitrary set of rules, made by a deity that is a cosmic "killjoy," we can harden our hearts in defiance. Our God is a loving, gracious, and good God Whose commandments are for our welfare.

God's rules are for our protection. Abiding in Him and following His commandments produces joy. Violating the rules produces chaos and unhappiness in our lives. Think about this: God the Father, through His Son, Jesus, wants us to be full of Joy. Does that fit in your paradigm of God? If not, you had better rethink what you believe.

June 30
Faith, God, and Country

"Posterity who are to reap the blessings will scarcely be able to conceive the hardships and sufferings of their ancestors." Abigail Adams (1744-1818) wife of John Adams, second president of the United States, and mother of John Quincy Adams, the sixth.

We live in the land of the free because many sacrificed their very lives. Have we become so spoiled that we don't appreciate the blessings of God? If we are not careful, we can lose God's blessing by our indifference to Him and His ways.

America came to be by men who sought to live out their faith without government interference. They sacrificed much because they understood the importance of what they were seeking to create. Our founders understood that for our nation to succeed, it would take a people who lived under the values of a higher authority than themselves. God's Word would be needed to curb the destructive powers of human nature.

Today, we see those destructive natures at work trying to create a new and different America. You also see an outright assault on God's Word. As we move towards the 4th of July and the celebrations of our country, we need to return to our roots by putting our hope and trust in God. If we return to God, He promises to return to us and heal our land. See 2 Chronicles 7:14.

07
JULY

July 1
Independence Day – the Pursuit of Happiness

"We hold these truths to be self-evident, that all men are created equal, that they are endowed by their Creator with certain unalienable Rights, that among these are Life, Liberty and the pursuit of happiness" part of the Declaration of Independence, 1776.

The words in the phrase "pursuit of happiness" were carefully chosen by the Founders and mean that as citizens we have the right to **pursue a state of flourishing in life for the purpose of living a virtuous life.** It is not about pursuing the emotions of happiness. It has in mind a high moral value for the good of all.

Freedom is not the right to do whatever I want at the expense of anyone else. It is the freedom to pursue happiness so that others may also benefit. The Founders believed that the best way this new government would work was with self-government. This was revolutionary. The ability of people to govern themselves and to keep themselves in check from the evil devices that have corrupted and destroyed other nations was a lofty experiment.

The First Amendment in the Bill of Rights ratified in 1791 guaranteed the Freedom of Religion. Our Founders knew that people who believe in God are more likely to govern themselves to a high standard. For America to survive, we must remind ourselves exactly what America stands for and the reason why she was birthed. Celebrate the freedom that our forefathers fought and died for. There is no other country like the United States of America.

July 2
Self-governed

Soon we will celebrate the 4th of July, the date of our declaration of independence from the rule of Great Britain in 1776. What our Founding Fathers gave us was a fresh, bold idea for how a people should be governed – self-governed.

John Adams, our second president, said, "Our constitution was made only for a moral and religious people. It is wholly inadequate to the government of any other." Biblical morality is the necessary foundation for our nation to be free. A religious people tend to realize self-control is necessary to be a free people.

Freedom isn't getting to do whatever I want. Freedom is a great responsibility. It is the power to choose the right thing to do in every situation without having to submit to a government authority that would control our daily life. Only God and His word have the power to help us live with moral integrity and character.

As we celebrate this 4th of July with our barbeques and family gatherings, let's take time to remember and thank God for this great nation and the freedom to celebrate as we so desire.

Holidays are a time to remember and be thankful.

July 3
Lives, Fortunes, and Relationships Lost

Tomorrow, we celebrate the day our country declared its right to independence from the rule of Great Britain. This led to the Revolutionary War, which lasted nearly 8 years. From April 19, 1775 to September 3, 1783. Our independence came at a heavy cost. Lives, fortunes, and relationships were lost.

Our Founding Fathers wanted freedom. Not reckless abandon or what today might be called "doing our own thing" with no one to answer to and no sense of responsibility to anyone else. Our Founders wanted to create an entirely new form of government based on the highest virtues. They wanted a representative form of self-government and the right to express worship of God without government influence and control. This cost so many so much. It cost some everything, including their lives.

These freedoms are slowly being stripped away, and our religious freedoms are disappearing. We need to remember and celebrate but also realize that it's time to fight. We can't sit by and watch as the America we once knew is dismantled by those who do not fear God.

Freedom demands sacrifice, sacrifice of our time and resources, and, as our Founding Fathers discovered, even our very lives. God has equipped and blessed us, and if we do not return to His ways, we will lose His blessing and forfeit our future. This Independence Day, let's remember what we are celebrating but also remind ourselves that it can be lost if God does not intervene in our future. God Bless America!

July 4
In Congress July 4, 1776

"The unanimous Declaration of the thirteen united States of America, When in the Course of human events, it becomes necessary for one people to dissolve the political bands which have connected them with another, and to assume among the powers of the earth, the separate and equal station to which the Laws of Nature and of Nature›s God entitle them, a decent respect to the opinions of mankind requires that they should declare the causes which impel them to the separation.

We hold these truths to be self-evident, that all men are created equal, that they are endowed by their Creator with certain unalienable Rights, that among these are Life, Liberty and the pursuit of Happiness.--That to secure these rights, Governments are instituted among Men, deriving their just powers from the consent of the governed, --That whenever any Form of Government becomes destructive of these ends, it is the Right of the People to alter or to abolish it, and to institute new Government, laying its foundation on such principles and organizing its powers in such form, as to them shall seem most likely to effect their Safety and Happiness. Prudence, indeed, will dictate that Governments long established should not be changed for light and transient causes; and accordingly, all experience hath shewn, that mankind are more disposed to suffer, while evils are sufferable, than to right themselves by abolishing the forms to which they are accustomed. But when a long train of abuses and usurpations, pursuing invariably the same Object evinces a design to reduce them under absolute Despotism, it is their right, it is their duty, to throw off such Government, and to provide new Guards for their future security.--Such has been the patient sufferance of these Colonies; and such is now the necessity which constrains them to alter their former Systems of Government." Preamble of the US Declaration of Independence.

July 5
God Bless America

We hear these words spoken by so many, from politicians to every-day Americans. That being said today is something to be thankful for. But, for God to truly bless America, we must invite Him back into every aspect of our lives. Doing so may come at a cost. We need to examine our hearts and ask God to show us where we fail to yield to His Lordship in our lives.

God does not just arbitrarily bless because we invoke the blessing at the end of a speech or conversation. It takes a nation of individuals willing to return to Him and seek His will and way.

As a nation, we have strayed from His moral and ethical commandments. If we follow God and obey His Word, blessings will inherently be a part of our lives.

Only through the transformational power of the Gospel of Jesus Christ can a nation change and become great once again. There are many ills that our nation faces and we do, in fact, need God's blessing. As we say these words, let's recognize that we can be the conduit through which God may work.

Let us return to Him so that He has reason to Bless America.

July 6
Thank You to All Freedom Fighters

Since the birth of our nation, so many have sacrificed so much for the freedoms that we easily take for granted in this great country.

Unfortunately, we have become more obsessed with our rights than our responsibilities.

Whenever the focus becomes "what I can get" over "what I can give," we create a people of entitlement.

Sacrificing for the betterment of future generations has been at the heart of this great country. It's time for us to return to the values that make us great, including hard work, self-sacrifice, and love of God.

If we, as a country, can stop focusing on ourselves and our rights and instead focus on creating a better world for our children, we can once again be the country that our forefathers envisioned.

God bless America! We sure need it!

July 7
A City on a Hill

The early colonial settlers of our country wanted freedom. They wanted a new way of living, a new way of being governed, and new freedoms in how they could serve God according to their understanding of God's Word. They wanted to be free to explore and be creative. What an adventure they began so long ago.

Fast forward 200-plus years, and look at us now. Have we been good stewards of God's blessing on America? Have we personally been faithful with the abundance of opportunities that living in this country affords us? We can find it easy to point fingers at others, but are we living a life as a City on a Hill, as a shining example to the world?

The colonial settlers risked it all for a new way to live. Have we settled for just living? Let's raise our expectations of what can be achieved because God is still enabling anyone who will put their trust in Him and because so many gave so much so that we could be free.

Let's live so that future generations can enjoy the same freedoms we have had, and let's no longer so casually take for granted.

July 8
Let's Celebrate

"The first fact about the celebration of a birthday is that it is a way of affirming defiantly, and even flamboyantly, that it is a good thing to be alive." G.K. Chesterton (1874-1936) American author.

Birthdays and anniversaries are special days to be eagerly anticipated and wholeheartedly celebrated.

God instituted special Holy days into the calendar so His people would stop their daily routines and remember all that God had done in the previous years by giving thanks and celebrating.

The Bible encourages us to "Rejoice evermore. Pray without ceasing. In everything give thanks: for this is the will of God in Christ Jesus concerning you" (1 Thessalonians 5:16-18 KJV).

We don't have to wait for special occasions to remember and celebrate those around us. Enjoying life and giving thanks must be intentional behaviors we incorporate into our everyday lives. We celebrate that which we want to encourage more of.

Choose to rejoice and celebrate. Enjoy this life while looking forward to heaven in the next.

July 9
Self-centered Religion

"You cannot give without loving. You cannot love without giving." Amy Carmichael (1867-1951) Irish missionary to India.

We all have religion. One definition of religion is a pursuit of interest to which someone ascribes supreme importance. Religion may or may not center around a supreme being. Self can be a religion. Self can replace the supreme being.

Self-worship will never be satisfied, will not unify, nor will it make the world a better place –quite the opposite. Self-worship is entirely selfish. Self cares only about its own thoughts, opinions, feelings, and values. Anyone who doesn't worship us is intolerable. Self-worship is so demanding of others that it is hostile to opposition of any kind.

As a nation, we have become so opinionated that we have lost sight of what is best for the community, the nation, or the family. Today's credo is *do your own thing* no matter who is harmed.

Any nation, community, or people that make Self their religion is setting themselves up for destruction. Life just doesn't work when we are focused on ourselves. Sorry folks, but the best religion is one centered on God and His Love. The God of the Bible loves unconditionally and requires us to do the same. It's amazing the difference it can make. Give it a try.

July 10
Love God and One Another

Jesus told us in the gospel of John that He was giving us a new commandment: that we should love one another. Jesus also narrowed down the Bible for us. He said the two greatest commandments were to love God and love one another.

I have watched two movies lately that make the case that love is what life is all about. *Collateral Beauty* and *Wonder Woman*.

In *Collateral Beauty*, Will Smith meets a character who is Love. Love tells Smith some incredible truths, "I am love. Don't try and live without me." And "I'm Love. I'm the fabric of life." During his pain over losing a child, Love tells him, "I'm the reason for everything. If you can accept that, then maybe you get to live again."

In the movie *Wonder Woman*, as the plot has life spin out of control, the film reveals that love is the answer even then.

Love can be very powerful both to heal and to destroy. God's perfect love and acceptance heal the deepest wounds we can experience in this life. We have the power through our love to bring healing and life back to those around us.

Let's believe it and make the world a better place.

.

July 11
Summertime Blessings

What a gift God has given us called Summer. The delights of more daylight hours and warmer weather usher in many outdoor activities we can do in the summertime.

Make the most of these summertime blessings. Enjoy a backyard barbeque. Take a stroll in the neighborhood or visit a park. Dust off the bicycle and take it for a spin. Plan a picnic or roll around in the grass with the kiddos.

Remember when you were a kid and got some cardboard to slide down a hill-and then had to pull the stickers out of your socks? Some of your kids don't even know what that's like.

Enjoy the beauty of His creation. Visit the ocean, and watch a sunset ,or go up into the mountains and gaze at its beauty. Get out and thank God by enjoying His wonderful gift to us.

Enjoy the rest of your summer because school is only 6 weeks away.

July 12
Restoring Order

It's hard to find the answers to all the problems we are facing today. Social unrest, a pandemic that won't go away, and economic hardships are just some of the major issues staring us down. There are many opinions on what should be done. People want to scream about the problems. But it's hard to find anyone in leadership who wants to work on resolving the issues honestly.

The solution is simple but not easy. Jesus said about Himself, "And I, if I be lifted up from the earth, will draw all men unto me" (John 12:32 KJV).

He said this in reference to the type of death He was going to suffer. He was lifted up from the earth on the cross to die for the sins of humanity. As people look to the cross to solutions for the ills that plague humanity, we are drawn to Him, and His love provides answers.

Jesus provides salvation and deliverance. And if we would stop communicating about the problems and begin to lift up Jesus, He will bring reconciliation to all of humanity.

Spending time exalting the name of Jesus results in finding peace and unity in the love of God.

We may not be able to get the world to exalt Jesus, but the church should certainly recognize the truth and come together to lift up the name of our Savior.

July 13
We Are the Storyteller

The writer of Psalms declares, "Now also when I am old and grey-headed, O God, forsake me not; until I have shewed Thy strength unto this generation, and Thy power to everyone that is to come" (Psalm 71:18 KJV).

Isn't this the responsibility of all Christians? We are the story-tellers of all God has done in and through us. We are to pass on to the next generation the goodness and faithfulness of God. What is your salvation story? Have you told your family?

My Portuguese great-grandmother was born in the late 1800s and immigrated to the US in the early 1900s. A Christian woman prayed for Grammie, and she was miraculously healed of cancer and became a Christian. As a result, her husband deserted her and their 12-year-old daughter – my grandmother – leaving them destitute. As a result of that, her immigrant community turned its back on her. Her faith cost her everything. She didn't quit. God provided for her through His people over and over.

When families tell their faith stories, others come to know God's faithfulness and the cost we sometimes pay to stand with Jesus. If those who know the Lord don't speak up, how will others know? If we do not tell our story about how God rescued us, there will be multitudes of people who will go into eternity without the Lord. Be your family's storyteller.

July 14
Thank God for Children

Children are a blessing from the Lord. Psalms 127 tells us that children are a gift ,and blessed is the man who has many of them.

Children live their lives in simple and cute ways. The smiles, creativity, frank comments, simple outlooks, and hugs from a child warm the heart and brighten our day. Let's not get too busy to notice those precious moments. Childhood is fleeting.

The Bible tells us that unless we become like little children, we will miss the Kingdom of God. The simplicity, trust, and honesty of the little ones are lessons that we could learn again.

There was a time when children in America were seen as our greatest treasure. A treasure that needed to be cared for and developed. Train up a child the Bible tells us. What an awesome responsibility we have! Let's value the gifts that God has given us and renew our passion for raising children in the fear and admonition of the Lord.

July 15
He Is Our Protector

Life can be a matter of inches. Winning and losing can come down to inches. Life and death can hang by the thinnest of margins. How many close calls does one have in a lifetime? Only God and His angels know. I just heard a story of a bullet piercing a windshield and lodging in the headrest next to the driver. Stories like these should make us appreciate life.

Often, we don't recognize the near misses of the divine protection of almighty God. When we hear near tragedies, we stop and give God thanks for His blessings of protection.

"I will lift up mine eyes unto the hills, from whence cometh my help. My help cometh from the Lord, which made heaven and earth. He will not suffer thy foot to be moved: he that keepeth thee will not slumber. Behold, he that keepeth Israel shall neither slumber nor sleep. The Lord is thy keeper: the Lord is thy shade upon thy right hand. The sun shall not smite thee by day, nor the moon by night. The Lord shall preserve thee from all evil: He shall preserve thy soul. The Lord shall preserve thy going out and thy coming in from this time forth, and even for evermore" (Psalm 121 KJV).

When we put our trust in God and ask for His protection, we can rest even though we know there will be many near misses. For some, that means His angels might have to work overtime.

Live life knowing He's got your back. That's a good reason to sing some joyful praises.

July 16
God Never Gives Up on Us

"Faith is deliberate confidence in the character of God whose ways you may not understand at the time." Oswald Chambers (1874-1917) Scottish Evangelist to India.

Child of God, there is nothing we cannot face with complete confidence in victory in Jesus. Not even death. God lives in us and responds to us through praise and prayer. God does not abandon us, and He never gives up on us. Ask God for strength and grace. He will help you navigate through whatever situation you are in right now. He will guide you through the choices and decisions you need to make. He absolutely loves you. If you don't feel love for Him, ask Him to give you a heart full of love for Him. He loves to answer that prayer.

July 17
Only God

Only God! When life is beating you down, Only God. When things seem to be spiraling out of control, Only God. When times are tough, and money is tight, Only God.

"We are troubled on every side, yet not distressed; we are perplexed, but not in despair; Persecuted, but not forsaken; cast down, but not destroyed; Always bearing about in the body the dying of the Lord Jesus, that the life also of Jesus might be made manifest in our body" (2 Corinthians 4:8-10 KJV).

When we are at our end, that is the opportunity God is looking for, if we invite Him into the situation. God's strength is made perfect in our weakness. The next time you find yourself struggling, look up and remember Only God.

July 18
God Doesn't Change

Times, they are a-changin,' but the Bible tells us that God is the same yesterday, today, and forever. In this world where everything is turning upside down, we can put our confidence in a God that changes not.

God's character doesn't change; what He said He would be, He will be. His character isn't fickle or impulsive. He loves us and isn't caught up in the changing winds of culture. He doesn't compromise His holiness. What was sinful or wrong yesterday is still wrong today.

The amazing thing is that if we do what the Bible tells us to do, our lives actually work better. If we love one another and treat each other with respect, racism has no foothold. If we seek to better the other person, selfishness dies. If we don't lie, cheat, or steal, integrity and trust will grow in us. Instead of trying to change the world, let's start at home. Let's endeavor to be the person we want the world to be.

We can only change one person; it's the one you see every morning staring back at you in the mirror. Change doesn't have to be a bad thing.

"Jesus Christ the same yesterday, and today, and forever" (Hebrews 13:8 KJV).

July 19
Watch and Pray

Jesus spent His last hours in a garden spent in prayer. He took 3 of His disciples deeper into the garden to pray with Him only, only to find them sleeping. He challenged them with this: "Keep watching and praying, so that you do not come into temptation; the spirit is willing, but the flesh is weak." He went away again, a second time, and prayed, saying, "My Father, if this cup cannot pass away unless I drink from it, Your will be done" (Matthew 26:41-42 NASB).

Jesus instructed His disciples to stay alert and pray. We need to heed that advice to be aware of what is happening to us, around us, and most certainly in the social, spiritual, and political realms of our time. Pray for wisdom and discernment for God's purposes to be fulfilled.

"Watch ye, stand fast in the faith, quit you like men, be strong. Let all your things be done with charity"(1 Corinthians 16:13-14 KJV). Paul also told them to devote themselves to prayer with an alert mind and a thankful heart.

We cannot be lulled into a false sense of security nor be intimidated into submission. It is not enough to see what is happening all around us; we must then pray, pray, and pray for God's divine intervention for our families, communities, and nation. Talk is not enough; action is required. Let us be about our Father's business and pray!

July 20
Pressure Reveals Weaknesses

If you want to find out the strength of something, you must put it under stress to see if any weaknesses develop. If you want to see the strength of someone's character, you must observe them in stressful situations. Difficult situations will cause people to do all kinds of things to escape the pressure. Some will hide, pretend that everything is alright, escape through drugs and alcohol, lash out at those closest to them, quit, blame others, or play the victim.

Strong leaders and emotionally strong individuals rise to the occasion in difficult circumstances. Over the last few months, we have been through extraordinary circumstances that have created stress, and there does not seem to be an end in sight.

What has been revealed in you during stressful events? Have any weaknesses been exposed that you were unaware of? Have fear and anxiety taken you down roads that you never thought you would travel? Does life seem overwhelming and confusing? With the bombardment of news and information, it is easy to get overwhelmed by it all.

Jesus said, "These things I have spoken unto you, that in me ye might have peace. In the world ye shall have tribulation: but be of good cheer; I have overcome the world" (John 16:33 KJV).

Our only hope in times of difficulty and the only place we can go to experience peace is into the loving arms of Jesus.

July 21
We Need a Savior

We are slowly removing Biblical Christianity, faith in God, from our cultural conscience. American culture says we can believe and practice any religion other than Christianity.

As Christians, we have slowly been cooked in the pot of compromise. We have fallen for the world's justification for sin and have adopted some of its values, and called it tolerance.

It's time to stop drinking at the wells of human desire. We need to come back to Jesus, who offers us living water.

The problem is that Christian disciplines that lead us to those waters have become foreign to us as we offer up our time to the god of busyness.

Only God can satisfy the thirsty soul. Apart from Him, we can do nothing.

It's time to break down our alters to the idols we give ourselves to and return to worshipping the one true God – no more games. Let us get holiness back in the house of God and give Jesus a chance to do what only He can do.

We need a Savior, and I know the perfect one. His name is Jesus!

July 22
More Love to Thee

I'm afraid I am a better complainer about life than I am a practitioner of expressing joy in my relationship with Jesus. Is it possible we are not experiencing more joy in our lives because we fail to realize how much joy God has in loving us? Even though we know He is a God of love, that truth has a hard time getting through our filter of brokenness, and we live as though Jesus loves everyone else.

Elizabeth Prentiss (1815-1878) American author, was the wife of a pastor in New Bedford, Massachusetts in the 19th century. She had a life of brokenness that began with the death of her father when she was just nine years old and the deaths of two of her children. Her beautiful hymn still sung today, "*More love to Thee*," begs God to give her more love for Him. Talk about being honest! Her book, "Stepping Heavenward," is a classic still sold today. Written as a journal over many years it conveys growth and maturity through pouring out to others.

It might be time to be as honest with the Lord as Mrs. Prentiss and admit that we don't feel His love through our brokenness. We can ask Him to fill us with a true sense of His love for us and His joy in us as if we are the only ones in the world.

July 23
Inspiration

What inspires you? For some people, it is the desire to make a difference in someone's life. For George Mueller (1805-1898) English evangelist, it was daring to trust God to show how God and God alone would provide through prayer and prayer alone for orphans in Bristol, England. He made his requests for the needs of the orphans to God alone. He never solicited donations.

How did it go? Time and time again, the little orphanage he began with would be down to a lack of one thing or another, and God would provide. Once, there was no milk for the children. They gathered at the table and prayed for milk. There was a knock at the door, and a milkman brought them an overage of milk that met their needs and that would have been discarded. This type of miracle happened again and again.

Over time, Mueller cared for over ten thousand orphans and gave them a Christian education. In fact, in that class-conscious era, he was criticized for raising the poor above what was thought to be their station in life. He established over one hundred schools, and in all, he gave a Christian education to more than one hundred thousand students in over 100 schools that he established.

The unsolicited donations amounted to hundreds of millions. He never went into debt and never took any government funds. Sometimes, funds would appear within hours of a critical need.

It is inspirational what faith and trust in God can accomplish. God, grow our faith in You and You alone to meet our needs.

July 24
The Fear of the Lord

"The fear of the Lord is the beginning of wisdom: and the knowledge of the holy is understanding" (Proverbs 9:10 KJV).

The Fear of the Lord sounds a little strange to our modern ears because we associate nothing good with the word "fear." But fear is taking God's word as deadly serious. To fear the Lord is to believe His word. It is to focus with awe on the Lord. We arrive at this by taking the time to read His word with thoughtful, pondering, and meditation on what we are reading.

When we do, we get smart! More accurately, we get wise, which is far better than smart. Wisdom is transformative.

In God's way of doing things, when we fear God, we fear nothing else. This kind of fear is an awakening to a deep spiritual truth that strikes our hearts. This fear develops awe, respect, belief, and devotion in us. This fear is a deep conviction that God is God, and we believe Him about everything He says and we worship Him.

King David, writing in the Psalms, said there were things too deep for him to understand until He went into the temple and meditated on God. If we set aside our distracting technology, and focus on God, and ponder the richness of who He is, it will be life-changing.

July 25
Some People

We have all been given a gift of potential. Psalm 139, verses 13-15 talks about God creating us in our mother's womb. Our giftedness is from the Lord. Yet, some of us attempt to power on in our own strength.

Some people have had very negative learning experiences and feel like they are the dummies who can't learn.

Some have had an easy time with book knowledge but have a hard time making the transition to the real world, so they think they can't make it.

Some people have had such a rough go at life that they believe life has nothing more to offer than heartache and misfortune.

Can't learn, can't make it, misfortune. But God.

God created us with gifts of potential. The first step is to believe that with His help, anything is possible. Then chart a course. It may take you higher and farther than you thought possible.

There is an old saying that goes something like this: "I would rather shoot for the stars and hit the top of the fence, than shoot for the top of the fence and never get off the ground."

With God, all things are possible. Ask Him to help you use the gifts He gave you to fulfill His purpose in giving them to you.

July 26
The Three Most Important Questions

How did I get here?

Why am I here?

Where will I end up when life is over?

My guess is that many people wonder about these questions at some point in life, but unless they have some type of belief system, they don't want to investigate them because they may not like the answer. Imagine living in the fear or apathy of not knowing the answer to these questions.

The answer to the first two questions gives our life meaning and purpose. The answer to the last question determines how we live.

The prevalent answers to the first question are that either God created us, or we evolved from some cosmic soup. Either answer requires faith. It's easy to accept cosmic soup because it doesn't require anything of us. But if we believe that we were created by a God, then we must be beholden to that God.

If you bet on cosmic soup and there is a God, you lose a lot. If you bet on God and it's cosmic soup, what have you lost? It is just something to ponder. Pssst, it's God.

July 27
A Person's Worth

How do you determine a person's worth? Do we look at their bank account, job title, or education? Is a person's worth based on the accumulation of material possessions? Is it based on friends, popularity, or the number of followers on one's social media account? Or is it determined by productivity, personality, looks, behavior, or talent?

If worth is based on temporal conditions, what happens when they are lost or taken away?

What about the worth of the unborn, the aged, the terminally ill, the disabled, the mentally ill? If we evolved meaninglessly from a cosmic soup, then the healthiest survive, and everyone else be damned. From that view, life is hard, cruel, and pointless.

We have been created on purpose by our Creator, God. There are no mistakes or junk. Everyone is a gift from God and gifted by God. Everything has a purpose. Christianity sees everyone with intrinsic value because everyone is made in the image of God.

"So God created man in His own image, in the image of God created He him; male and female created He them" (Genesis 1:27 KJV).

July 28
Prayer

There are many forms of prayer, including thanksgiving, petition, intercession, and relational conversation. There are so many amazing benefits of prayer.

Prayer helps us focus on God. Prayer is a process, not to get God to work on our behalf but to move us into alignment with God's heart.

Prayer helps us mentally. We can be overwhelmed by emotional turmoil in our situations. Spending time in prayer helps to calm our emotions and clear our heads to get us into a better position to hear God's wisdom and reassurances.

Prayer helps us physically. Many situations we face require a fair amount of time in the throne room asking for God's will to be done. There are physical benefits of quieting ourselves.

Prayer helps us emotionally. As we pray and talk to God, our hearts are being surrendered to God, and it gives God an opportunity to bring change in us before He changes our situations. Prayer develops patience as we sit in His presence talking with Him.

Prayer helps us spiritually. The Bible is full of examples of individuals in crisis calling out to God for help and deliverance.

"Prayer does not fit us for the greater work; prayer is the greater work." Oswald Chambers (1874-1917) Scottish Evangelist to India.

July 29
Change

Someone defined insanity as repeatedly doing the same thing the same way but expecting a different result. It does sound nuts. But change is risky business. Change comes at a cost.

If we want things to be different in ourselves, our marriages, our children, or our jobs, but we keep doing things the same way, let's ask ourselves _why_. There are sensible reasons why we might not risk change. Change is uncomfortable, requires effort, and can feel futile.

But God loves us too much to leave us as we are, and He will help us make needed changes. And He will even help us when the changes we painstakingly make, especially in relationships, don't immediately turn out well. Change can happen very slowly. He will be with us in the struggle. Lean on Him.

Change is holding our tongue. Change is returning a blessing for a rude comment. Change is having the perfect snarky comeback, but not. Change is attending to the things we have let go of in the house, the car, our health and fitness. Change is caring about others by seeing them as placed in our lives by God. Change is humility. Change is possible with God's help.

2 Timothy 4:6 describes how Timothy saw his life as an offering to be poured out to God. <u>That is an elevated but very realistic view that honors the Lord.</u> God gave us life. How we live our lives can be a gift back to Him.

July 30
Why Is Life so Hard?

Why does it seem like whenever I want to do something, a Goliath is standing in my way?

I thought that if I accepted Jesus Christ into my life that life, life would be a little easier. Success would come a little faster. I would at least get a fast pass like you do at Disneyland to bypass all the non-Christians who want the same things that I am going after.

I've discovered that God isn't as interested in my success as I am. It isn't that God is opposed to people being successful; He just has a different idea of what success is.

He wants sons and daughters who are more interested in being in a relationship with Him and trusting Him to mature us into Christ-likeness. He allows a Goliath to show up so that we have no recourse but to turn our hearts back to Him.

Why is life so hard? If you're like me, God is usually my second choice.

July 31
Be Blessed by God

Psalm 84 tells us that the man who trusts God is blessed and that God won't withhold good things from those who do what is right.

We all want to be in the divine flow of God's blessings, and we all want to experience good things in our lives. The problem is we want them all right now and every day. We don't want pain, problems, or bad circumstances. When we do experience the negative aspects of life, we tend to wonder why God has forsaken us.

Pain and problems are a part of life. The truth is that what God allows, He will use for our good. Suffering is never pointless. He will never forsake us.

The blessings of God and the good things that He bestows upon His followers happen over a lifetime. When we look over the course of our lives, we see the hand of God and His blessings. We see Him carrying us through trials and suffering.

The psalm writer declares his observations concerning those who put their lifelong trust in God. In the end, they will declare God's faithfulness. They don't look for immediate gratification; they continue to be faithful, live right, and have a blessed life through hard times and easy times. They are blessed by God. Be among them.

08
AUGUST

August 1
Facing Uncertainty

"My Hope is Built on Nothing Less," is a beloved hymn written in 1836 by Edward Mote (1797-1874) English Pastor.

"My hope is built on nothing less Than Jesus' blood and righteousness. I dare not trust the sweetest frame. But wholly lean on Jesus' name. On Christ the solid rock I stand, All other ground is sinking sand, All other ground is sinking sand.

When He shall come with trumpet sound O may I then in Him be found. Dressed in His righteousness alone Faultless to stand before the throne. On Christ, the solid rock, I stand All other ground is sinking sand."

There is a solid foundation on which we can build our lives that can withstand the uncertainty of our days. Hope is confidence in a future reality. When we put our hope in temporal conditions, we can find ourselves discouraged and hopeless. Jesus was victorious over death, hell, and the grave, and we can put our hope and trust in Him to see us victorious no matter the circumstances that challenge us.

Jesus told us that in this life, we would have struggles and trials, but we could be of good cheer because He has overcome the world. In the changing landscape of our world, we can live in peace and have hope for the future because we have put our confidence in the unchanging love of our God. On Christ, the solid rock we stand!

August 2
Remember Who God Says He is

When life is chaotic, confusing, and stressful, the best thing to do is slow down and simplify. Go back to the basics of what you know and believe. There is so much noise right now from social media, the news, friends' and co-workers' opinions, and our own thoughts and fears that it is hard to focus on what is true. For those who believe in Jesus Christ as our savior and the answer to the world's problems, let me remind you of who God says He is.

"The Lord is good to all: and his tender mercies are over all his works" (Psalm 145:9 KJV).

"The Lord is merciful and gracious, slow to anger, and plenteous in mercy" (Psalm 103:8 KJV).

"O taste and see that the Lord is good: blessed is the man that trusteth in him" (Psalm 34:8 KJV).

"Enter into His gates with thanksgiving, and into His courts with praise be thankful unto Him and bless His name. For the Lord is good; His mercy is everlasting; and His truth endureth to all generations" (Psalm 100:4-5).

Do not let the events move you into a place of fear and panic. Trust in His unfailing love and steadfast kindness. Remember who He says He is and not what your circumstances are telling you. Go back to the basics.

August 3
Emotional and Spiritual Maturity

"My Dear Son...remember that you are accountable to your Maker for all your words and actions." Abigail Adams (1744-1818) wife of John Adams, second president of the United States and mother of John Quincy Adams, our sixth president.

God wants us to be emotionally and spiritually mature in all our words and actions. From James Chapter 1, we see that trials are allowed in our lives to produce patience, and that patience is to have its perfect work. That perfect work causes us to grow into complete maturity, lacking nothing.

The Bible also tells us that God's plan from the beginning is that His children would be fashioned into the same form as Jesus and that we would grow to be more like Him. Jesus is completely balanced in His approach to life. On earth, He was whole and complete, emotionally and spiritually. He didn't need or use people. Jesus loves at all times. It is God's desire for us to experience His love so profoundly that it causes us to grow into wholeness to love others out of that completeness.

Are we loving better and deeper than we ever have? Are we treating everyone we encounter with a love that leaves them wondering? Are we growing in our awareness of God's love? If not, why not? Ask God to help you. He will.

August 4
We Can Be Agents of Encouragement

Johann Wolfgang von Goethe (1749-1832) considered to be the last "polymath" – a person who knew just about everything about all the academic subjects of his day – stated, "When we treat man as he is, we make him worse than he is; when we treat him as if he already were what he potentially could be, we make him what he should be."

God gives us opportunities to rise to the occasion – or not. Cain's response to God's inquiry as to where his brother Abel might be: *Am I my brother's keeper?* was not an example of rising to the occasion. Yes, we are our brother's keeper. Jesus answered this question in the New Testament when He said, "Greater love has no man than this, than to lay down his own life for his friends" (John 15:13 KJV). Not just keepers but ready to die for one another.

It's easy to pick on others' weaknesses, faults, blemishes, and differences because, somehow, it makes us feel superior. God challenges us to see past the surface and see someone made in His image, someone He loves, and to humble ourselves and love others.

We are our brother's keeper, and we have an incredible opportunity all around us to brighten someone's day with just a kind and encouraging word. You never know whose destiny you could change.

August 5
"Wisdom Is the Principal Thing

Through King Solomon, the wisest man who ever lived, God gave us some of the wisest advice we can ever receive.

"My son, forget not my law; but let thine heart keep my commandments: For length of days, and long life, and peace, shall they add to thee. Let not mercy and truth forsake thee: bind them about thy neck; write them upon the table of thine heart: So shalt thou find favour and good understanding in the sight of God and man. Trust in the Lord with all thine heart; and lean not unto thine own understanding. In all thy ways acknowledge him, and He shall direct thy paths. Be not wise in thine own eyes: fear the Lord, and depart from evil" (Proverbs 3:1-7 KJV).

We are blessed to have extremely convenient access to this wisdom. We can read it in our Bibles, on a Bible app on our cellphones, or online from a digital device. Another way is to associate with people who habitually seek to learn and apply God's wisdom to their lives. Those are people who live and breathe wisdom, and we can learn a lot from them. To obtain Obtaining God's wisdom has never been more accessible.

The benefits of wisdom are clear. The pitfall of attempting to live our lives in the darkness of our own thinking is also clear. We must be willing to seek after wisdom like one who is looking for buried treasure. Wisdom will enrich our lives.

August 6
Pride Blinds

"Pride goeth before destruction, and an haughty spirit before a fall" (Proverbs 16:18 KJV).

Haughty means disdainfully proud or scornfully arrogant. Pride blinds us to the truth about ourselves and our situations. The Bible warns us that pride sets us up for destruction.

We can get ourselves into a dangerously prideful state of mind when we convince ourselves that what we are doing is okay, that nothing can go wrong, that we don't need help, and that we can handle things on our own. We think the best about ourselves, and we are suspicious of the motives of those around us.

The Bible instructs us to live humbly and to think soberly about ourselves. To see ourselves correctly, and compare ourselves to God's standard and not comparing ourselves among others. Pride refuses to admit blind spots. Be warned: When we are prideful God Himself resists us. We do not want to be in that position.

"God resisteth the proud, and giveth grace to the humble.

Humble yourselves therefore under the mighty hand of God, that He may exalt you in due time" (1 Peter 5:5b-6 KJV).

Humility begins when we begin to realize who we are in relationship to a Holy God. The more I see myself in relation to Him the more I realize how much I need God. When we humble ourselves before God, He promises to lift us up and help us stand strong.

August 7
It's All About Jesus

It is all about Jesus. "For as by one man's disobedience many were made sinners, so by the obedience of one shall many be made righteous" (Romans 5:19 KJV).

The Apostle Paul explained to the church in Rome that in the very beginning, Adam disobeyed God's instructions, causing humanity to be at odds with a Holy God.

The remedy was when Jesus Christ came to humanity. He was obedient even to the point of death on the cross. The crucifixion was an extremely cruel way to die. Jesus endured taking all our mistakes, failures, and sins upon Himself so that all who put their trust in Him can begin anew with a clean slate.

Most don't give any thought to what Jesus did and how it might impact their own lives. Some can't believe that Jesus can make a difference. The Bible says that if we believe with our hearts and confess with our mouths, we shall be saved. It is a free gift; all we must do is accept it.

Jesus opened the door for us to have life a life-changing relationship with the Holy Trinity. Give God a chance. You will be amazed at what He can do.

August 8
God's Two Witnesses

In His infinite wisdom, God gave mankind two witnesses to draw us to Him. The heavens declare the glory of the Lord, and His Word declares who He is. As we look at all of creation and the intricacies that are around us, how can we say that all the created world is by cosmic chance? The detailed order of our world is created by design, by a God who put it all in motion. Its very design was to cause us to look up and declare there is a God. Then seek Him out. To go on a quest and discover who this God is, which leads us to the Bible.

Let me just say that the Bible is the all-time best-selling book in history. It has been under attack to be discredited and annihilated, even to this day, but to no avail. God has protected and preserved His Word. His Word is His love story with His creation. It is our manual on how to best live, which is why it is under attack.

His word tells us what will happen if we try to suppress the knowledge of God. We will get exactly what we see happening in our world: a downward spiral of decadent behaviors. Let us look at God's two witnesses and allow them to lead us back to Him.

August 9
What a Mess We Have Made

King David wrote, "O Lord, our Lord, how excellent is thy name in all the earth! who hast set thy glory above the heavens. When I consider thy heavens, the work of thy fingers, the moon and the stars, which thou hast ordained; What is man, that thou art mindful of him? and the son of man, that thou visitest him?" (Psalm 8 verses 1, 3, and 4 KJV).

The psalmist was looking up at the stunning night sky, considering its created beauty, and then he looked at life as he knew it. I can imagine him shaking his head as he asked the question of why God would even bother with us and the messes we make. The answer is that God has chosen to love us and has made us His focus. Not because we are deserving but simply because we are His creation.

When we look around the world at all the confusion and chaos offering no real answers, people must wonder how we are getting out of this mess. Politicians cannot agree on what is best for the nation. Agendas are driving the social media narratives. Individuals are doing their best to navigate changing social, educational, and economic realities.

We, too, need to lift our eyes up to the sky and marvel at the greatness and vastness of His universe and remember that the God who made it all loves you. He has promised never to leave us nor abandon us. When life seems out of control, remember who controls it all. He will make a way where there seems to be no way.

August 10
God's Transformative Power

God has an amazing way of taking life's challenges and working them to our good if we let Him. When you read about the characters in the Bible, God takes them and molds them through the journey of their life. When you see the finished product, you see an incredible story of brokenness and redemption.

All of us are in the process of discovery. Discovering our brokenness, our frailty, the fact that we don't have all the answers, and that we need someone bigger than us. When we surrender to God and accept the sacrifice of His Son Jesus, it opens the door for God to take and redeem our life's purpose.

It doesn't ensure that we will not struggle or have difficulties, but through those trials, something beautiful emerges, like when a caterpillar turns into a butterfly. Life must be lived one day at a time, and it isn't always easy to see what God is doing. When you look back over the years, you begin to see things that you didn't see at the time.

God is always faithful and is always working to give us the best life possible. At the end of our time here, will our life be a testimony of God's grace and love working in us?

August 11
Learn to Articulate What We Believe

In the 2014 film, "God's Not Dead," a college student is challenged by an intimidating professor to defend what he believes about God. The professor requires all his students to sign a written declaration stating that God is dead in order to pass his class. Only one student refuses to sign. The professor requires the student to debate the topic with him and further requires the entire class to determine who is the winner of the debate.

We see pressure, force, intimidation, and open hostility widely used against believers today. It is acceptable to believe just about anything else and get a free pass, but if we mention Jesus, the PC (politically correct), police come out in force.

Sadly, very few can defend what they believe intelligently – on either side! They know what they believe but have a hard time articulating it. Blind faith isn't attractive, but a reasoned faith draws others. Evil is spreading, and Jesus is still the answer.

It's time to do the work to prepare ourselves to stand up and proclaim truth intelligently, even in the face of opposition but with love and compassion for those who are blinded by the god of this world. "But sanctify the Lord God in your hearts: and be ready always to give an answer to every man that asketh you a reason of the hope that is in you with meekness and fear" (1 Peter 3:15 KJV).

August 12
Living on the Edge

"Dare to be a Daniel. Dare to stand alone,
Dare to have a purpose firm. Dare to make it known."

Today, when we think about living on the edge, we may picture outspoken, daring men and women. But Phillip P. Bliss (1838-1873) a hymn writer and evangelist, was probably not a mighty figure like we imagine such figures to be. He was mightily used by God, writing Hymns like "Dare to be a Daniel." When his daring moment came, he knew what to do. On a train trestle 70 feet above a ravine, the train went off the track. Phillip's wife, Lucy, was caught in the ironworks. He was free and could have gotten away. He stayed with her, and they died together. What a Daniel-like, daring, yet Christ-like, loving way God chose for Bliss to "make it known."

Inventor,Thomas Edison, chose the hymn, "I Will Sing of My Redeemer," which was written by Bliss, to be one of Edison's first-ever recordings in the world. Other hymns by Bliss include Almost Persuaded, Hallelujah, What a Savior!, Hold the Fort, Jesus Loves Even Me, Once For All, Whosoever Will, Wonderful Words of Life, and The Light of the World is Jesus.

"Many mighty men are lost. Daring not to stand

Who for God had been a host. By joining Daniel's band

In using his talents to write inspirational hymns, and in being a hero who died with his wife when he could have spared his life, Mr. Bliss lived on the edge and glorified the Lord.

August 13
Worshipping God

Do we Worship God or just go through spiritual calisthenics?

As Christians, we are called to worship God. We all know the word "Worship," but what exactly does it mean? Is it a type of service at church? Is it an attitude that we are supposed to have? Is it singing or raising our hands to God? Is it a mental, emotional, spiritual, or a physical discipline?

We all have an idea about it, but if we really don't understand what God is expecting of us, how can we be sure it's pleasing Him? Is it possible to do all the motions of worship and still not actually worship God?

We can go to church, sing the songs, play on the worship team, raise our voices and our hands, bow in reverence, sit in quiet reflection, and still not participate in worship.

The dictionary defines worship as reverent honor and homage paid to God, and adoring reverence or regard. Nice definition, but what does it mean? What does adoring reverence look like? Is it our facial expression? The Westminster Shorter Catechism states, "A man's chief end is to glorify God and to enjoy him forever." Worship starts with our desire to give God glory.

I've asked a lot of questions about worship. What are your thoughts on worshiping God?

August 14
Look up and Ask

There is an old Sunday School song that went something like this: "If you want joy, you must ask for it, jump for it, clap for it," etc. It's an action song that gets the kids moving and singing. The truth of the song is that the joy of the Lord is our strength, and when we need it, we should ask for it.

Asking is such a hard thing to do. Most people want to be self-sufficient and try to figure things out on their own or believe that there isn't a God that can be called on for help.

In the book of James in the Bible, its author, James states, that if anyone lacks wisdom, we can ask, and God will give wisdom liberally. He also states that we have not because we ask not or ask wrongly.

There are times in our lives when we need to look up and ask for help, such as when we need strength, wisdom, joy, peace. love, help with finances, direction, or purpose. God hears and desires to give us what we need.

The answer comes when we activate faith. We must believe that God exists and that He rewards those who diligently call out to Him. Let us not be filled with doubt so that our calling out to God is as if we are wishing upon a star, just hoping something works.

The person who, in desperation looks up, and believes will ultimately find the answer they are seeking. Look up and ask!

August 15
Love and Accept Others

God did an incredible thing when He gave man free will. God does not use manipulation, control, or intimidation when dealing with us. He gives us a choice to either accept what He has to offer or reject it. He loves us regardless, as a parent would love their child regardless of the choices that child makes. God does not sit in the heavens and whine and cry over our rejecting what He has to offer. He doesn't pout and promise to make us pay for our bad choices. He doesn't make our life hell because we choose to do it our way (we invite hell into our lives by the choices we make).

If God doesn't use control, manipulation, and intimidation in our lives, then neither should we in our relationships with others. God created us to be free, and only the free can choose to do the right things.

We are to love and allow others the right to their free will. The actions of your free will could cause me not to be in a relationship with you. Love and accept others for who they are and be the person you would want to be friends with, and your life will go well for you.

August 16
A Great Promise

At the end of his life, Moses told the children of Israel, "But if from thence thou shalt seek the Lord thy God, thou shalt find Him, if thou seek Him with all thy heart and with all thy soul" (Deuteronomy 4:29 KJV).

Moses reminded them that the key to following God is to seek Him with all their heart and soul and follow His commandments. He wants all of us. Not a half-hearted, "tip of the hat" acknowledgment. Moses said that if they were to ever break the covenant given to them by God and serve other gods, Jehovah would turn them over to foreign nations to be taken captive. But Moses said that even if they did allow that to happen, the way back to God and to be free again was the same: seek the Lord with all their heart and soul, obey His commandments, and He promises He will come to them. He would watch over them, protect them, and bless all their endeavors.

Many find themselves lost and feeling abandoned by their country, community, and family. God's promise is the same today: that if we will seek after Him diligently with everything we have, we will find Him. We can trust Him. Only God can fill us with His peace, love, and joy. He gives us a sense of purpose and fulfillment as we live out our lives in obedience to His Word.

August 17
Trust in the Lord

"Trust in the Lord with all thine heart; and lean not unto thine own understanding. In all thy ways acknowledge Him, and He shall direct thy paths" (Proverbs 3:5-6 KJV).

Trust means a firm belief in the reliability, truth, ability, or strength of someone or something. Trust is easy when everything is running smoothly. It is when our world gets turned upside down that our ability to trust is put to the test.

The writer of Proverbs instructs us to put our complete trust in the reliability and strength of God and not to put confidence in our own ability to reason things out.

We are mostly people of action, and we want to fix problems and negotiate our way out of circumstances. But putting our confidence and trust in God keeps us from giving in to fear and making bad decisions. Trust in God keeps us grounded in the truth of His ability to deliver us from all circumstances. To acknowledge God in every step we take is to invite His help in everything we do.

Often, when the fear of uncertainty comes knocking at our door, it is good to make trust declarations. <u>Lord, I trust you, even though I see no way out of this mess.</u> As you declare in faith, trusting God for answers, He always comes through. Most of the time, trusting God involves patience. Waiting and trusting are not easy to do when our world is crumbling, but God has promised that He will direct our steps. Put your confidence in the Lord, and you will not be disappointed.

August 18
The Priority of Love

What if the final test of our lives is how well we've loved others?

We were made in the image of God, and we know that the Bible tells us that God so loved the world that He gave His only Son. We know that the Son willingly gave His life to redeem mankind out of love.

We are uniquely created to represent God on earth. I Corinthians 13 describes what love is to look like in our relationships. It is a high standard that can only flow out of us as we surrender to God. He has instructed us to love our neighbors, and Jesus gave us a new commandment that we should love one another.

It sounds to me like love is a high priority, and He expects us to love others well.

Love isn't about feelings. It's about a decision to love others even when they choose not to love in return. Loving requires risk, and sometimes there is pain involved. Hurting people sometimes hurt other people, but love covers a multitude of sins. Love is the final answer. God has invested Himself in us, so let us live up to our high calling and love as He loves.

August 19
Preach the Gospel to My Own Heart

"For as he thinketh in his heart, so is he" (Proverbs 23:7 KJV). Oh, the power of our thought life, our self-talk. "A man is literally what he thinks, his character being the complete sum of all his thoughts." And "Every action and feeling is preceded by a thought." James Allen (1864-1912), British Author.

Negative, faithless self-talk: It's no wonder they don't like me. Things will never change. He/She will never change. That's too hard. I'll never be able to break this sinful habit. I don't have the time to make that, fix that, do that, learn that. Life is so hard. The people in my life make it impossible. Why can't I trust God more? I'm terrible at XYZ. It's hopeless.

Instead, preach the Gospel to ourselves: Jesus loves me so much He died for me and I'm precious to Him. Prayer changes things. I trust God and I step out in faith to do new and hard things for His glory and my good. This hard trial has purpose and I'm excited to see what God is doing in me through this mess. I can approach God's throne of grace boldly because of Jesus Christ I'm forgiven. I love God, I trust God. I roll all my care upon Him because He cares for me. I thank God for everything. God sees me, is with me, is in me!

"Good thoughts and actions can never produce bad results; bad thoughts and actions can never produce good results." E. M. Bounds (1835-1913) American Author and Attorney.

August 20
Healing Words vs Harming Words

In Proverbs, the great wisdom book of the Bible, we often see a teaching technique of contrast and comparison. In the verses below, we see truth about the power of our speech – good and bad.

"There is that speaketh like the piercings of a sword: but the tongue of the wise is health" (Proverbs 12:18 KJV).

"The mouth of a righteous man is a well of life: but violence covereth the mouth of the wicked" (Proverbs 10:11 KJV).

We can say things in a way that either violently cuts our listener like a sword or extends to our listener a sense of healing, like a wellspring of life. These verses ascribe words that bring life and healing as characteristic of the wise and words that cut people as acts of violence and wickedness.

That's a lot of power.

In matters of our speech, we can't excuse ourselves on the basis of our good intentions. We must take ownership of our responsibility to speak in a healing, life-giving manner all the time.

It's a matter of life and death to our listeners.

August 21
The Problem Isn't Problems

"Is the church relevant anymore?"

"Are we making a difference in any area?"

It is so easy to focus on problems. Jesus prepared us for it: "In the world ye shall have tribulation: but be of good cheer; I have overcome the world" (John 16:33b KJV). We shouldn't be surprised by hardships and difficulties. If we are breathing, we are going to have problems.

The answer isn't even the church. Hopefully, you will find the answers there, but we must remember that the church is made up of people with problems. Hurt people tend to hurt other people, so we must give the church and its people some grace.

The problem isn't problems. The problem is, where are we looking for the answers? If it isn't Jesus, *that's* a problem.

We look to Jesus and His instructions to us. If we want the church to be relevant and make a difference, we must remember we are the church, so if the church isn't relevant, we must ask ourselves: Are we relevant? Are we making a difference? We as believers must be authentic in our faith, not just what we believe but what we practice. We must be what Jesus tells us to be and do what He tells us to do.

Jesus is the answer! Believe it.

August 22
Blessed Are the Peacemakers

Over the recent months, there seem to be more and more demonstrations and even people using their vehicles as weapons to spread messages of hate. What is our role as Christians?

Jesus, teaching the masses in the sermon on the mount, gives us our role. "Blessed are the peacemakers: for they shall be called the children of God" (Matthew 5:9 KJV).

God's peacemakers are to show people by our own example how to cooperate instead of fighting.

Our role is to be peacemakers wherever God has us: in the home, on the job, in our church, and in the community. Wherever there is tension and discord, we should do our best to mediate peace.

Someone once said that we all carry two pails in any conflict. One pail has gasoline, and the other pail has water. We can either help put out the conflict or throw gasoline on it making it hotter and bigger.

In our world today, I see people throwing gasoline instead of working to relieve the situation. We don't have to follow the crowd. We need to do our best to live up to the words of Jesus and be peacemakers.

August 23
Self-Examination

Personal evaluation and reflection are good for us if done constructively and prayerfully. "But let a man examine himself" (1 Corinthians 11:28a KJV). It is not for the purpose of just focusing on the bad and beating ourselves up.

I have found that there is usually more going on in my life than I'm aware of. I can get a kind of tunnel vision by being so focused on getting an array of things done. We need time to stop and examine the path of life we are on. If we bring the Lord into this process of self-examination, it can be insightful and transformative.

"Search me, O God, and know my heart: try me, and know my thoughts" (Psalm 139:23 KJV).

August 24
To God Be the Glory

When was the last time you stopped and consciously gave God all the glory?

- Glory means high renown or honor.
- Renown means the condition of being known or talked about by many people, fame.
- Honor means regard with great respect.

There is grandeur in the meaning of the word "glory." God, the Father, Jesus, His Son, and the Holy Spirit are worthy to be regarded with total respect, honor, and glory. Let's bring this understanding to our worship, songs, and prayers.

"Wherefore David blessed the Lord before all the congregation: and David said, Blessed be Thou, Lord God of Israel our father, for ever and ever. Thine, O Lord is the greatness, and the power, and the glory, and the victory, and the majesty: for all that is in the heaven and in the earth is Thine; Thine is the kingdom, O Lord, and Thou art exalted as head above all. Both riches and honour come of Thee, and Thou reignest over all; and in Thine hand is power and might; and in Thine hand it is to make great, and to give strength unto all. Now therefore, our God, we thank Thee, and praise Thy glorious name" (1 Chronicles 29:10-13 KJV).

Give God all the glory and wait and see what only God can do with a heart that seeks to honor Him.

August 25
A Return to Holiness

As we tune into the news in whatever format that might be, we hear the experts and politicians speaking their version of truth.

I was reminded of a television show I recently watched. It was an old episode of "Bones." In this episode, there was a group of people who decided to speak only the truth, no matter how rude, painful, or destructive it might be. At first, it all seemed liberating to speak only what was true. As time went on, it was discovered that many of the participants had hidden lives of deceit that contradicted their vows to be truthful.

I cannot help but feel the same thing is going on as I watch the talking heads spout out their version of the truth. I fear that concern for integrity, honesty, and the greater good has gone the way of the Kodak FotoMat, Sambo's Restaurant, Blockbuster, and Toys R Us. As far as I can tell, they are non-existent.

If we are going to fix the social, political, and relational problems of our day, we are going to start with a return to eternal Biblical values.

There once was a day when our culture insisted that doing the right thing was a virtue. Not anymore.

I am not advocating; I am only speaking the truth, no matter the consequences. I do believe it is time to raise the bar on holiness. It starts with each of us and requires the same from our leaders.

August 26
How Do We Glorify God

Question: "What is the chief end of man?"

Answer: "The chief end of man is to glorify God, and to enjoy Him forever."

The above is the first question, and its answer in the Westminster Shorter Catechism. God's whole point in creating us, our "chief end," is so that we can glorify Him and enjoy Him forever.

How do we do that? It is in a million small day-in and day-out attitudes of the heart in response to what comes into our lives.

We glorify God when we clean our home. He is a God of order. Cleaning our home reflects who God is and brings Him glory if that is our heart attitude.

But we don't glorify God when we clean our home if we clean our home in anger that people living there don't help us. We don't glorify God if we clean our home out of pride that we are better than others who don't keep a tidy home. It's all about the attitude of the heart. We glorify God from sincere hearts that love Him and want to please Him.

God wants our hearts. Let's glorify Him now and enjoy Him forever.

August 27
How Do You Want to Be Remembered

"Let us endeavor so to live so that when we come to die even the undertaker will be sorry" Mark Twain , (1835-1910) American author and humorist.

First, let's realize none of us are getting out of here alive. We are all dying. It is inevitable, unless Jesus returns before we die, that we will all pass into eternity through death.

This is not a party conversation topic. In fact, most people do a really good job of living so as not to be bothered with such thoughts.

Because, at some point, our light will go out, let me give you something to ponder: How do you want to be remembered?

You can control the conversation as they gather to talk about you based on the way you live your life. What are the one or two dominant characteristics that you want to be known for? That you loved others well? That you were family first? That you put others first? That you served God?

How do you want to be remembered? Start living backward toward that end goal.

August 28
Love is Demonstrated in Obedience

"It is inbred in us that we have to do exceptional things for God: but we have not. We have to be exceptional in the ordinary things, to be holy in mean streets, among mean people, and this is not learned in five minutes." Oswald Chambers (1874-1917) Scottish Evangelist to India.

God helps His children to be exceptionally obedient in all kinds of situations and with all kinds of people. But He gives us extraordinary help. He gives us the indwelling Holy Spirit and His word, and He gives every man and woman, and every boy and girl a conscience to know right from wrong in the majority of situations. He works through His people to help one another. He knows that our growth takes time.

God understands the complexity of life and wants the absolute best for His children. He knows we operate well in loving obedience and submission to His plans and purposes. As lost and broken children, we often find ourselves reaching for the proverbial "hot stove" and suffering the inevitable consequences.

Life has many moral and ethical forks in the road. His Word is our guide to navigate challenges with wisdom and discernment. God gives us what we need for the most in life. As a loving Father, He wants to see us thrive.

August 29
To Trust, or Not to Trust

"If the highest aim of a captain were to preserve his ship, he would keep it in port forever." Thomas Aquinas (– 1274) Christian thinker and writer.

If our faith were a ship, would we sail the high seas in it trusting in God, or would we keep it in port? To trust or not to trust, that is the question. It is getting harder to answer.

We may be called upon to take a dangerous stand trusting in God and if we don't take that stand, we aren't just parking our ship in port to preserve it; in not taking that stand, we are abandoning our trust.

We are living in a time when the culture is increasingly hostile to Christianity and absolute truth. Even speaking observable truth that would have been widely agreed upon only a few decades ago has become ideological and political. Some objectively false man-made rights and wrongs are being forced on us as truth with a threat of retaliation if even questioned, let alone rejected. Will we trust God to stand? Will we fold?

Unfortunately, we can't choose to sit it out. The only choice we have is to trust in God or to trust in ourselves. The battle is raging. Who are you trusting in?

August 30
Time to Evaluate

Do those who know you the best respect you the most? We may be able to talk a good game and fool most people with our charm and wit. We usually can't fool the ones we live with.

We can say we believe this or value that, but does our lifestyle back it up? What are our priorities? Does our life reflect what we say is important to us?

Here are a few things to consider as we evaluate our life.

- What do you believe about God, and how does that effect how you live?

- What are your priorities in life? Do the ones closest to you know how much you love and care about them?

- How do people respond to you? Do people want to be near you or try to get away from you?

- Are you just living life, or are you trying to make a positive difference to those around you?

A life lived in selfish ambition is no life at all. When we get to the end of our life, what's going to matter is the people standing by our side. Time to evaluate!

August 31
The Christian Life Is a Life of Repentance

"Repent ye therefore, and be converted, that your sins may be blotted out, when the times of refreshing shall come from the presence of the Lord" (Acts 3:19 KJV).

There is a biblical word that used to be understood a lot more than it is today. The word is repent. It means more than apologizing for a wrong. Repent conveys the idea of agreeing with God that something is wrong and turning from that wrong. It is not a one-and-done. We may have to repent multiple times over the same behavior.

To repent is not to apologize. We apologize for something accidental, like stepping on someone's foot waiting in line.

True repentance means we take the time to confess to God and ask Him to help us see what meant more to us at that moment than doing what is right. Did we feel snubbed? Did we want to feel seen? We tell God we are sorry and repent, remembering that He never snubs and never puts us down. He sees us. We tell the person we hurt, I'm sorry and I want to make it up to you. And then we do something to make it up to them. Their heart may or may not soften. They may or may not forgive us. That part isn't in our control. Our repentance is in our control.

Repentance is hard. Embarrassing. Humbling. It honors God, and it matures us into more Christlikeness. It won't feel good in the moment. Repent anyway. Becoming more like Jesus is worth it.

09

SEPTEMBER

September 1
Living by Faith

"My faith rests not upon what I am or shall be or feel or know, but in what Christ is, in what He has done, and in what He is now doing for me." Charles Spurgeon (1834-1892) English Preacher.

The Bible tells us "We live by faith and not by sight" (2 Corinthians 5:7 KJV). The object of that faith matters. It is not merely an unspecified, so-called, faith that is placed in nothing other than a willingness to think things will all be okay. The object of our faith must be solidly in Jesus Christ, our Lord and Savior, from Whom we get our true identity.

The enemy of this world is the ultimate identity thief. He would have us believe false messages about our identity, who we are, our worth, and who to blame. Blame your parents, your environment, or your past for your lot in life. Or he plays on our need to be in control with messages to just put on our big boy pants and push through all the negativity.

The Bible tells us to take hold of the truths written in the Word of God and to put our trust in what it says about us. This takes faith, trust, and living not just by what we see and hear around us. The Bible tells us that we are loved, accepted, and chosen. We are His special creation and have high honor and value. We are fearfully and wonderfully made. We are special because we are made in the image of God. Our faith rests in Jesus Christ Who gives us our identity in Himself. Hallelujah.

September 2
Trust in the Lord

"Thou wilt keep him in perfect peace, whose mind is stayed on Thee: because he trusteth in Thee" (Isaiah 26:3 KJV).

Peace: something we all want. Trust: the way to peace.

We have all been burned by someone we thought we could trust. When someone lets us down, we build walls to protect ourselves from disappointment. It may have started with a parent consistently disappointing us by not coming through after repeated promises. It may have been a relationship that ended in pain. Whatever the case, we find it hard to trust others with our love, hopes, and even our fears. Our hearts scream at us that we are the only ones we can depend on. We travel through life in protective mode to avoid disappointment and rejection.

The creator of heaven and earth calls to us, inviting us to trust Him. At this crossroads, will we choose trust and faith, or will we continue on the pathway of fear and doubt? Trusting God doesn't mean that life is going to be all rainbows and butterflies. Trusting God allows us to relax in confidence, knowing that no matter what we go through, God will be there to walk through it with us. Deciding to trust Him brings peace.

"And the peace of God, which passeth all understanding, shall keep your hearts and minds through Christ Jesus" (Philippians 4:7 KJV).

September 3
Forgiveness

"Forgiveness is the fragrance that the violet sheds on the heel that has crushed it" Mark Twain (1835-1910) American author.

Forgiveness has the power to keep our hearts free of bitterness and resentment. When someone hurts us through words or actions, we have a choice to make. We can let it go through forgiveness, or we can hold onto the offense and let it eat us up from the inside out.

When we are hurt, we usually want our offenders to suffer like we have. We are afraid to let go of the hurt because we are afraid they will never find out how badly they hurt us. When we hold onto it, we are the ones who suffer. We are the ones chained to an event in our past that we can't move on from.

I'm not saying it's easy or that what someone did wasn't painful or destructive. Forgiveness isn't some 1, 2, 3 formula that makes everything better. But forgiveness is the best medicine for us. Sometimes we must repeatedly declare our forgiveness until our minds and emotions catch up to our confession. To forgive is to place them in God's hands and let Him deal with them. He is much better at that than we are. Forgiveness allows us to move on with our lives and enjoy all the blessings God has for us.

September 4
Great Expectations

"Now, I return to this young fellow. And the communication I have got to make is, that he has great expectations."

In _Great Expectations,_ published in 1861 by Charles Dickens (1812-1870) English author, the main character, Pip, went from poverty to wealth and from trust to disappointment with moral lessons along the way.

As Christians, our greatest expectation is expressed in The Gospel in a Nutshell: "For God so loved the world, He gave His only begotten Son, that whosoever believeth in Him should not perish, but have everlasting life" (John 3:16 KJV).

In addition:

Delayed Expectations: "Hope deferred maketh the heart sick: but when the desire cometh, it is a tree of life" (Proverbs 13:12 KJV)

Redemptive Expectations: "In whom we have redemption through His blood, the forgiveness of sins, according to the riches of His grace" (Ephesians 1:7 KJV)

Unrealized Expectations: "When a wicked man dieth, his expectation shall perish: and the hope of unjust men perisheth" (Proverbs 11:7 KJV)

Expectation of good from God: "My soul, wait thou only upon God; for my expectation is from Him" (Psalm 62:5 KJV)

Today we hear that a person has "great prospects" rather than "great expectations." Our ultimate prospects are eternal, and for those in Christ, they are great, indeed!

September 5
Count Your Blessings

"When upon life's billows you are tempest tossed. When you are discouraged thinking all is lost. Count your many blessings, name them one by one. And it will surprise you what the Lord hath done." *Count Your Blessings*, Written in 1897 by Johnson Oatman (1856-1921) considered one of the most prolific American hymn writers worldwide.

This great old hymn advises that when things look grim, stop and count the many blessings in our lives given to us by God. It is timeless advice.

We can so easily take things for granted. Life moves so fast that it is hard to notice the small changes in our children as they mature into adulthood, the acts of kindness by our family and friends, the thoughtful caring of our brothers and sisters at church, the roof over our head, the food on our table, and life itself.

God created us to be in relationships. Sometimes, we need to stop and enjoy the people around us. They may not be perfect, and they may have some quirks that bug us, but I'm sure we have some that bug them. We can't know how long they will be in our lives, so let's appreciate them while they are. Don't wait until family and friends are gone before we say how much they mean to us. Be careful not to allow the speed of life to rob you of the blessings of family and friends. Stop and enjoy the beautiful bouquet of people in your life.

September 6
Let the Church Arise

Jesus said, "I will build my church; and the gates of hell shall not prevail against it" (Matthew 16:18b KJV). There have been many attempts to suppress the church of Jesus Christ, and every time it grows stronger.

Dictators, governments, and evil regimes have done their best to silence and destroy the church, but to no avail. All the power of earth can be leveled against her, but she will not be destroyed. She may not be perfect and has made many mistakes, mostly because churches are filled with broken people who do not always adhere to God's Word.

Even with its broken history, the church is still the agency God uses to reach the world. God has not given up on the church and continues to do great things through her. Even now there are many attempts to shut her down and silence her voice, but God always has the last say on her future. This hour in history demands that the church find its place and voice as she aligns with the will and purposes of almighty God.

The voice and purposes of the church should be demonstrated through love and compassion, not criticism and judgment. The church may lose some battles, but she will not lose the war. Let us arise as one and let our enemies be scattered as we worship the King of Kings and Lord of Lords. Let the church of Jesus Christ Arise.

September 7
A Cry for Help

It was perfection when God created the Garden of Eden and placed Adam and Eve there to live. They had all that they could ever want: the perfect environment, everything they would need to sustain life, animals for their pleasure, and most of all, a relationship with God Himself. Then, disobedience threw it into chaos. Creation worked against them. Their relationships with God and each other fractured.

Thousands of years later, humanity is still in chaos, and life seems to be falling apart all around us. Marriage and families bear little resemblance to the pattern ordained by God. Materialism and greed are the idols of today. Addictions are a plaque in the land. Depression and unhappiness are rampant. Few are willing to ask for help. People go about their lives doing their best to make it in their own strength.

We were not created to go at life on our own. We need each other and God for a happy, healthy, and successful life. King David knew what to do when He was in difficult times, "In my distress I called upon the Lord, and cried unto my God: he heard my voice" (Psalm 18:6a KJV). David did not let pride or self-sufficiency stop him from asking God for help. We all need help from God and each other. Let us not wait until it is too late before we ask.

September 8
It's Time to Be Salt and Light

"Ye are the salt of the earth" (Matt 5:13a KJV).

"Ye are the light of the world" (Matt 5:14a KJV).

How did our nation get into such a mess? If a person has enough money or political clout, they can get away with just about anything, while those who stand up for right values get arrested.

Jesus declared that His followers would be salt and light. The darker the days become, the brighter His children *should* shine. I say should. If we don't know the truth, it will be easy to be deceived into doing the wrong things, thinking we are doing right.

God's children cannot sit idly by while evil rises. It's time to get involved, to make our voices heard. I believe God is allowing America to be insulted by its politicians to see if His Children will rise up. The place to start is on our knees but then we must stand up and stand together for what is morally right.

We need to get behind those who will stand for the values that made America great. If God is going to bless America as He has since the beginning, it will take the same kind of leaders it took to found this great nation – Godly, principled leaders willing to stand for what is Biblically right. It is time to be the salt and light.

September 9
Delicate Balance

Today, we hear about "Life and Work Balance." The idea is not to become extreme in either area. Believe it or not, there has never been a better time as a country to have an ideal balance in our personal and work lives. Let's look at history.

During the Colonial Period in our country, 1607-1776, people worked "from first light to dark," which could be 12 or more hours depending on the time of year. In the 1800s, a typical factory day was 10-12 hours, 6 days a week including children. There were no home appliances, indoor plumbing, or electricity. Everyday tasks were done with intense physical labor and strain.

Today, our work weeks are typically 40 hours long. We have the benefits of modern innovations: home appliances, automobiles, and medical care that would have been unimaginable centuries ago. Our homes are constructed for better function and insulation from the weather. Our labor is nothing compared to the past.

Yet, we observe the hectic frenzy of life today. Some work themselves to exhaustion. Some don't seem to have a work ethic bone in their body. We need a delicate balance of work and rest.

God's way is always the best way. He made us to be like Him. He worked and then He rested. We are at our best when we follow His example. Let's keep the balance, and everybody wins.

September 10
The Cost of Being a Disciple

Luke records Jesus' words to a large crowd:

"If any man come to me, and hate not his father, and mother, and wife, and children, and brethren, and sisters, yea, and his own life also, he cannot be my disciple" Luke 14:26 KJV.

Is Jesus really telling us that if we don't hate our own families and our own lives, we cannot be His disciples?

Jesus is cutting to the heart of our excuses about following Him. We will use our relationships as an excuse not to obey His commands. We will choose our own desires over serving Him. We must be willing to choose Him over our families and our own desires. Our desires will bring us into conflict with His purpose for our lives. If we are unwilling to lay our desires down, we will find ourselves at odds with Kingdom purposes.

Following Jesus means obedience and dependence on Him. We lay down our self-sufficiency and control. We must not fool ourselves into thinking that we can be His disciples and serve ourselves.

September 11
America Under Attack

Where were you and what were you doing when *"The World Stopped Turning"* on September 11, 2001? I had just arrived at work, and a coworker informed us that America was under attack. We quickly went into an office that had a television, and we all sat in silence as we watched the events of that morning unfold.

New York City rebuilt, but the scars of that day remain. There are many stories of heroism. Many people sacrificed their future health to save the lives of others. Many died by rushing in to save lives, as many were running out to save their own. Flight 93 didn't reach its destination because the passengers decided if they were going to die, they were going to die fighting.

The acts of heroism remind us that we all have a choice when things become difficult. We can either cower in the corner, or take action and fight back.

Today, as we recount the events of that day, let us remember and honor the heroes, but let's also remember what makes America great – the willingness of her people to lay down their lives to save the lives of other people both on foreign soil and domestic. God bless America!

September 12
Influence Through Service

God has given everyone the gift and responsibility of influence. Our influence may be big or small. It can affect a few people or many people, depending on our circumstances. But we all have an impact whether we see it at the time or not. Influence is powerful.

Followers of Christ influence through our primary ministry – serving others. How we treat others impacts anyone around us who overhears or watches us. People can't help but watch our lives, just as we can't help but watch them. Jesus taught us to do unto others as we would like them to do unto us in the same circumstance. This principle, called "The Golden Rule," is drawn from the Lord's teaching in Matthew 7 in the Sermon on the Mount.

We influence others by serving them, by showing grace and patience to the rude checker, the arrogant bank officer, the thankless spouse, the annoying co-worker, and the inconsiderate neighbor. We don't retaliate. We don't expect thanks from them. We don't withhold our hearts from them. We treat them as we wish they would treat us. Regardless of the response in the moment, God works in those moments and drives home the impact He wants for their hearts and minds.

Influencing others through our service glorifies God and makes lasting impressions on lives that we may never see. God sees. As we serve others, God changes us, too.

September 13
Trust and Obey

"When we walk with the Lord in the light of His word

What a glory He sheds on our way

While we do His good will, He abides with us still

And with all who will trust and obey

Chorus: Trust and obey, for there's no other way

To be happy in Jesus, but to trust and obey."

Trust and Obey. Written in 1887 by Daniel B. Towner 1850-1919

It's easy to trust God when everything is going well. But are we trusting God at all? We don't depend on God for the necessities of life. We have good paying jobs to take care of our basic needs and wants. We have credit cards if something breaks, or if we just want something now. We have medical insurance if we get sick. If things get bad, we have the government to help take care of the basics. The only time we look to God is when something catastrophic hits. We then expect God to jump in and deliver us from whatever evil circumstances has befallen us.

I have some news for you. God is more like American Express (Never leave home without it) than Capital One (What's in your wallet?) God isn't something we pack away in our wallet and pull out only when we need Him. We should never leave home without trusting in Him for everything that might come our way. Trusting God is a daily dependence on Him no matter how good or bad our circumstances. Our world doesn't need to get rocked when bad news hits because we know who controls the future. We declare our trust daily believing God will provide everything we need in all situations.

September 14
A Heart of Worship

"Thou shalt have no other gods before me" (Exodus 20:3 KJV).

The first of God's ten commandments is to treat nothing as more important than Him. We are to worship Him and Him alone.

A heart of worship is cultivated by worshipping God. Worship can happen any time and place. Our heart attitude is key.

Our worship reflects the value we place on our relationship with God. We can place value on things that keep us from giving God the glory and honor due to Him. God gave the command because He knows the tendency of humanity to be distracted and to develop idols. Psalm 139:23-24 instructs us to pray for God to search our heart, reveal its condition to us, and deliver us from anything that may compromise our full worship of Him.

Developing a heart of worship is something we must work on while we go about our daily duties. Worship is a heart attitude that longs to be in His presence by giving ourselves to Him. It is a cry that longs for intimacy with our Creator. Worship expresses itself through song, prayer, quietness, reading the Bible, and in our emotions.

Our world reminds us daily that we need a savior. Worship brings us into His presence and releases kingdom realities into us and our circumstances.

September 15
Isolation and Division Hurt Us

The small minority expressing their views can say and do anything they want if it goes with their social narrative. Those with belief in God and what the Bible says is right or wrong are declared as the minority. I do not believe this to be true at all.

I believe most people still have a firm grasp on right and wrong. He has written His laws on our hearts. He gives everyone a moral conscience. When evils are declared as good, it is time to take a stand. "Ye that love the Lord, hate evil: He preserveth the souls of His saints; He delivereth them out of the hand of the wicked" (Psalm 97:10 KJV).

Standing for truth, we can be isolated. We can be overwhelmed by feeling all alone in the fight. Let's remember what is true. We are never alone. God is always with us and will never forsake us.

Those who love the Lord, it is time to stand up to the evil being presented as good. We see the few who are trying to dictate to the majority. Corporate sponsors are bankrolling agendas that fuel the few. We, the majority, need to fight with our prayers and our wallets. We, the majority, can have an impact and make a difference if we do not allow ourselves to be isolated and will come together. We must have the courage to stand up to the divisive tactics and come together, raise our voices, and stand against evil. The Lord will deliver us from the wicked.

September 16
Learning to Live in His Presence

Proverbs 3:5 says, "Trust in the Lord with all thine heart; and lean not unto thine own understanding" KVJ. This one verse sums up the struggle we all have between putting our trust in God and not putting all our confidence in ourselves.

God's ways are much better than our own, but we are so impatient and think we know what's best. Even if we get our best, it is so much less than what God wants to give us. The best God has for us is Himself.

We settle for trinkets from this world, bright, shiny things that grab our attention and distract us from the ultimate prize. Jesus came and opened the door back to God.

The problem with either the so-called "Prosperity Gospel" or the "Poverty-is-a-Sign-of-Humility-Gospel" is that God is seen as either blessing or pounding His children.

Trusting in the Lord is learning to live in His presence. In His presence, we will find everything we need no matter what happens around us. It's learning to walk with God in the cool of the evening, just like Adam and Eve. He's waiting to give us Himself. *"Fear not I am with thee, peace be still, in all of life's ebb and flow."* The hymn "He Keeps me Singing" written in 1910 by Luther Bridgers (1884-1948) American hymn writer.

September 17
"The Same Flame That Melts the Butter Hardens the Steel"
Clara Olive Silva, my great-grandmother.

We are confronted every day with challenges. Challenges at work, at home, in relationships, in our faith, in marriage, with finances, and with parenting. We have a choice to accept responsibility for our part of the problem or bury our heads in the sand. We can blame others or complain and do nothing. *We change when the pain of our circumstances becomes greater than our fear of the work involved to change.*

"We are not made for the mountains, for sunrises, or for the other beautiful attractions in life - those are simply intended to be moments of inspiration. We are made for the valley and the ordinary things of life and that is where we have to prove our stamina and strength." Oswald Chambers (1874-1917) Scottish Evangelist to India.

"Change takes effort, and most people are not willing to put in the necessary work to achieve it." Thomas Edison (1884-1948) inventor of the incandescent light bulb in 1879. Edison said many things about the hard work needed in challenges, including:

• "I didn't fail a thousand times. The lightbulb was an invention with a thousand steps."

• "There is no substitute for hard work."

• "When I have finally decided that a result is worth getting, I go ahead on it and make trial after trial until it comes."

• "The successful person makes a habit of doing what the failing person doesn't like to do."

• And "All progress, all success, springs from thinking."

September 18
Spend Time With Jesus

Here are the words of a beloved old hymn that remind us to spend precious time with our Savior.

"In the Garden" composed in 1912 by C Austin Miles (1868-1946).

"I come to the garden alone, While the dew is still on the roses, And the voice I hear, falling on my ear, The Son of God discloses,

Chorus: And He walks with me, And He talks with me, And He tells me I am His own, And the joy we share as we tarry there, None other has ever known,

He speaks and the sound of His voice, Is so sweet the birds hush their singing, And the melody that He gave to me, Within my heart is ringing, I'd stay in the garden with Him, 'Tho the night around me be falling, But He bids me go; through the voice of woe, His voice to me is calling,

Chorus: And He walks with me, And He talks with me, And He tells me I am His own, And the joy we share as we tarry there, None other has ever known."

We all need the gentle nudge to slow down and spend time with Jesus. When we do, there is something precious and life-changing. If it has been a while since you made time to walk and talk with Him, take some time and find a place without distractions and have a little chat with Jesus. It might be the cure for what ails you.

September 19
Come Unto Me

"Come unto me, all ye that labour and are heavy laden, and I will give you rest. Take my yoke upon you, and learn of me; for I am meek and lowly in heart: and ye shall find rest unto your souls.

For my yoke is easy, and my burden is light" Matthew 11:28-30 KJV.

Jesus extends an invitation to all who are worn out and tired to come to Him and find rest. Jesus isn't inviting us to join religious endeavors. He is inviting us to come to Him.

Spiritual disciplines help us prioritize. Church attendance provides spiritual growth. These things have an important place in our lives. And when we are dry, tired, and worn out, let's turn directly to Jesus, meek and lowly, for the kind of rest that heals, restores, and leaves us at peace.

We believe that to be happy and successful, we must keep up the rat race and keep all our plates spinning. Jesus' invitation is to let some of the plates come crashing down and to jump out of the hamster wheel.

He invites us to turn things over to Him in prayer, talking to Him, asking for help and wisdom and then listening for answers and direction. Everything tends to work together instead of falling apart. Even better is that *we* tend to work better without coming apart.

September 20
Present Your Bodies a Living Sacrifice

"I beseech you therefore, brethren, by the mercies of God, that ye present your bodies a living sacrifice, holy, acceptable unto God, which is your reasonable service.

² And be not conformed to this world: but be ye transformed by the renewing of your mind, that ye may prove what is that good, and acceptable, and perfect, will of God.

³ For I say, through the grace given unto me, to every man that is among you, not to think of himself more highly than he ought to think; but to think soberly, according as God hath dealt to every man the measure of faith" (Romans 12:1-3 KJV).

We try to present the best of ourselves without giving sober thought to sinful patterns that can either kill or enhance our relationships. We talk of love but gossip and tear down others. We want to extend grace and kindness yet are judgmental and critical. We tell our children not to lie, cheat, or steal, but we exaggerate stories and distort details. We sneak food into the movie theaters and justify it because the prices are outrageous. We harm our witness and effectiveness by being inconsistent.

The world will press in and conform us unless we always present ourselves to God as a living, sacrificial servant of the Lord. He will renew our minds, and be with us and help us.

September 21
Navigating Relationships Successfully

"But let no person say what they would or would not do, since we are not judges for ourselves until circumstances call us to act." Abigail Adams (1744-1818) wife of John Adams, the second president of the United States, and mother of John Quincy Adams, the sixth president.

We think, we plan, we pray, and we have a level of confidence about how we would certainly act in a circumstance. But when the time comes, we can totally blow it. Abigail nailed it.

People, beautiful people. When you bring life back to the basics, it's all about people. Relationships can be wonderfully frustrating and wildly fulfilling. No matter how difficult they are, relationships are a necessity. Why is it so hard to get along? Why are relationships so hard to navigate? People, especially family, can bring the greatest joys and deepest sorrows. We must be careful not to allow our desires to sabotage our deepest needs.

The Bible teaches in Matthew 7:3-5 that we easily see the tiny splinter of fault in our brother's eye, but we are ignorant of the enormous beam of fault in our own eye. If we see our beams at all, we minimize them. Christians serve well when we lead with love and work on our own relationship deficiencies instead of trying to fix others. Relationships have a way of drawing out our deficiencies and exposing our limitations. So, we tend to ignore or hide from others. But we hide in plain sight for all to see. Father, help us. We know this matters to You. We need You.

September 22
Unshakable

"Whose voice then shook the earth: but now He hath promised, saying, Yet once more I shake not the earth only, but also heaven. And this word, Yet once more, signifieth the removing of those things that are shaken, as of things that are made, that those things which cannot be shaken may remain. Wherefore we are receiving a kingdom which cannot be moved, let us have grace, whereby we may serve God acceptably with reverence and godly fear: For our God is a consuming fire" (Hebrews 12:26-29).

The writer to the Hebrews is reminding us that kingdoms may come and go, governments rise and fall, dictators may achieve power and be replaced, but the kingdom of God cannot be shaken or removed.

Our personal lives may have difficulties, and the world around us may be shaken literally and figuratively, but those who have placed their trust in God can never lose because we are founded on the rock, Christ Jesus. We receive God's grace – His unearned favor – enabling us to come as we are and serve Him with reverence and godly fear.

Because of what He has done for us, out of His loving kindness, we come to Him reverently serving Him, knowing that He is a consuming fire. It does not matter the circumstances of our lives; those that serve God have come to the unshakable mountain. The foundation of His throne is strong enough to withstand every attack, and therefore, we can stand strong knowing that He has it all under control. Do not lose heart; though the world is shaking, we will not lose the inheritance God has promised.

September 23
You Are Not Alone

It's common. When things are as crazy as they are these days, we feel isolated and alone and even as if we are the only ones left fighting for what is right.

Elijah also felt that way. He was being hunted down by the King and Queen of Israel because he had given them a word from God they did not like. Elijah ran for his life, complaining to God that Israel's leaders had killed all the prophets and destroyed all the places of worship, and Elijah thought he was the only one left to defend God's name. God reassured Elijah that God Himself had preserved 7,000 people in Israel that had not surrendered to the false gods in Israel. See 1 Kings 19.

The battle can seem overwhelming, and that there are too few fighting to make a difference. I have good news for you. You are not alone. God is raising an army who have not bowed down to the false gods of this world and will not be forced into submission. It is not the size of the army that makes a difference, but those who have put their faith in the size of their God. Remember, Gideon had 300, David had a slingshot, the 3 Hebrew children had Jesus walking with them in the flame, Esther had favor, and Daniel trusted in his deliverer. "The sacrifice of the wicked is an abomination to the LORD, But the prayer of the upright is His delight" (Proverbs 15:8 KJV). You are not alone, and God delights in your prayers. Keep fighting and keep praying.

September 24
Waiting on the Lord Is Always Worth the Wait

"For this is what the Lord God, the Holy One of Israel, has said:

"In repentance and rest you will be saved,
In quietness and trust is your strength."
But you were not willing" (Isaiah 30:15 NASB).

When God offers advice, we would do well to accept it. God gave Israel advice. But they did not take it.

God gives us this literal advice. Come to Him and be saved, rest in Him quietly and confidently as He strengthens us.

We run around trying to save ourselves and fix our problems. God is waiting for us to return to Him for His help.

Waiting is just that – waiting and surrender. We can wait upon the Lord anywhere – in the quietness of our home or in a bomb shelter. He wants us to want His salvation and show it by coming to Him in rest and quietness to find strength. Giving our problems and situations to Him and waiting for His deliverance. Trust Him to do exceeding, abundantly beyond what we could ask or think.

September 25
What Is Freedom?

Our national anthem declares that we live in the "land of the free and home of the brave." How free are we?

Are we free to walk away from our jobs right now? Are we free from guilt? Are we free of any kind of addiction? We have the illusion of being free because we live in the greatest nation in the world.

Freedom is the ability to make the right choices for the right reasons. Freedom is a heart issue, not a behavior. I can think I'm free because I can choose to do whatever I want when I want. Is that really freedom, or is it selfishness?

True freedom is the ability to love and serve others with no other agenda. To give our best to others with no expectation of reciprocation. To grow in freedom is to grow in love and to choose to lay down our lives for others.

The moment we start to object to this kind of life is an indication we are not free. Only Jesus gives us the opportunity to truly be free and to live a life of freedom.

"And ye shall know the truth, and the truth shall make you free" (John 8:32 KJV). Jesus is Truth. "Jesus saith unto him, I am the way, the truth, and the life" (John 14:6 KJV).

September 26
Because He Lives

"Because He Lives," Is an inspirational and comforting song written in 1971 by the husband-and-wife team Bill and Gloria Gaither. It speaks of the reason to have hope in uncertain times; the reason is the title – because He lives.

The period from the late 1960s to the 1970s was a time of great disunity in our nation. There was distrust in government and traditional values. The American way of life itself was being challenged. Customs and social norms changed. New influencers arose. Shortages and price hikes on food, household goods, and gasoline put nerves on edge. Bumper stickers with "Question Authority" appeared on cars. People carried protest signs saying, "H--- No! We Won't Go!" in reaction to being drafted by the military to serve in Vietnam. There was an atmosphere of fear and distrust.

And that's when the Gaithers wrote a song about why we can face each new tomorrow without fear – because we know He holds the future. Because He lives. Because even though He was crucified and died, on the third day, He arose from the grave and forever lives at the right hand of the Father. Death was not strong enough to hold Him. He was victorious over death, hell, and the grave. This means there is no problem we face that heaven can't handle. Because He lives, we can keep going through the hardest difficulty. Because He lives, it adds meaning to all our days, and there is no reason to fear. God holds your future. That's good news, my friend!

September 27
Uniquely Created

God has uniquely created each one of us. We are as different from each other as each snowflake is unique to any other. Children born to the same parents can have a lot of similarities and yet be polar opposites.

It is a shame anytime someone's unique characteristics are put down and made fun of. It can cause the person to look at themselves as less than others and wish that they were more like others instead of being content with the uniqueness of how they were created.

Have you ever celebrated yourself just being uniquely you? God created you uniquely to fulfill a specific purpose. Accepting ourselves as we are and knowing our loving Creator God made us as we are on purpose can help us recognize the purpose He has for our uniqueness.

Discover your particular gift mix, and let God lead you to the opportunities He has for you. Celebrate the uniqueness of your children and all those around you. Help those around you to be who God created them to be.

Release the power of encouragement on others and watch them blossom into the beautiful creation God intended.

September 28
Speak Life into One Another

Solomon was the wisest man who ever lived. He left us a record of his wisdom in the book of Proverbs. In chapter 18, Solomon wrote, "The spirit of a man will sustain his infirmity; but a wounded spirit who can bear" (Proverbs 18:14 KJV)?

When we are ill and feeling miserable, there is something inside of us that has the ability to cope with the circumstances and we can persevere through it. However, when a person's spirit has been wounded it's nearly impossible to cope with life's difficulties.

Solomon writes a little later: "Death and life are in the power of the tongue" (Proverbs 18:21 KJV). The words that we speak to others either bring encouragement or can wound the spirit of a person. Most wounded or broken spirits are caused by words spoken to us in vulnerable moments.

We need to speak life and bring encouragement to others. Only God can bring healing to a broken spirit, but often, He uses people to undo what others have done.

We all have the ability to speak life; it's a matter of choice.

September 29
Practice Greatness...Be the Servant of All

Jesus said, "Greater love hath no man than this, that a man lay down his life for his friends" (John 15:13 KJV). Then He went out and did it. He also said, "For even the Son of man came not to be ministered unto, but to minister, and to give his life a ransom for many" (Mark 10:45 KJV). Jesus came to show us how to live the best life possible which is opposite of the way most of us do life.

Today the emphasis is on getting not giving. Jesus said to gain our life we must lose it, and that if we try to hold on to our life, we will lose it. If I make my life the central focus and make sure that I'm taken care of, in the end I won't have had much of a life in the areas that matter. However, if I make loving and serving others the central focus, I will find a fuller more beautiful life than I ever could have imagined.

The ability to live a comfortable life is a wonderful blessing, but if we aren't attentive, it can rob us of the best possible life – a life that is oriented on others and not just self. Comfortable can lead to complacency, which can lead to boredom, which can lead to stagnation. Stagnation stinks and no one wants to be around someone that is a taker and has nothing to give.

Jesus showed us the way to live by His actions. His way is the best and only way to experience the best possible life. "Remember the words of the Lord Jesus, how He said, "It is more blessed to give than to receive" (Acts 20:35b KJV).

September 30
We Need a Move

Paul writing to the church at Rome gives this truth, "But where sin abounded, grace did much more abound: That as sin hath reigned unto death, even so might grace reign through righteousness unto eternal life by Jesus Christ our Lord" (Romans 5:20-21 KJV).

When people are increasingly forsaking God's way and committing every kind of evil, God's grace is even more present to deliver and redeem all those that would call out to Him. When we see the evidence of crime and evil progressing, we need not despair. We can trust that God is about to move in a fresh way upon the earth. Trust in the almighty power of God to change the world.

Paul writing to his young protege encouraged him with this truth,

"The Lord is not slack concerning His promise, as some men count slackness; but is longsuffering to us-ward, not willing that any should perish, but that all should come to repentance" (2 Peter 3:9).

As we witness the events of our day with increasing chaos all around us, let us look to heaven and cry out to God, "we need a move." We need a fresh move of God's Spirit upon the earth, opening eyes that cannot see or understand the greatness of God's love and forgiveness A fresh move of God's healing, delivering, power and a spiritual revival bringing life and power to His church. We need a Move.

10
OCTOBER

October 1
Come Boldly to the Throne of Grace

"Let us therefore come boldly unto the throne of grace, that we may obtain mercy, and find grace to help in time of need" (Hebrews 4:16 KJV).

Because Jesus, the sinless son of God, took the penalty for our sins and iniquities, when we confess our sins, we are forgiven, and we can come boldly to God the Father and obtain mercy and grace to help in our time of need.

Mercy is not getting what I deserve, and grace is getting what I don't deserve. Instead of getting punishment from a holy and righteous God, I get mercy. He lavishes on us His unmerited favor. This is a promise that when we have a need, a problem, a situation or difficulty, we can come straight to God, and we will find mercy and grace.

"Or what person is there among you who, when his son asks for a loaf of bread, will give him a stone? Or if he asks for a fish, he will not give him a snake, will he? So if you, despite being evil, know how to give good gifts to your children, how much more will your Father who is in heaven give good things to those who ask Him (Matthew 7:9-11 NASB).

God waits for us to come boldly and to ask largely. Do we believe it? Then put action to your belief. He's waiting.

October 2
Who Is Better Off for Having Known You

"God's purpose for my life is that I have a passion for God's glory and that I have a passion for my joy in that glory, and that these two are one passion." Jonathan Edwards (1703-1758) American preacher who believed that joy is a central part of God's nature and of what it means to be a Christian.

He was a prolific writer of over one thousand sermons in addition to notebooks, printed materials, and correspondence. Edwards is still read today.

As a result of Jonathan Edwards knowing and embracing his life purpose, the lives of untold thousands of people have been made better off over the last three hundred years and still counting.

During our lifetime, it is estimated that we will encounter eighty thousand people. How many of those will we influence? And of those, how many will then influence others over the next three hundred years?

Let's live so that the people we influence in our lives are better off for having known us.

October 3
Temporal Versus Eternal

This world is not all there is. It seems to have so much to offer that it is hard to keep ourselves from acquiring as much as we can. If we train our hearts to keep an eternal perspective, we will invest ourselves in people for eternity more than in things for the here and now. It requires a heart devoted to the Lord. This life seems so important; we can live as if this is all there is.

Jesus said it like this, "Do not store up for yourselves treasures on earth, where moth and rust destroy, and where thieves break in and steal. But store up for yourselves treasures in heaven, where neither moth nor rust destroys, and where thieves do not break in or steal; for where your treasure is, there your heart will be also" (Matthew 6:19-21 NASB).

Christ is our treasure. Christ is our identity. Our identity must be our motive for investing in others – not pride, guilt, or any other motive because they won't sustain us or honor Christ.

We invest in others with our time, resources, and prayers. Every time we act like Jesus, we are teaching the gospel. When we come along side someone and help them to grow in Christ, when we respond to a need even though we are tired, when we serve when it is convenient and when it is not convenient, when we do these acts of service, we are honoring and worshipping God. We are investing our hearts in work that has an eternal impact and that will live on whether we live to see it or not.

October 4
Them Before Us, With Caution

Jesus sent out His disciples with this instruction, "Behold, I send you forth as sheep in the midst of wolves: be ye therefore wise as serpents, and harmless as doves" (Matthew 10:16b KJV).

Jesus warns us not to expect anything but potential hostility like that of a pack of wolves as we live for Him and minister to others in this world. He tells it like it is without sugarcoating. He makes it clear that we are to use our heads, and that includes being careful about what comes out of our mouths. Words can wound.

Even a vicious wolf can get injured. We must understand the hurt and pain of those God puts in our lives to help. Jesus knows the best way to get past people's defense mechanisms is through genuine love and service. He demonstrated how to connect with the pain and loss of Martha and Mary when their brother died. Jesus wept. Sometimes, we comfort others by weeping with them.

We have been instructed to lay down our lives for the sake of the cross and for others. We must identify with the pain of others and do what we can to assist them by discerning what they need in their pain. We can be the connection that overcomes the pain of past hurts from treatment that was not Christlike.

Jesus did not commission His followers to go and judge the world but to love and serve it. What an incredible opportunity the church has to love and serve others in the hour in which we live. Let us put them before us in both word and deed.

October 5
Jesus Showed Us How to Live

There is a wonderful old hymn based on Psalm 40:1-3:

"He brought me out of the miry clay, He set my feet on the Rock to stay; He puts a song in my soul today, A song of praise, hallelujah!" Hymn published in 1898, text by Henry Jeffreys Zelley (1859-1942) American minister and producer of hymns and poems.

God calls us up and out – out of the miry clay and up on a solid foundation so He can clean us up and then send us out. Notice who is making it all happen: God. God wants us to receive His work of grace and rest in His love. No earning it, working for it, or performing for it. Saved by grace alone, through faith alone.

God wants us to surrender to His plans and purposes. How do we surrender when everything in our world is saying faster and more of it? Life may keep us busy, but God wants us to slow down and let Him work. He calls to all who are weary and burdened down with the pressures of this world to come and learn from Him because His way is easy, and His burden is light.

Jesus showed us how to live contrary to the popular opinions of the day. He was never in a hurry. He waited on God before doing anything. Might we be so patient and trusting!

October 6
He Works from the Inside Out

"When he hurts, I bleed." Said about her husband. Abigail Adams (1744-1818) wife of John Adams, the second president of the United States, and mother of John Quincy Adams, the sixth president.

Everyone has a story. The events of our lives make us who we are. We can love someone so much that when they hurt, it feels like we are the ones bleeding in sympathy. We can have been hurt so much in life that we inflict our pain on others who feel like they are bleeding in pain caused by us.

Only God can redeem the hurts and pains caused by the sins of others or us. God works from the inside out, washing away the guilt and shame of our past. He makes us clean in a way that is indescribable. Then God heals the hurts, setting us free to experience life with peace and a whole new perspective. He fills us with a love so powerful that it changes every relationship.

It truly is amazing grace. If that isn't your story yet, it can be. Come to Jesus. He wants to heal your wounds, forgive your sins, and give you peace and eternal life with Him. Tell Him all about it. He loves you. Receive Him today.

October 7
The Great Common Denominator

What is it that can be had, used, saved, watched, stopped, marked, flown, wasted, abused, ignored, and found? Time. Time is the great common denominator. We all have the same amount of it each day. What divides us is the way we use it.

"Time is what we want most and what we use worst." William Penn (1644-1718) Religious writer. Mr. Penn was a Quaker and founder of the Province of Pennsylvania. He endured persecution in England for his faith. So, he established freedom of worship for all in his North American colony. Even someone as accomplished as Mr. Penn identified with the difficulty of time management.

Being busy doesn't mean being productive. We can do a lot of busy work but never accomplish anything. There are endless types of time-wasting opportunities that rob us of more meaningful and fulfilling endeavors.

What separates the successful from the mediocre is the way time is utilized.

"Beware the barrenness of a busy life." Socrates (469-399 BC) Ancient Greek Philosopher. And don't we know it. The fact that someone who lived 400 years before the birth of Christ and was successful enough to be quoted today struggled with this issue means that it is as universal as time itself.

"So teach us to number our days, that we may apply our hearts unto wisdom" (Psalm 90:12 KJV).

October 8
Bring Honor to Those Around Us

We live in a time when we are told by our culture what to think, what, and who is important. What determines a person's worth? Is it their productivity? Is it their looks or intelligence? Is it their position, status, wealth, or the accumulation of possessions? Does a person's past have to continually contaminate their present reality?

We are all on a journey of discovery, and at each stage of life, we discover more about ourselves and how we interact with the world around us. Life is about learning – learning from our mistakes, learning through our experiences, and learning through the experiences of others. We must ask ourselves: With all the information we are being bombarded with, is it making us a better person, a better people?

It's easy to go along with the crowd or the popular opinion, no matter who gets destroyed in the process. God's word tells us to stand for what is right and for justice. We are all made in the image of God and that is what gives us our value and worth.

Any other criteria with a hierarchy of value that can bring us to do away with anyone that doesn't measure up – Heaven forbid!

Let's bring honor to each individual and not succumb to the spirit of this age that seeks to destroy because we don't see eye-to-eye. There is a better way to live. Let's learn from our mistakes and grow in love and forgiveness.

October 9
God Makes Himself Heard

"For the Lord gives wisdom; From His mouth come knowledge and understanding" Proverbs 2:6 NASB).

When we find ourselves in a tough spot and don't know what to do, this verse promises that when we call out to God, He will help us. It isn't always instantaneous, but He will give us what we need.

They are times when we are faced with choices and we don't know which way to go. We can turn to the best source of wisdom there is. God will always come through. He has come through in my life, and I know He will in yours. The key is to be patient. Someone once told me that it is not in my ability to hear but in God's ability to make Himself heard. God has no problem making Himself heard. It is usually us that have a hard time believing that God actually cares about us and our situation.

My friend, He cares a lot and wants to help us in the smallest details of our lives. We just have to believe and trust. Next time you need wisdom on what to do, take a little time and ask for help. You'll be amazed at God's timing and response.

"But if any of you lacks wisdom, let him ask of God, who gives to all generously and without reproach, and it will be given to him" (James 1:5a NASB).

October 10
Whom Do You Say I Am

How the time flies. I got a notice recently inviting me to my high school reunion. It can't be true that many years have passed since I graduated, but it is. These milestones get our attention.

If you knew you only had a short time to live, what would be your biggest priorities? Whatever your answer is, for the rest of your life, start there and cut back on everything else. I know for me, it would be God, family, and friends.

At some point, everyone asks whether this life is all there is. That leads us to the God questions – is there a God? Who is He? How can I know Him? Jesus prompted this discussion with His disciples. "He saith unto them, But whom say ye that I am? And Simon Peter answered and said, Thou art the Christ, the Son of the living God" (Matthew 1:15-16 KJV).

Who do you say Jesus is? Time is ticking away, don't lose another minute on things that won't matter 100 years from now.

October 11
Back to Basics

When life is confusing, we can become overwhelmed. Being overwhelmed can be emotionally paralyzing. That's when it is essential to narrow things down and focus on what we know to be true at basic levels and stick to those basic principles: save our money, take care of ourselves emotionally and physically, stay close to family and friends, and make sure we are staying connected to our heavenly Father.

Getting back to basics spiritually means putting an emphasis on spiritual matters. It means not relegating spirituality to the lowest priority but elevating it to the highest. Jesus came to bring us back into an intimate relationship with God so that we could navigate through life's difficulties connected to almighty God.

Sticking to the basic things can bring us peace and contentment in a chaotic and turbulent world. Things like watching the sunrise or sunset, listening to ocean waves, or a baby's laugh can restore order to a perplexed soul. Talking to God can bring a peace that does not always make sense. Spending time in a church service with other people has a way of building faith that sustains us through the next obstacle.

Sometimes, we look for the big answer or seek relief from unhealthy places when most of the time, it is getting back to the basics of life that will bring us to tranquil waters. Slow down, take a deep breath, and invite God into your situations. He is there waiting for you to ask.

October 12
Arise Shine

The prophet Isaiah wrote concerning Jerusalem, "Arise, shine; for your light has come, And the glory of the Lord has risen upon you. For behold, darkness will cover the earth. And deep darkness the peoples; But the Lord will rise upon you And His glory will appear upon you" Isaiah 60:1-2 NASB).

God's call to His people is to arise and shine and let the glory of the Lord be upon you. If there ever was a time in our most recent history for the church to arise and shine, it is now. We cannot get caught up in all the turmoil of the hour, and there is much to get caught up in.

God is calling us to arise, not in our own power or strength but in His. God is with us, in us, and all around us. We cannot be intimidated by the darkness covering our nation and its citizens. The promise of Almighty God is that His glory will be upon us, and it will be seen.

We must not shrink back in this hour but seek God for His direction. God will provide all that we need at this time to impact the world around us.

Arise, Shine, for His Glory is upon YOU!

October 13
Time to Get on Our Knees

There are two prominent themes being pushed by today's influencers. One is how important it is to have self-love. The other is how bad narcissists are. Self-love is virtually being in love with ourselves and giving ourselves a pass for all our flaws. A narcissist is someone preoccupied with themselves to the point that they put themselves before others. It seems obvious that the first can lead to the other, does it not?

Our culture places a high value on beauty and being physically fit and little value on character. We can idolize musicians, athletes, and the famous, regardless of their lifestyles and morals.

We can elect officials who promise to give us what we want without having to work for it, regardless of what values they stand for, so long as it doesn't personally affect us. But it always does personally affect us. Character matters. We need to spend more time on our own character and understanding our value before God instead of our vanity.

This country was founded on principles that are being forgotten and sacrificed to the god of "feel good," so-called "self-love," and entitlement. It's time to return to our rich heritage of Godly principles and stop all this political correctness.

We are drowning in a sea of moral relativity while losing our children to the devil. It's time to get on our knees and take our country back. Can I get an Amen!

October 14
Will We Be Hurt Again

The hurts and pains of life cause us to build walls of protection to keep us from being hurt again. The problem is that we can bury ourselves so deeply to protect our hearts that we end up losing touch with our hearts altogether.

God intends for us to connect heart-to-heart in our relationship with Him and with one another. But some find that either foreign or uncomfortable. If we allow the hurts from our past to keep us from experiencing God and enjoying deep and meaningful relationships with others, we may feel safe, but we are missing out on some of God's richest blessings.

Will we be hurt again? Probably. But to protect our hearts so we aren't hurt again causes us to hide and isolate even from those we love. And that, my friend, is no life at all.

"He heals the brokenhearted and binds up their wounds" (Psalm 147:3 NASB).

"Just as the Father has loved Me, I also have loved you; remain in My love" (John 15:9 NASB).

October 15
A House Divided

Jesus was accused of casting out devils by the power of the devil. His answer to the accusations was pure gold. He said, "No city or house divided against itself will stand" (Matthew 12:25c NASB). Any entity that uses its power against itself, will indeed destroy itself. Why would anyone purposely work against themselves? It happens all the time.

Political parties using their power to stay in power will eventually lose it. Marriages using the power given through love, trust, and respect, to turn on one another eventually destroy the power of unity, and inevitably, the relationship is terminated.

Recognize the power of unity in working through our differences and fighting for the common good. Our unity is to be in Christ. Our unity in Christ is more important than being right. Our unity in Christ calls us to sacrifice for the good of our country, families, and relationships. We can no longer be separated by our perceived differences. In His high priestly prayer, Jesus prayed that those who follow after Him would be one as He and the Father are one.

Unity is not conformity. Unity is oneness with and because of Christ. Today, in our country, we look more like a house divided than one working together to accomplish great things. Practicing unity begins in the heart, then in the home, and then it touches the world.

October 16
Thank God

"O give thanks unto the Lord; for He is good; for His mercy endureth forever" (1 Chronicles 16:34 KJV).

These are pretty simple instructions, but also easy to forget. Giving thanks for the good and the bad keeps our heads above the clouds of despair.

"Make a joyful noise unto the Lord, all ye lands. Serve the Lord with gladness: come before his presence with singing. Know ye that the Lord He is God: it is He that hath made us, and not we ourselves; we are His people, and the sheep of His pasture. Enter into His gates with thanksgiving, and into His courts with praise: be thankful unto Him and bless His name. For the Lord is good; His mercy is everlasting; and His truth endureth to all generations" (Psalm 100:1-5 KJV).

When you don't feel like it, Thank Him.

When life is hectic, Thank Him!

When you're having the best day ever, Thank Him!

The best way to live life, is to live life with God. The best way to ensure God is with you is to have a heart and attitude of thanksgiving. Have a Thanksgiving Day every day and see the difference it can make.

October 17
Coming Together in Times of Need

As fires raged throughout Northern California, families were displaced and had to run to safety. Sadly, many lost their homes, and worse, some didn't make it out. My daughter and her six children made it to safety as her husband stayed behind to do what he could to save and protect their property. I'm happy to report that they were spared the heartache of losing everything.

One of their children called their dad a superhero for having the courage to stay behind and fight to save the house. Hearing the word superhero, one of the little ones wanted to know if their dad could fly. Out of the mouths of children.

Courage is not the absence of fear in challenging situations; it's just not allowing it to control us. In the midst of so much heartache and loss, it's amazing to see people come together and support one another. For all the ugliness we see on the news, my faith in humanity has received a boost this week as people rallied to help those in great need.

I hope and pray that God will fill those suffering with strength for the journey, peace to endure, and hope for a better tomorrow.

"And do not neglect doing good and sharing, for with such sacrifices God is pleased" (Hebrews 13:16 NASB).

October 18
Pray Get Informed Vote

Don't believe everything you read and hear especially if it's on social media. God is still on the throne and He's still ruling and reigning despite what we hear and read.

Part of the reason why we are in this mess is that we have neglected our civic responsibilities to be involved in what our public servants are doing. We have become enamored with personalities over substance. This is more than Candidate A versus Candidate Z. We are fighting an ideological war, and we are unarmed.

We have been manipulated by the media and the PR people who spin everything to get us to believe what they want us to believe, and we have gone along for the ride.

Many really don't care if it doesn't mess with them personally. Well, guess what? It's at our doorstep, and we are ill-prepared to know what to do. We take the easy way out and leave it up to the politicians to fight it out. That is not how this country is supposed to be run. They answer to us. The only power they have is what we give them, and it's time to take it back.

Pray, get informed of the issues, and then vote. We ought not to be bullied into or out of our vote. This election is too important to just sit back and see what happens.

October 19
Kingdom Possibilities

In the book of Ecclesiastes, Solomon tells us that God has put a desire for eternity in man's heart. In the Lord's prayer, which appears in both Matthew and Luke, Jesus taught His disciples to pray, asking God for the realities of heaven to come here and now to earth.

"After this manner therefore pray ye: Our Father which art in heaven, Hallowed be thy name. Thy kingdom come, Thy will be done in earth, as it is in heaven. Give us this day our daily bread. And forgive us our debts, as we forgive our debtors. And lead us not into temptation but deliver us from evil: For thine is the kingdom, and the power, and the glory, forever. Amen." (Matthew 6:9-13 KJV).

Just imagine what it might that look like if everyone on earth hallowed – reverently respected God's name? What would it look like if His will was 100% done everywhere all the time on earth as it is in Heaven? If we trusted Him completely for our daily needs? If we forgive others as He forgives us? If we were not tempted but were delivered from evil, right now, on earth, all the time? His Kingdom is a reality of peace and godliness.

Kingdom possibilities await those who will passionately pursue His presence and align themselves with righteousness (doing things God's way). It is time to seek the kingdom and petition heaven for God's will on earth, like never before.

October 20
He Is Worthy

No matter who wins the election, God is still worthy of our adoration, trust, and thanks. When society turns on itself, God is worthy of our praise. When the finances come up short, God is worthy of being magnified and exalted.

God has proven Himself faithful time and time again. Jesus is the same yesterday, today, and forever! If we can develop a lifestyle of praise and worship even during our struggles, we will find God near and dear to us. It is imperative to keep our focus on who He is and what He has done for us.

God has promised to work all things for our good. That does not mean that all things that happen to us are good. It just means that God can give us a different perspective and outcome when we trust Him with the difficult challenges, suffering, and outright failures of our lives.

Thankfully, God is perfection. While we are made in His image, in our fallen humanity, we don't reflect Him as perfectly or as majestically as He is. He is perfect in all He does, and He is kind and generous in His blessings. God is faithful and cannot go back on His promises. This day, look up and give Him thanks; for He is worthy!

"Eye hath not seen, nor ear heard, neither have entered into the heart of man, the things which God hath prepared for them that love him" (1 Corinthians 2:9 KJV).

October 21
Love Like God Loves

To love and be loved is what life should be all about. Too bad it isn't.

God demonstrated His love by giving His son to die for mankind, only to be accused of holding out and not giving enough. We want prosperity, health, and a fulfilled life, and we blame God when it is not achieved.

Selfishness destroys love. Many are focused on what they can receive versus what they can give. We have become consumers of love. We take from the ones who give until we have squeezed everything out of them and then complain when they stop giving.

We move on to shopping for the next giver and then start the process all over.

God calls us to be like Him. He loves and gives extravagantly and then gives even more. The fullest life is one that is filled with loving others and providing for the betterment of those around us.

The saddest life is the one lived focused on itself. The world is slowly destroying itself because we have become selfish and want what we want, not caring how it hurts others.

It's time to love like God loves and give until it hurts.

October 22
Decisions

Once upon a time, a young man named Johnny approached a farmer for work. The farmer had him harvest potatoes in the hot sun with other field workers. Johnny was remarkable. The farmer had never seen such a productive worker. He did more than any other worker by a long shot.

"Well," the farmer thought, "He was putting his best foot forward, so I'd keep him on. He'll probably slack off tomorrow." To the farmer's amazement, Johnny was even more productive the next day. Johnny worked harder than anyone in the hot sun day after day. "Here, I'm rewarding you for your hard work." Said the farmer one day. "I am letting you work in the nice cool shade of this shed. All you do is sort these potatoes by throwing the culls over there and keeping the good ones here." At noon the farmer went into the shed. To his shock, he found Johnny passed out on the floor. "Say! Johnny! Wake up! What's the matter?" Coming around, Johnny looked up at the farmer and explained weakly, "Decisions!"

Decisions are exhausting, and we have so many of them. They can knock us for a loop. There are times when we are caught between two different desires, each with compelling reasons to do or not to do. If our choices don't involve breaking the law or being disobedient to God, then we should let ourselves off the hook and rejoice in the fact that God loves us regardless of the choices we make, and if there are negative consequences to our choices, then we learn the lesson and keep living largely.

October 23
The Ebenezers in Our Lives

God has put it in our hearts to celebrate our life milestones, such as birthdays and anniversaries ,just as He instructed Samuel to set stones in piles as "Ebenezers," which were to be reminders of His help in 1 Samuel 7:12.

In the very old hymn, "Come, Thou Fount of Every Blessing," we sing, "Here I raise my Ebenezer; hither by Thy help I'm come;" written in 1758 by Robert Robinson (1735-1790) English Preacher. Today, the word "Ebenezer" is associated with the stingy Ebenezer Scrooge, a character who undergoes a total transformation in Charles Dickens' "A Christmas Carol." It appears Mr. Dickens chose that name for its irony.

We give thanks to God for our lives, for each passing year, and for all His blessings. It is basic to His character that we celebrate these life milestones of His keeping and protecting us. We imitate Him in our Ebenezer's of celebration. It helps us to value our time and keep a proper perspective so that we don't miss out on the importance of each day.

When we invite God into our days, He has a way of weaving every experience into a beautiful tapestry. Each event in our lives serves to shape and mold us. A life must be lived to appreciate the full spectrum that life can bring. Don't waste or resent what time brings to us. Be thankful and grateful for each moment because you never know how much time we have. Live well!

October 24
Encouragement and Hope

"Therefore, encourage one another and build one another up, just as you also are doing" (1 Thessalonians 5:11 NASB).

Everyone needs a little encouragement and a little comfort. The ability to encourage someone doesn't take much effort. It's an investment of time and a few words. There are people all around us that need hope restored and some encouragement.

If the Holy Spirit prompts you to share an encouraging word with someone, please do. We never really know what someone is going through, and the Lord may use us to turn someone's despair into hope. Let's walk through life each day expecting to be an encourager to everyone around us.

The Bible exhorts us to "fear not" and to be "strong and courageous." Let me encourage you to find someone to encourage. Ask God to guide you to them. Help them to dream again. You never know the impact you can make on someone and the difference they could make on someone else.

You may just be the catalyst to ignite a fire in someone that changes the world. Be strong and courageous, and step out of your comfort zone to be a beacon of hope through words of encouragement.

"Behold, the eye of the Lord is upon them that fear him, upon them that hope in His mercy" (Psalm 33:18 KJV).

October 25
Speak Love

"A soft answer turneth away wrath: but grievous words stir up anger" (Proverbs 15:1 KJV). Proverbs exposes the effect our words have on those around us. We can either deflate a situation by talking softly, or throw gasoline on the conversation by harshly letting someone know exactly what we think. It comes down to who is in control of their words and emotions. If we can maintain control in a heated situation and learn to answer in a whisper, it has a way of calming the other person down so that the conversation can be productive rather than destructive.

Verse 4 states, "A wholesome tongue is a tree of life: but perverseness therein is a breach in the spirit." The ability to stay positive to speak loving and encouraging words brings life to those around us. However, to speak negatively or harshly, condescendingly or judgmentally crushes the mind, will, and emotions of those around us.

Those within our sphere of influence should be able to come to us and eat freely from the tree of life, knowing that they will get uplifted and encouraged. "The lips of the wise disperse knowledge: but the heart of the foolish doeth not so." Verse 7. Wisdom is rare, and it's hard to find people that dispense it. Wisdom is knowing the right thing to do at the right time. It is important to find people who are wiser than we are, and we should do our best to be influenced by them. Our words speak volumes about the kind of person we are. Wise or foolish? A Tree of Life or one who crushes the spirit of a person?

October 26
Finding God

God invites us to look for Him so that He can be found. In Jeremiah 13 verse 9 the Lord says that when we search for Him, with our whole heart, we will find Him.

The problem is that we have so many competing desires that we are easily distracted from our pursuit of God. He tells us that we must search with all our heart. Which means we must desire to find Him more than anything else. The evidence for God is so overwhelming that people must choose not to believe that there is a God even when presented with all the facts. God is full of compassion and mercy, waiting to receive all who seek Him. God desires for us to experience His love, grace, goodness, and provision when we come to Him with open, teachable, and hungry hearts. Begin the journey today and experience all God has prepared for those who seek Him.

"A truly humble man is sensible of his natural distance from God; of his dependence on Him; of the insufficiency of his own power and wisdom; and that it is by God's power that he is upheld and provided for, and that he needs God's wisdom to lead and guide him, and His might to enable him to do what he ought to do for Him." Jonathan Edwards (1703-1758) American preacher.

October 27
A Different Perspective

Living this life is all about perspective. When we surrender our life to God and seek to live obediently to His will and purposes, we must also change our perspective in our approach to life. The Bible instructs us that God's ways are not our ways, and His thoughts are not how we think. If we are going to get on board with God's program, we must change the way we think.

With all that is going on in the world right now, it would be easy to fall into the trap of wanting things to return to normal, whatever that is or was. We want peace and comfort, no more chaos or turmoil. The freedom to go do whatever we want without masks, fear of illness, or pressure to do anything we do not want to do. However, we must stop and ask, if this is God's thought or perspective.

God is working from a distinct perspective. His agenda might be bigger and higher than we are capable of thinking or perceiving. God works from an eternal perspective, which means He sees the end from the beginning and works all things accordingly. We must know what the Bible tells us about the future and God's involvement in all things. If we have indeed surrendered to His will and purposes, then we must be confident in His ability to navigate all things in our lives and trust Him. Trust is about having a different perspective on our lives and the things that are going on in our world. He will not fail, and His love is eternal.

October 28
Reflection

Reflection is a good thing. It allows us to look back and recognize how fast time is moving, to remember from whence we have traveled, to celebrate the victories, and to learn from the defeats.

Passivity does not slow down time; it just makes the passage of time unproductive. As we look to the future, we must be pro-active in our use of time. Sand will continue to fall from the hourglass of our lives regardless of our desire to slow it down.

We cannot let discouragement, past failure, passivity, and current circumstances keep us from getting the most out of our future. Through the prophet Jeremiah, God tells us in chapter 29 that He knows the plans He has for us, and that they are for our good, with a future and hope.

God is declaring over each one of us, that when we put our trust and hope in Him, He can fill us with purpose and make us hopeful for the future.

"For I know the thoughts that I think toward you, saith the Lord, thoughts of peace, and not of evil, to give you an expected end.

Then shall ye call upon me, and ye shall go and pray unto me, and I will hearken unto you" (Jeremiah 29:11-12 KJV)

October 29
To Love Is to Give

How is it that we can be so sure that what we are doing is right and turn out to be wrong? The litmus test is in our relationships with other people in our lives. It comes down to the kind of impact we have on those closest to us.

To love is to give. To give of our time, our words, and our hearts. If we are too focused on ourselves, we are unaware of the needs of those close to us. How do kids spell love? T-I-M-E! Spending time to know their hearts, what they care about, what they are involved in, who their friends are, and what kind of influences they allow into their lives.

How do marriages last a lifetime? They require an investment of ourselves into the relationship, which means investing our time into our marriage, seeking to know and serve the other person. What are their likes, wants, needs, and desires? Marriages disintegrate if either or both are focused on their own needs, wants, and desires, failing to notice their mate is drifting away.

Let's ask ourselves hard questions. Are the people in my life growing healthier because they know me? Do I put others first? Can my loved ones depend on me? Do my loved ones know I love them? If the answer is no to any of these questions, then we better change the way we live. If we don't change then our lives will be empty and meaningless.

October 30
Failure Isn't Fatal

For the most part, people despise tests. Tests are just tools to help us discover where we are lacking and what we haven't learned – yet. But we associate our self-worth with a grade. Poor grades mean we must retake the test, and we do not like that.

We fear failure. We don't like to have our weaknesses exposed. We are comfortable knowing that we might not be an Einstein, but we don't want evidence to confirm it. Life is a never-ending classroom with never-ending lessons and tests. There are lessons in relationships, money management, in what happens when we don't give our best effort, in morals, and in manners, that, if not learned, get retaken over and over and over.

Maturity is about learning how to pass these tests and excel in life. We shouldn't fear tests but learn from them. Fear not. Failure isn't fatal if we learn how to grow from our mistakes.

So, the next time you feel like you're struggling to do the right thing, realize you're in a test and you are about to learn a lot.

October 31
The Spirit of Adoption

I had the opportunity to witness the final court appointment for an adoption. Two families were increasing their size by adopting 6 siblings. One family was taking the older 2 while the 4 younger ones were being added to the other family.

It was a beautiful and emotional time watching the lives of 6 children and two families being forever changed. These children were being taken on by strong, loving, and invested parents. Their future trajectory has been radically altered for the better. When the judge made the final decree, cheers and tears flowed freely.

I was reminded of the scripture, "For ye have not received the spirit of bondage again to fear; but ye have received the Spirit of adoption, whereby we cry, Abba, Father" (Romans 8:15 KJV).

God has given each one of us the opportunity to be adopted into a relationship with a Heavenly Father who wants to be our Abba, our Daddy, and forever change the trajectory of our future. When we present ourselves to Him, He gladly receives us as sons and daughters.

The joy of getting to know our Heavenly Father awaits us. Listen for the cheers of Heaven's courts as we receive the Spirit of adoption and find ourselves in the loving embrace of our Creator.

11
NOVEMBER

November 1
Fear Not

One of the most spoken phrases in the Bible is "Fear Not." There can be much to be fearful about these days. The news continually paints bleak pictures of doom and gloom in seemingly every segment of our world. The pandemic's statistics are continually paraded in front of us. The political fighting makes it difficult to know what is best for our country. The day-to-day struggles of making ends meet produces its own set of fears. And it goes on and on.

In uncertain times that could produce fear, it is good to remember these words of Jesus, "These things I have spoken unto you, that in Me ye might have peace. In the world ye shall have tribulation: but be of good cheer; I have overcome the world" (John 16:33 KJV).

Also, Jesus said, "Peace I leave with you, my peace I give unto you: not as the world giveth, give I unto you. Let not your heart be troubled, neither let it be afraid" (John 14:27 KJV).

Life will always have problems, illness, societal issues, presidential elections, employment concerns, marital and family concerns, and hardships. In life, we can come to Jesus and rest in His peaceful presence. He can calm our fears and reassure us that He is in control, and we do not have to fear the future but can have hope for a better tomorrow. Jesus has triumphed over death, hell, and the grave so that we can be victorious as well. Fear not and be courageous, for the Lord Thy God is with you!

November 2
Have an Attitude of Gratitude

Stop whatever you are doing and reflect on all the good in your life. Let this approaching Thanksgiving Day holiday impact you by making you intentional about giving thanks all the time for everything.

We are bombarded with messages telling us we need more than we do, which leaves us feeling dissatisfied with what we have. Having an "attitude of gratitude" is a catchy phrase that reminds us of something we should practice every day.

The lack of gratitude is called ingratitude. Psalm 28:5 ingratitude can lead to our destruction. 2 Timothy 3:1-5 ingratitude is closely linked to pride.

If we are not careful, we will blow through this month and start the holiday rush, and before you know it, we're picking up wrapping paper and boxes, counting down to the New Year. The holidays can actually be a little depressing if we don't allow the power of gratitude to capture our hearts and be a reminder that God has truly blessed us. So, start today and take a few minutes every day to reflect on how blessed we are and give thanks to God for supplying all that we need.

"And with all his abundant wealth through Christ Jesus, my God will supply all your needs" (Philippians 4:19 KJV).

November 3
Fixing Our Country Starts at Home

Here in my heart, my happiness, my house. Here inside the lighted window is my love, my hope, my life. Peace is my companion on the pathway winding to the threshold. Inside this portal dwells new strength in the security, serenity, and radiance of those I love above life itself." Abraham Lincoln (1809-1865) The 16th President of the United States.

The family was the very first institution that God created. His idea for the family was that it would perpetuate His love and truth down through the generations. Parents would teach their children the truths about God and life as they had been taught by their parents.

Unfortunately, things got a little crazy over the years, and values and morals are not being taught, at least not absolute values. We have become kind of relative in our teaching, and it's become more; "Do what I say, not what I do".

Kids are left to themselves to figure things out, and there are a whole lot of voices speaking into them and pulling them to do things that prior generations would find unacceptable to say the least.

If we are going to fix our country, it must start at home. Parents need to get back to loving and caring for each other, setting a good example for their children, loving them unconditionally, and teaching them Biblical values.

Can I hear an amen!

November 4
For God so Loved the World

For any neglected and abused child, an adoption can be a lifesaver. It has been a beautiful thing to see the lives of children being changed by love. It takes a special kind of person to take on the challenges of children who have been taken from their families of origin. Patience and generous amounts of understanding go a long way to bring healing to their hearts and lives.

In much the same way, God takes us as we are and gives us generous amounts of love, grace, and patience to fix the brokenness in our lives.

Adoption is a beautiful picture of how God works in our lives. He extends an invitation to come to Him. He wraps us in a cocoon of love and truth and begins to heal us from the traumas of life. As we open ourselves to His love and grace, it begins to change us from the inside out. As children are exposed to unconditional love, it opens them up to embrace all they can be, so too, God's unconditional love brings healing and restoration to those who receive it.

In some cases, children, in their brokenness, cannot comprehend and receive unconditional love, and they rebel against it. It is also true that not everyone can comprehend and receive God's unconditional love. "For God so loved the world, that He gave His only Son, so that everyone who believes in Him will not perish, but have eternal life" (John 3:16 NASB). Will you receive His love?

November 5
How Desperate Are You

Jesus teaches us about the Kingdom of God and how to operate within it. In the 5th chapter of Matthew, He gives us keys. He gives us a list of attitudes we are to cultivate to unlock Kingdom blessings. Attitudes are hard to explain, but you can sure see one when it's manifesting in your teenagers.

The definition of attitude is a settled way of thinking or feeling about someone or something, typically one that is reflected in a person's behavior. Jesus tells us what kind of attitude we can carry and manifest that brings about Kingdom blessings.

In Matthew chapter 5 verse 3, God blesses those who are poor and realize their need for Him, for the Kingdom of Heaven is theirs. He is not talking about financial poverty but having a realistic view of ourselves and realizing how much we need Him.

What would the opposite attitude be? In America, we have an attitude of self-sufficiency. We really don't need God until things get so desperate that we can't fix it on our own. God wants us to live in a state of dependency on Him for everything. This isn't for God's sake but for ours.

Jesus taught that when we recognize our need and call upon Him, He tells us that we are blessed, and all the Kingdom of God is made available to us. Sounds like a good deal to me. How desperate are you?

November 6
Plan Intentionally

The holidays are right around the corner, and the next eight weeks are going to pass very quickly. Feasts, faith, family, and fun await. I hope we all enjoy each aspect to the fullest.

There is no other time of the year that can be so exhausting, yet so exhilarating. Family, friends, and loved ones gather together to spend time with one another, give thanks for all the blessings we have been given, and show love to each other.

The first Thanksgiving was to give thanks to God for preserving the lives of the Pilgrims from Europe through extraordinary hardships coming to America and founding a colony here.

Christmas is about remembering the holy event of God's son coming to earth as an infant to change the course of eternity.

It can get busy and even a little "crazy." Before the craziness begins, let us be intentional during these next eight weeks, not to allow the hectic pace of the holidays to rob us of the joy and happiness of this season. Give thanks to God, worship the One who has blessed us with His Son, and spend quality time with the ones you love.

It will be over before you know it, so love well.

November 7
Thanking Our Valiant Military

"And the angel of the Lord appeared unto him, [Gideon] and said unto him, The Lord is with thee, thou mighty man of valour" (Judges 6:12 KJV).

This week, we thank and honor the men and women who have served in the Military. They make sacrifices to protect us and to defend the freedoms we so richly enjoy. President Abraham Lincoln (1809-1865) the 16th President of the United States, set us a good example in his letter to soldiers, sailors, and citizens who honored and supported them in 1863:

"Honor to the Soldier, and Sailor everywhere, who bravely bears his country's cause. Honor also to the citizen who cares for his brother in the field, and serves, as he best can, the same cause -- honor to him, only less than to him, who braves, for the common good, the storms of heaven and the storms of battle."

--December 2, 1863

In 1782, our nation's first president, George Washington (1732-1799) created a badge of Military Merit in recognition of heroic acts. It was simply a heart made of cloth or silk. This eventually became the Purple Heart Award. President Washington gave this impassioned speech to his men: "My brave fellows, you have done all I asked you to do, and more than can be reasonably expected; but your country is at stake, your wives, your houses and all that you hold dear. You have worn yourselves out with fatigues and hardships, but we know not how to spare you."

God bless America, and God bless those who serve in our military.

November 8
Brokenness

There are two types of brokenness. One we try to hide from, and the other we seek to fight against. The Bible tells us that "He healeth the broken in heart, and bindeth up their wounds" (Psalm 147:3 KJV).

God heals the brokenhearted and bandages their wounds. We have all experienced the pain of living. Words and deeds done that leave a soul bruise that most carry for a good portion, if not all their lives. We try to push past it, ignoring its implications on our lives and doing our best to put on our happy face.

God cares deeply about the hurt and brokenness brought into our lives. He offers to heal us if we will trust Him with it. Most do not want to relive their past and bring it all out into the open. The Word of God instructs us to confess our faults (sins, brokenness) to one another, that we may find healing. The brokenness that we run from is the one that God seeks to bring healing to in all of us who desire to do His will.

We have all heard the phrase in child rearing that we must break the child's will but not his spirit. God must also do that to His children, and this is the type of brokenness we must submit to. Moses spent 40 years in the desert learning humility. Joseph spent 13 years sold into slavery to learn forgiveness and submission. Jesus learned obedience through suffering. No one likes the pain of brokenness. The brokenness we hide from is the pain that we need to be healed from. The brokenness we fight against is the pain that we need to submit to.

November 9
Eternal Governing

Speaking about the coming Messiah, the Savior and Deliverer of Israel, Isaiah gives us these characteristics,

"For unto us a child is born, unto us a son is given: and the government shall be upon his shoulder: and his name shall be called Wonderful, Counsellor, The mighty God, The everlasting Father, The Prince of Peace. Of the increase of his government and peace there shall be no end, upon the throne of David, and upon his kingdom, to order it, and to establish it with judgment and with justice from henceforth even forever. The zeal of the Lord of hosts will perform this" (Isaiah 9:6-7 KJV).

Jesus Christ, the sovereign Lord, is ruling and reigning over all of creation. Nothing escapes His attention. His government will increase and never end. We do not have to fear the affairs of man and their governments. Our peace and security come from the one who has created all things. Let us raise our Hallelujah amid our enemies and struggles, knowing that we have a savior and deliverer who has declared His love for His children and watches over and protects those who are His.

Do not allow fear to rob you from trusting in the Mighty God, Everlasting Father, and The Wonderful Counselor. God's Kingdom and Government cannot be overthrown or voted out. Praise the Lord.

November 10
Growth Means Change

"But grow in grace, and in the knowledge of our Lord and Savior Jesus Christ. To Him be glory both now and forever. Amen" (2 Peter 3:18 KJV).

"I want to tell you a growing conviction with me, and that is that as we obey the leadings of the Spirit of God, we enable God to answer the prayers of other people. I mean that our lives, my life, is the answer to someone's prayer, prayed perhaps centuries ago. It is more and more impossible to me to have programmes and plans because God alone has the plan, and our plans are only apt to hinder Him, and make it necessary for Him to break them up. I have the unspeakable knowledge that my life is the answer to prayers, and that God is blessing me and making me a blessing entirely of His sovereign grace and nothing to do with my merits, saving as I am bold enough to trust His leading and not the dictates of my own wisdom and common sense." — Oswald Chambers (1874-1917) Scottish Evangelist to India.

Growth means change. God is constantly growing and stretching us, going the extra mile in service to others. To be in Christ requires that we move through our promised inheritance, taking more and more territory, in other words, developing our potential into reality. To plateau when God has more to do in us and through us keeps us from knowing Him and ourselves.

November 11
Thanking Our Military on Veterans Day

November 11 is Veterans Day. This is a day to honor all Veterans, living and dead, who have served our country in the military, both in peace time and in times of war.

On the last Monday in May, we celebrate Memorial Day, a day set apart to remember those who died in military service, particularly in battle. We immensely appreciate the ultimate sacrifice paid to defend our deeply cherished freedoms.

We are proud of the American tradition of honoring the people who have surrendered their freedom to protect ours. We owe them a debt of gratitude and our deepest respect.

Freedom isn't free, and the physical and emotional price that is paid so that we can enjoy the freedom and privileges of this great country can never be calculated.

Sacrifice to the point of death so that others can live a free and noble life is what the Bible calls love.

Thank you to the men and women of our Military who live sacrificially to protect and defend our freedoms.

November 12
Growing in Faith

Faith is both what we believe and our ability to trust. Growing in our faith involves time, patience, and problems. Problems or difficulties expose what we believe and our level of trust.

Someone once said that we don't really know what we believe until that is all we have to depend upon. Growing in our faith requires an investment of time in reading and studying God's Word. "So then faith cometh by hearing, and hearing by the word of God." (Romans 10:17 KJV). We cannot grow or be challenged in our understanding of God without learning His Word.

People may have a lot of opinions about God, but what matters is whether they align with who God says He is in His Word. To grow in our ability to trust God, we must learn how to believe God and His promises in the face of our problems. It takes time and patience, things that are usually in short supply when we are facing struggles. When we see God meet our needs in ways that only He could have brought about, our faith strengthens. When we do this over the course of a lifetime, we become people of faith. Most believers want to be people of strong faith; they just don't want to go through the struggles and difficulties that help them grow. "My brethren, count it all joy when ye fall into divers temptations; Knowing this, that the trying of your faith worketh patience. But let patience have her perfect work, that ye may be perfect and entire, wanting nothing" (James 1:2-4 KJV).

November 13
It's Time to Hit Our Knees and Pray

"These are the times in which a genius would wish to live. It is not in the still calm of life, or the repose of a pacific station, that great characters are formed. The habits of a vigorous mind are formed in contending with difficulties. Great necessities call out great virtues. When a mind is raised, and animated by scenes that engage the heart, then those qualities which would otherwise lay dormant, wake into life and form the character of the hero and the statesman." Abigail Adams (1744-1818) wife of John Adams, the second president of the United States, and mother of John Quincy Adams, the sixth president.

Abigail was right. Great necessities do call out great virtues. Evil is causing chaos in our cities, and natural disasters are hitting our nation with increasing force and destruction. I have lived in California for most of my life, and I have never seen fires hit so close together and cause so much destruction. In a matter of hours, the town of Paradise Ca was completely wiped out.

Jesus told us that we will have difficulties, but we can take comfort that He was victorious against all the things that were thrown at Him. We have a God who understands what we are going through and He doesn't leave us hanging.

What can we do in times like these? First, pray earnestly for those who are suffering. Second, be thankful for all that you have. Third, find out what you can do to help.

November 14
The Most Wonderful Time of the Year

Christmas music can be heard in my home and car. It's never too soon to get into the holiday spirit. Christmas music reminds us to be home for the holidays, to dream of a white Christmas, to listen to angels singing, to get down to a little Jingle Bell rock, and to enjoy one another's company. No other time of the year brings people together like the holidays.

The reason Jesus came to earth was to reconcile man to God and bring peace to our relationships with others. God is all about family. He wants to bring fullness and joy to our interactions with one another.

Jesus modeled for us how to bring peace to our families:

Be willing to be a servant and be quick to ask and give forgiveness. Most difficulties and problems stem from selfishness and brokenness.

We tend to want those closest to us to meet all our needs, and hurting people tend to hurt others, but not always intentionally. Let the grace of this season bring compassion to those who would seek to rob us of our joy. Put on some Christmas music and be reminded that we serve a great God and what a great time of year it is.

November 15
Give Thanks

November, the month we celebrate Thanksgiving. It has been almost 400 years since that first Thanksgiving celebration. The times may have changed, but the spirit of it still remains. The spirit of giving thanks, stopping and reflecting, and having a grateful attitude for all we have been blessed with.

The Bible encourages us to be thankful: "O give thanks unto the Lord; for He is good: for His mercy endureth forever" (Psalm 136:1 KJV).

The first settlers had to overcome hardships and difficulties to get to that first celebration of giving thanks. We, too, must lift our hearts heavenward and give thanks.

We as a country have drifted from our religious foundation and have stopped looking to God as the source of all blessings. Thanksgiving has become centered around food and football and maybe a family gathering.

This Thanksgiving, let's remember our roots and stop and honor God with grateful hearts. Appreciate family and friends as they gather around the Thanksgiving table. Happy Thanksgiving!

November 16
The Key to Revival

After Solomon dedicated the temple, God spoke to Solomon and said, "If my people, which are called by my name, shall humble themselves, and pray, and seek my face, and turn from their wicked ways; then will I hear from heaven, and will forgive their sin, and will heal their land" (2 Chronicles 7:14 KJV).

God puts the burden of responsibility on His people to repent for our sins and the sins of our country and to seek God on behalf of the people.

When John the Baptist came on the scene to prepare the way for the Lord Jesus to begin His ministry to the people, John began by calling the people to repent and turn away from their sins. When Jesus started His earthly ministry, He began by proclaiming, "Repent ye: for the kingdom of heaven is at hand" (Matthew 3:2 KJV). The essence of repentance is to turn away from our selfish and self-centered ways, which are in rebellion against God and His ways, and to return to the Lord in complete obedience to His Word.

The key to revival in our own hearts and in our country is for God's children to recognize how much we have sinned against the holiness and purity of the Word of God and to realign ourselves through the act of repentance. Repentance is more than receiving forgiveness. Repentance is forsaking our sins and seeking after God until we see change in us and through us. Repentance is the key to revival. We must not delay!

November 17
The Promise

With our feet planted firmly in this life, it is almost impossible not to be consumed with all of life's complexities. The life we find ourselves living can be full of joy and sorrow or somewhere on the path between those destinations. This year has been like no other; the speed at which life has changed for many of us and the uncertainty of the future landscape brings their set of fears and anxieties.

The disciples of Jesus knew a thing or two about hardship and difficulty. Their lives were on the line for spreading the good news of Jesus Christ. The apostle Paul, writing to believers to encourage them during their struggles, reminded them of this truth, "But as it is written, Eye hath not seen, nor ear heard, neither have entered into the heart of man, the things which God hath prepared for them that love him" (1 Corinthians 2:9 KJV).

This life is not the ultimate prize. God has given each person a longing and desire for what He has prepared for us after this life is over. Our roots go deep into the soil of this life, which makes it difficult to think and believe that there could be anything more than this life.

Do not be seduced into thinking that this is all there is. Humankind cannot comprehend the things that God has for those who love Him. Rejoice because this too shall pass, and there really is an eternal reward. God's Promise!

November 18
We Can't Escape Eternity

"If Christianity is false, it cannot be saved by theology. If it is true, it cannot be destroyed by science." E. Y. Mullins (1860-1928) American Preacher.

We all must make a decision about the claims of Jesus. Christianity is more than a religion; it is more than a list of should-not and do-not. Unfortunately, that is all some people know about it.

Jesus taught that we will all live for eternity; it's just a matter of where it will be. We can live our lives and go about our busyness and try not to think about eternity, but the closer we come to the end of our lives, it begins to knock on our consciousness.

The Bible tells us that God has put eternity in our hearts. We can't escape it. Jesus said, "I am the way, the truth, and the life: no man cometh unto the Father, but by me" (John 14:6 KJV).

There is only one way to spend eternity with God, and that is by accepting what Jesus did for us.

Christianity. Eternity is hanging in the balance.

November 19
By the President of the United States of America
A Thanksgiving Proclamation

"During the last year the Lord has dealt bountifully with us, giving us peace at home and abroad and the chance for our citizens to work for their welfare unhindered by war, famine or plague. It behooves us not only to rejoice greatly because of what has been given us, but to accept it with a solemn sense of responsibility, realizing that under Heaven it rests with us ourselves to show that we are worthy to use aright what has thus been entrusted to our care. In no other place and at no other time has the experiment of government of the people, by the people, for the people, been tried on so vast a scale as here in our own country in the opening years of the 20th Century. Failure would not only be a dreadful thing for us, but a dreadful thing for all mankind, because it would mean loss of hope for all who believe in the power and the righteousness of liberty. Therefore, in thanking God for the mercies extended to us in the past, we beseech Him that He may not withhold them in the future, and that our hearts may be roused to war steadfastly for good and against all the forces of evil, public and private. We pray for strength, and light, so that in the coming years we may with cleanliness, fearlessness, and wisdom, do our allotted work on the earth in such manner as to show that we are not altogether unworthy of the blessings we have received. Theodore Roosevelt"(1858-1919) 26th US President on October 31, 1903."

November 20
Be a Witness

Some of the final instructions from Jesus to His disciples included these words, "But ye shall receive power, after that the Holy Ghost is come upon you: and ye shall be witnesses unto Me both in Jerusalem, and in all Judaea, and in Samaria, and unto the uttermost part of the earth" (Acts 1:8 KJV).

Jesus was telling all His followers that they needed to be evidence for the case of Christ in their hometowns, throughout the state of their residence, in locations that they might want to go to, and eventually throughout the whole earth.

Being evidence for the case of Christ means that by our words and actions, we should be testifying of the saving grace of Jesus Christ. Our very lives should be on display, demonstrating a life transformed by the love of Jesus.

We would accomplish this through the power of the Holy Spirit, not in our own ability or ingenuity. As we surrender our lives to God and are open to the many opportunities around us, God will fill our mouths with the words to communicate the good news of Jesus. The great thing about God is that He knows what little we know and can use what we know to help someone else. He's not looking for theologians or even a know-it-all. He looks for anyone whose life has been changed to speak on His behalf. The world needs the love and delivering power of Jesus. Let someone know what He's done for you. It starts with someone close to home.

November 21
Prayer, Praise, and Thanksgiving

"Prayer, praise and thanksgiving all go in company. A close relationship exists between them. Praise and thanksgiving are so near alike that it is not easy to distinguish between them or define them separately The Scriptures join these three things together. Many are the causes for thanksgiving and praise. The Psalms are filled with many songs of praise and hymns of thanksgiving, all pointing back to the results of prayer. Thanksgiving includes gratitude. In fact, thanksgiving is but the expression of an inward conscious gratitude to God for mercies received. Gratitude is an inward emotion of the soul, involuntarily arising therein, while thanksgiving is the voluntary expression of gratitude." E. M. Bounds (1835-1913) American author and attorney.

Our traditional American Thanksgiving is a wonderful thing that happens once a year. The habit and practice of being thankful can happen every day. Cultivating a daily habit of thanksgiving is a healthy habit. When we read scripture daily, our hearts are touched by the Holy Spirit, and we give thanks to the Lord for what He is doing in our lives. When we sing hymns, we can't help but be thankful for the loving God we sing about and worship. When we pray, we give Him our cares and troubles, and as He lightens our load, again we give thanks.

We have much to be thankful for. The people in our lives, the church we attend, the home we live in, the needs that are met, the kindness of friends and strangers. Most of all, the gift of eternal life freely given to us, but it cost our Heavenly Father His only Son's life.

November 22
Let the Peace of God Rule Your Heart

"Things which matter most must never be at the mercy of things which matter least." Johann Wolfgang von Goethe (1749-1832) Polymath.

This holiday, let's remember to keep the main thing, the main thing. The main thing is giving thanks to God for and with the people around our table at the Thanksgiving meal and the loved ones who may be missing.

It is easy to focus on the details of the meal and lose sight of the reasons why we are doing what we are doing. The preparations for Thanksgiving can become all consuming. We can become short and irritated with interruptions from the very ones we are working so hard for.

Pray as the apostle Paul said, "And let the peace of God rule in your hearts, to the which also ye are called in one body; and be ye thankful" Colossians 3:15 KJV.

Heavenly Father, we love You, and we are so thankful for You. Help us have Your peace in our hearts, on our faces, and in our smiles as we gather with the ones we love. Make lasting, loving memories in all the gathered hearts. Amen.

Love well, and Happy Thanksgiving!

November 23
Thanksgiving Focus

This week we participate in the oldest shared American experience, Thanksgiving Day.

Originally, Thanksgiving was a distinctly Christian celebration of giving thanks to the God of the Bible for His many blessings and for His protection through hardships. In modern times, it can also be a day of feasting, family, friends, and football watching on television.

Over the last several years, "Black Friday" has encroached on "Giving Thanks Thursday." The significance of that is that the focus quickly turns to sales and discounts and not on the special people you are spending time with.

Let's not miss the significance of modeling gratitude to those around us. If we are not grateful for all we have, we will never have enough.

This Thanksgiving, don't let food, football, and sales rob us of the true spirit of Thanksgiving. Give thanks to God for what we already have, celebrate the people closest to us and share our blessings with others.

Happy Thanksgiving!

November 24
Happy Thanksgiving, Rejoice Evermore

What can we say about Thanksgiving or the giving of thanks that we do not already know? Like most things in life, it is not about learning new facts or information about a subject. What we need to do is put into practice what we already know.

A portion of our day is filled with negative news and information. Social media is filled with a representation of everyone's best life and leaves us filling depressed because our lives are not so great. We come to this holiday every year to be reminded to be thankful. We have much to be thankful for, and the fact that most have a tough time recognizing it speaks volumes about our condition.

Giving thanks and being grateful must be a quality that is practiced every day and not just once a year. This year, let us take time to appreciate everything about this holiday season. The people we see, the food we eat, and even the presents we receive next month. We do not know what the future holds, and from the way things are progressing, it may not get better or brighter.

Start now to give thanks in all things. "Rejoice evermore. Pray without ceasing. In everything give thanks: for this is the will of God in Christ Jesus concerning you" (1 Thessalonians 5:16-18 KJV).

November 25
Happy Thanksgiving in Lock Down

It's time to slow down and give thanks.

In a year of forced isolation, lock downs, and illness, it is easy to lose the attitude of giving thanks. But we still have a lot to be thankful for.

We must push past the fear and the negativity to see the beauty that is all around us. We need to be intentional in giving thanks to God for our families and the people in our lives. Do not let the events of 2020 suck the life out of our holiday experiences.

This year has been harsh for a lot of people, and it would be easy to give in and give up. As we practice the giving of thanks in all our circumstances, may we lean on that power greater than ourselves to carry us through these days.

Holidays are a great opportunity to see life for the joy that it can be. Let us wind down this year celebrating God's blessings and prepare our hearts to be filled with all the wonder and joy of Christmas.

November 26
The Exercise of Giving Thanks

In 1 Thessalonians, chapter five, Paul encourages believers to give thanks in every situation because it is God's will. God knows what is good for us. Modern studies show that people with gratitude are characterized by calmness and good health.

The giving of thanks during hardship is never easy and almost humanly impossible. Paul wasn't saying that everything that happens is good and that we should be thankful for it. What he was saying is that "in" the situation we should give thanks not "for" the situation.

Giving thanks in the situation helps us lift our eyes off the problem knowing that we have a God who loves us and has promised that He can turn every situation to our good, and for that we can be thankful. Giving thanks helps us to let go and let God move and work in every situation. The giving of thanks is a muscle that must be exercised in the good times so that when difficult times come it's an automatic reflex. Whether you find yourself in good times or difficult times this holiday season, still find reasons to give thanks. Happy Thanksgiving.

November 27
Give Thanks With a Grateful Heart

We enter the week of Thanksgiving either excited for the Holiday or dreading the work that is required. Thanksgiving should be more than just a 4-day holiday with lots of football and massive amounts of food. Now, there is nothing wrong with all those things unless that's all there is to the celebration.

It is a time to reflect, and count our blessings, and give thanks to God, from whom all good things flow. A very ancient hymn called The Doxology provides a comprehensive framework for thanks:

> Praise God from Whom all blessings flow
> Praise Him all creatures here below
> Praise Him above ye heavenly host
> Praise Father, Son, and Holy Ghost

Thanksgiving was established to stop normal routine and give thanks to God for the blessings of the harvest, for who He is, and for all His provision and protection.

To give thanks is, by its very nature, a way to move us from a focus on the negative things in our lives and force us to look at all that is good and positive. It is a season to focus on God and the fact that He gave us a reason to celebrate. Let's enter into this Holiday season with thanksgiving – for the best is yet to come. His name is Jesus!

November 28
The Good Meal of Wise Words

In a topsy-turvy world, fear and anxiety are always right below the surface, ready to pounce on every piece of news that comes our way. How do we stay levelheaded and functioning on all cylinders amid such chaos? The longer we focus on the craziness all around us, the easier it is to give in to it. This week is a reminder of how to rise above it all and stay emotionally strong.

This week, we celebrate Thanksgiving. It is a time to remind ourselves and to give thanks for all the good things in our lives. The Bible reminds us continually to give thanks to God for His blessings. "With the fruit of a person's mouth his stomach will be satisfied, He will be satisfied with the product of his lips. Death and life are in the power of the tongue, And those who love it will eat its fruit" (Proverbs 18:20-21 NASB).

What comes out of our mouths reflects our thinking. Having an appreciative and thankful mindset will influence the words that come from our mouths and can help give us a life that is satisfying.

Life and death are in the tongue. We need to be careful what we say and how we say it. Our words don't create the difficulties we deal with, but they sure do shape our attitudes towards them.

This Thanksgiving, focus on what is going right and give thanks. Happy Thanksgiving!

November 29
Spreading the Christmas Spirit

The Thanksgiving train is leaving the station, and the Polar Express will soon be coming down the tracks. The child in all of us can feel the excitement of the season.

"For it is good to be children sometimes, and never better than at Christmas, when its mighty Founder was a child Himself." From "A Christmas Carol." Published in 1843 by author Charles Dickens (1812-1870).

This is a special and wonderful time of the year. As families make plans to be together and special thought goes into gift giving, it tends to bring out the best in people. No other time of the year causes us to dedicate a whole month to family and friends.

I think God is pleased when we honor His Son and love on one another. Christmas brings many messages, but the most important is the baby in the manger. Let us come and bow down and give honor to Jesus. If we really want to capture the Christmas spirit, it is giving out of a heart of love. Something that really can be done each month. Don't be a Scrooge this Christmas, perpetuate the spirit of the season and love well.

"For God so loved that He gave...." (John 3:16 KJV).

November 30
Get Your Christmas On

T'was the month before Christmas and all throughout the house, no one was talking because they were all on their electronics buying presents on Amazon and looking for the best deals.

My, how the times have changed. Is it for the better? We have become more isolated in our homes with less and less human contact. We barely speak to those who live under the same roof.

Christmas is all about demonstrating love. God started it, when, out of love for His creation, He sent His son to us. "For God so loved the world that He gave His only begotten Son, that whosoever believeth in Him should not perish, but have everlasting life" (John 3:16 KJV).

Love seeks to give the best of ourselves to those around us. Love causes us to go out of our way to make sure others know they are loved. Love seeks the best interest of those we say we love. Let the God of love, who started Christmas by giving, lavish upon you His amazing love so that you have an endless reservoir to draw from to lavish on others.

Instead of disappearing through electronics, step away from your devices and spend some quiet time with God. Then, you will be ready to get your Christmas on.

Love well and Merry Christmas!

12
DECEMBER

December 1
Looking Back and Looking Forward

Writing to the church at Corinth, the apostle Paul gave instructions on Communion. He said as often as you eat the bread and take the Lord's cup you do this in remembrance of Him until He returns.

Communion is both a looking back and a looking forward. Jesus took all the wrath of God, for our disobedience, so that we could be reconciled back to God. The good news is, we don't have to fear God. No matter how big of a mess we may have made of our lives, God is waiting with open arms to receive us into His loving embrace.

By looking back and receiving His grace and forgiveness we then can look forward with anticipation of His return. Jesus is going to return and deliver fallen creation once and for all. What a glorious day that will be.

I imagine on the day He returns there will be a lot of surprised individuals. People who heard but didn't believe will be left holding onto their excuses while the rest will be celebrating His return.

Christmas is the beginning of the story of redemption. As we celebrate the birth of the Savior, communion is a reminder of why He came. Tell the story and celebrate it with communion. Merry Christmas.

December 2
This Christmas Be Jesus to Someone

Christmas is a time of caring and sharing. Many people of all ages are struggling to have some level of normalcy in their lives. This can be a rough time emotionally for many families, and especially children. They don't always understand the complexities of life. They just see what's missing for them and they feel forgotten.

It's easy to blame parents for the situations they are facing. Sometimes, due to their poor decisions and choices, we conclude that it is their own fault. When God looked at humanity, He could have taken the attitude that we deserve everything that happens to us. Instead, He made a choice that has impacted both heaven and earth. Out of love, He gave His Son to come to hurting humanity. He didn't come to judge us for our mistakes and bad choices. He didn't even come to bring a new religion. (Religion gives us rules with no help to live them out.) He came to walk with us and give us power to live a new life. God invites us to come to Him during difficult seasons, and because of Jesus, we don't have to fear rejection.

Look around this Christmas season and see if there isn't someone in your sphere that you can help by bringing a little Christmas joy into their lives. Don't judge their situation as to whose fault it is; be Jesus to them. Merry Christmas.

December 3
Come and Receive Christ, the King

In the gospel of Luke, you will find the most detailed narrative of the birth of Jesus. In Luke chapter two, we read, "And the angel said unto them, Fear not: for, behold, I bring you good tidings of great joy, which shall be to all people. For unto you is born this day in the city of David a Saviour, which is Christ the Lord" (Luke 2:10-11 KJV).

The angels appeared to shepherds out in the fields and declared to them that a Savior had been born. In our politically correct environment, it's not fashionable to admit that we need saving. The truth is we do. We are broken and flawed human beings. God came to demonstrate to us real love and acceptance by living among us and dying to save us from our failures, mistakes, and sins. He came to deliver us from the lies that plague us and to teach us the truth about two things that are not very popular today: all have sinned and there is truth that doesn't diminish just because some choose to ignore it.

Jesus declared of Himself, "I am the way, and the truth, and the life; no one comes to the Father except through Me" (John 14:6 KJV). To be set free, seek out Jesus and the truth that He teaches. We need a savior, and Jesus comes to save us. This Christmas season, let's come and receive Christ the Savior and King" Merry Christmas!

December 4
Childlike Wonder at Christmas

Do you remember the awe, the wonder of Christmas morning? The can't-sleep-excitement of not knowing what was coming. The early morning rush to wake your parents, wondering if they would ever get out of bed?

Now it's relived watching our kids and grandkids experience the raw excitement of Christmas. There is something to be learned from watching their trust, hope, and excitement as they anticipate what's coming.

Faith produces the same excitement as we put our hope and trust in God. Christmas is a big reminder that what seems impossible is possible with God. A baby born to a virgin came to save the world from their sins. Impossible, you say. But not to God.

This Christmas, remember that whatever you're facing, whatever circumstances seem impossible, and whatever mountain of problems seem too big to go away, God can make a way when there seems to be no way. Put your hope and trust in His ability, and let the anticipation of Christmas morning live in you once again. Merry Christmas.

December 5
What is Man That You are Mindful of Him

David the psalmist penned these words, "When I consider Your heavens, the work of Your fingers, The moon and the stars, which You have set in place; What is man that You think of him, And a son of man that You are concerned about him" (Psalm 8:3-4 KJV)?

David, reflecting on the beauty and grandeur of the observable universe, contemplates the God who created it all and wonders aloud: Why would a God so powerful be considerate of humanity? David is in awe that this God would have anything to do with mankind.

Little did David know that years later, that very God would take on human flesh and come to live among us. God has made us in His image and has committed His love to us. He does not abandon us to the problems that plague our world but has come to be with us and help us through them.

Christmas is a reminder that the God of creation came to us in the form of a baby to show us His love and compassion. Jesus grew up to be the example we all need of who God is and what He is like. God took the first step; it is up to us to move toward God. Do not be confused; Jesus did not come to fulfill our every desire. He came to change our desires. He came to show us the way to God and how to walk in obedience to the God of creation.

As we abide in His Word, we find the life we are meant to live. Celebrate the gift of Jesus, given in love to a lost and hurting humanity. Celebrate Jesus!

December 6
Open the Gift

This season, we celebrate the ultimate gift that was given by God to all of us. It's a gift that some refuse to open or even acknowledge being offered. We can get lost in the clamor of activity that this season brings and fail to recognize what exactly we are celebrating.

I love this time of year with the family gatherings, decorating, the parties, the food, and the giving of expressions of love.

Some would say it has become too commercialized, and maybe it has; however, I still get excited for several reasons. It's a reminder of how much God loves us because He willingly gave us His son. It takes me forward to Easter and why He came, which was to redeem us and bring us back into fellowship with our Creator. Lastly, Christmas is an example that with God, nothing is impossible.

There are a lot of people who don't have time for the whole religious thing. I want you to know neither does Jesus. Jesus offers Himself as a gift and leaves it up to us to accept Him by faith or reject Him through unbelief. This Christmas, let's open the gift and discover the incredible love, peace, and joy that only Jesus can give! Merry Christmas.

December 7
The Holidays: Timeless Traditions or Time for Change?

"If you always do what you've always done, you'll always get what you've always got." Henry Ford (1863-1947) Founder of Ford Motor Company.

How would you like to celebrate this Christmas season? Do you like keeping long-held traditions? Or would that feel like living out the Henry Ford quote? Do you like trying something new, or would that feel like a break from tradition that would be uncomfortable?

The season is about love and giving. Scripture says that because God so loved us, that He gave and that to give is better than to receive.

Do something different this Christmas. Start a new tradition of celebrating the birth of Christ by giving to those that are in need or serving someone that you wouldn't normally. You would be surprised the joy it brings when we step out of our traditional patterns and act more Christ-like. Change it up and do something different. You might get something new yourself. Merry Christmas.

December 8
Wise Men Still Seek Him

In the telling of the story about Jesus, the God-man, coming to dwell among us, we find out about the wise men coming from afar to worship the newborn king. Captivated by the sight of a new and brilliant star, they believed the star appeared to point them to the arrival of a king. Determined to go on a journey to discover the king, they set out bearing gifts and fully expected to find what they sought. What a picture of faith!

During this holiday season, we search for the perfect gift to be given. All the while, an eternal gift has been offered and is waiting to be received. God so loved us that he gave us His son that anyone who would believe in Him would find life and live it abundantly.

Why do we fight so hard to reject what is offered so that we can do life on our own terms? We struggle to find happiness and contentment while living lives of frustration and sadness.

Maybe, just maybe, it's time to stop and ask about this baby in the manger. Maybe there is more to it than you've been willing to admit. You have nothing to lose by investigating the reason for the season. Merry Christmas.

December 9
Immanuel: God With Us

This is the season to remember and celebrate God's gift to the world of the Messiah, Jesus. In Matthew's account of Jesus' birth, an angel appeared to Joseph and told him not to fear but that Mary had conceived a child by the Holy Spirit. He said this had been done as was spoken by the prophet Isaiah. "Behold, the virgin will conceive and give birth to a Son, and they shall name Him Immanuel," which translated means, 'God with us'" Matthew 1:23 NASB).

We can know the story and even believe it, however, we can lose the impact of what it means – God is with us. The prophet wasn't just referring to a specific point in time that only lasted for the thirty-three years Jesus walked on earth. God with us is a reality for today. When we are hurried and harried, God is with us. When we are confused and uncertain about life's direction, God is with us.

God is with us when we feel unworthy, unlovable, and lonely. When we are afraid, unsure of ourselves, battered and scarred, God is with us. The promise is real, and the possibilities are endless for those who believe and live then. Immanuel, God with Us! What an amazing gift.

December 10
What's Right in Front of Us

There was a woman who was born in a state known for its majestic mountains. She married and had children in a Great Plains state known for its big sky. Years later, she was excited to take her children to her home state and let them enjoy the beautiful mountains. To her surprise, the children were not impressed. "Mom, it's so crowded you can't see anything. Those mountains are in the way."

We can become locked in our thinking and miss what is right in front of us. This can happen in the month of December. As we make our plans to celebrate Christmas with family and friends, we can miss the significance of what we are supposed to be celebrating.

If we aren't careful, it can become about a man riding in a sleigh, delivering presents or other modern-day attractions, and not about God coming to us as an infant to change the course of history.

It's easy to dismiss the infant in the manger because of the distractions of Christmas. Don't miss out on what's right in front of us. Jesus wants to be the best gift of all this Christmas. Open your heart and home and let Him live there, with you ... He's there, right in front of you.

December 11
Christmas Is Centered in Love

The story began a long time ago. Driven by love and a desire to be reconnected, a bold and audacious plan was conceived and initiated.

The object of His love had been taken captive and needed to be rescued. Unfortunately, the object of His love had been captive for so long that their affection had also been taken captive, and they had forgotten the One who had promised to love them forever.

Nevertheless, the rescue was underway at a huge cost to the One driven by love. He was willing to make every sacrifice to bring the object of His love back to himself. Because of love, the plan succeeded, and the object of His love was no longer held captive. He waits for His love to return to Him and be lavished in His love.

Every year, we set aside time to retell the story of Love – how the King of Glory initiated the rescue of mankind by sending His son to deliver the object of His love. Who is the object of His Love? That would be you and me. He waits for us to return to Him and express our affection and gratitude for all He has done.

Celebrate Jesus! Celebrate Love! Spread the joy of Christmas to all that you know. Merry Christmas.

December 12
Faith

There are some things that only God can do. God waits to be invited into our lives so He can take ordinary people and do extraordinary things through them.

We have bought into the philosophy of science and materialism. We only trust what can be proven by science and what we can discern with our senses in the material world. If it can't be proven or handled, it can't exist. This thinking keeps us from believing that there is a supreme God who supersedes science and the material world.

The book of Hebrews states that it is impossible to please God apart from faith. Why? Because anyone who wants to approach God must believe both that He exists, and He cares enough to respond to those who seek Him. The secret to seeing God do what only God can do requires faith. To choose to trust someone we can't see, or touch requires faith. Faith says, I know He's there, and I know if I keep asking, God will respond.

What do you need to be done that only God can do? Trust that He is there, and He's waiting to be invited. Jesus said, "Ask, and it shall be given you; seek, and ye shall find; knock, and it shall be opened unto you" (Matt 7:7 KJV). He's waiting for us. Need faith? Here is God's Promise: "So faith comes from hearing, and hearing by the word of Christ" (Romans 10:17 NASB). Need faith? Read God's Word.

December 13
The Hope of Christmas

Every child and even some adults dream of what is under the Christmas tree – hoping for the latest and greatest toy, tech device, or gaming system. All these things are good and bring joy to the person receiving them and the person giving them by hoping to fulfill the wishes of loved ones. Christmas is about so much more. Toys break, gaming systems become obsolete, and within a short time, the joy of receiving fades.

Christmas, for most, has lost the true importance of the season. We should be mindfully celebrating the greatest gift ever given. Jesus Christ came as a babe to liberate humanity from the tyranny of sin and selfishness. Jesus came to us to be with us, to restore a pattern that started in the garden of Eden – God walking and talking with His creation. Christmas is not about religion. It is so much more. Only through Jesus can we find the life we were meant to live. The hope of Christmas is for every person to experience the love of God and be set free from the hurt, pain, and damage of living in a fallen world. Only when we come to Jesus humbly and sincerely, desiring to know Him as He is, will we find the joy and happiness we so long for.

Coming to Jesus will not be experienced in religious observance or duty-bound performance; it is found through simple trust and faith. May you find "The hope of Christmas" during this Christmas season.

December 14
The Baby Lying in a Manger

As we zero in on Christmas, we take in all the reminders of the principal elements of the Christmas story. A star, wise men from the east, shepherds out in the fields, angels declaring and singing, animals, Joseph and Mary, a manger, and baby Jesus.

Who does not love everything about a baby? This was no ordinary baby; this was the Son of God. God's gift of love to us all wrapped up in swaddling clothes lying in a manger. It can give you that warm fuzzy feeling.

But do not be fooled by the cute little baby. One day, this baby will return to us in furious love and set down all those who oppose Him. He will once and for all destroy all the enemies of God. He will restore all things and set up His kingdom to rule and reign on earth. No one will be able to oppose Him. He will come with legions of angels and all the redeemed to carry out His purposes on earth.

We honor and celebrate His coming to us over two thousand years ago and all He accomplished. However, we need to be alert and ready because we never know what tomorrow holds. The angels told the disciples that this same Jesus that they watched ascend into heaven was going to return in the same way.

People, get ready; Jesus is coming!

December 15
The Baby Jesus

Babies are cute, welcoming, and approachable. We are drawn to them by their sweetness and vulnerability, making it easy to drop our defenses and draw near.

It is easy to welcome babies right into our hearts.

God so desires a relationship with His creation that He sent His Son to earth as a newly born, welcoming, approachable, vulnerable baby. The baby Jesus shows us a side of God that we may have otherwise missed.

God wants us to know that He is approachable and tells us to boldly approach His throne of grace. Jesus demonstrates His vulnerability by giving us the ability to reject His love. Jesus extends the hand of grace and opens the door to welcome us to receive God's unconditional love.

Jesus makes it easy to welcome Him right into our heart.

December 16
What Are We Celebrating?

How is it that we can celebrate a season that completely rearranges our schedule, causes us to spend more money than we should, and give gifts that our kids will be bored with before the year is over?

What, exactly, are we celebrating? A fat guy in a red suit, family, love, tradition, and even the Nativity can just be part of the decorations.

I used to dread the emptiness after the holidays because it all seemed like a lot of effort for missing the point.

"For unto us a child is born, unto us a son is given: and the government shall be upon his shoulder: and his name shall be called Wonderful, Counsellor, The mighty God, The everlasting Father, The Prince of Peace" (Isaiah 9:6 KJV).

Jesus isn't just the reason for the season; He is the reason for everything.

He is the same Jesus who one day will come back and establish His kingdom rule. It's time to look past all the decorations and come face to face with the One who is the Way, the Truth, and the Life and decide exactly why we were given a babe in the manger.

Are you ready to meet Jesus?

December 17
The Gift of Jesus.

Two thousand years ago, the times were very much like today. Uncertainty hung in the atmosphere. Government control and religious oppression caused the hope of a better life to fade and be replaced by resignation to a less hopeful way of life.

The people had long awaited a Messiah whom they thought would come in divine power and overthrow their enemies to rescue them and set up a new kingdom of military might on earth.

God's answer for their situation was not to overthrow the political and religious hierarchy. His was a promise of "God is with us." He was giving Himself to them amidst their struggles. God wasn't going to change their situation. He was going to change them from the inside out.

God wanted them to learn how to live in any situation, even in a world of chaos, and yet be at peace within themselves based on their identity in Him. To live in a world of brokenness and pain yet be healed and restored by His presence and love.

Just like two thousand years ago, today we want our problems fixed, and we want to be given a good and easy life. God's gift to us is still Himself. Typically, it is not the gift everyone is looking for, just as they were not expecting a baby in a manger.

Let's accept the gift of Jesus and allow Him to penetrate our hearts of stone and receive His love and forgiveness. It is a gift of grace received by faith.

December 18
Jesus Is Still the Best Gift

What is it that makes a gift a good gift? Is it because the gift is useful and practical, like a robot vacuum or a wireless drill? Or is it because it is just something impractical but highly desired? Is it truly in the eye of the beholder because one man's junk is another man's treasure?

God gave us a perfect gift in His Son Jesus. What we do with His gift is determined by how valuable we think the gift is. Some dismiss the gift as if it is some burden we must live up to. Others are initially excited by the gift but then do nothing with it. A few understand the gift and embrace it as if their lives depended on it.

Jesus came to be the best gift we will ever receive. His love for us has the power to transform our lives – not merely motivate or inspire us but literally transform us. He takes the broken parts of us and restores us back to our original purpose.

This Christmas, don't look past this amazing gift to see what else is under the tree. To get the most out of God's gift to us, we need to read the owner's manual and not just play around with it for a few weeks and then discard it because it's not doing what we thought it would.

If you give Him your all, you will be surprised to find that Jesus really is the best gift. Merry Christmas.

December 19
Love Creates Memories for Life

"Love is the only force capable of transforming an enemy into a friend."-- Martin Luther King, Jr.

Christmas is the celebration of love. Giving is an act of love. God gave His son. We give to demonstrate love to our friends and family. Love breaks down walls of hurt and pain and gives hope to those crushed by rejection. Sacrificial love fills us up and warms the heart.

Love creates memories that we carry for the rest of our lives. Think back to your childhood and the special times spent with your family during Christmas. This Christmas, receive the love that God has for you by opening your heart to the gift of His Son.

Be sure to make some love-filled memories for others to cherish, including sharing God's son, Jesus, with others.

December 20
Love Them Like Jesus

Last night, I had the opportunity to spend some time with my granddaughters. Man, I sure do love them. There isn't anything I wouldn't do for all my grandkids.

I want to protect them from every injustice and lavish on them every good thing this world has to offer. I want to teach them about a God who loves them even more than I do. I want them to know what Christmas is all about and who Jesus is. I want them to live Godly lives full of grace and truth, and I want them to spend an eternity with God.

I want them to know that their Papa will always be there for them and believe in them. The truth is we all make mistakes, and no mistake can separate us. This is the message of Christmas.

God loved us so much that He sent His son to lavish on us all that heaven has to offer. He fights against every injustice and wants us to spend eternity with Him.

This Christmas, give the gift of Jesus to those you love and even those you don't. Love your family well, and make sure they know that you do. Merry Christmas.

December 21
Merry Christmas

"John 1:1 In the beginning was the Word, and the Word was with God, and the Word was God" (John 1:1 KJV).

"He was in the world, and the world was made by Him, and the world knew Him not. He came unto His own, and His own received Him not. But as many as received Him, to them gave He power to become the sons of God, even to them that believe on His name" (John 1:10-12 KJV).

In the gospel of John, we are told the beautiful and loving story of one member of the Godhead coming to dwell among humanity. Over two thousand years have passed since the first Christmas, and we still struggle with its message. Jesus came to be with us and to show us who the Father is and how He loves us.

People rejected Him and His message. The world is still rejecting the message of Jesus Christ. Like the media of today that seek to distort the truth, the world tries to paint such an ugly picture of Christians and Christianity that bears no resemblance to the truth.

Be open to the simplicity of His message. Christmas is a time of remembrance and celebration. Let's remember what God did for us by coming to us and remember the beauty and love of friends and family. Celebrate the greatest gift of all, and then share His love with those around you. Merry Christmas!

December 22
Christmastime

At no other time of the year can you look all around and see the message of God so prominently declared.

Yes, I know the message gets obscured by all the commercialization and panicked Christmas buying. However, if you stop and look around, you see Jesus and the message of Immanuel, "God with us."

God came to us, to be with us and to demonstrate His love, compassion, and kindness. Every Christmas tree, wreath, light, ornament, and nativity scene speaks to us of God's love for us.

Gift giving started with God giving us His son, and we demonstrate our love by giving to each other.

As we move toward Christmas and the end of the year, let us keep our eyes on the beauty of Christmastime. It will soon be over, and all the promises of a New Year will be upon us.

We need the reminder of the gracious gift of Jesus. Let's allow the message of peace on earth and goodwill towards men to invade the craziness of the hour to settle our hearts.

Merry Christmas to all!

December 23
Celebrate Jesus With Family and Friends

Christmas is about celebrating Jesus. It is also about family. Family can be the biggest blessing or the biggest challenge. Jesus can make all the difference in a family because Jesus came to reconcile relationships. What is humanly impossible, God can make possible.

I think we have lost that old-fashioned family Christmas celebration. Families aren't as close as they once were. I can remember the Christmas Eve and Christmas Day family trips to visit grandparents and aunts and uncles. We got to spend time with cousins that we only saw once or twice a year but always at Christmas. Now families are scattered all over, and it's hard to get together. It's a shame that Christmas Day is one of the biggest movie theater days of the year because after the presents are opened, families don't know what to do with each other.

This Christmas, celebrate with family and friends. If you are not close to your family, invite friends over to celebrate Jesus by enjoying a meal or playing games. Christmas is about expressing love and giving. The highest expression of giving is our time. Love Well. Merry Christmas.

December 24
God Made the First Move

It started with a baby. God made the first move. An angel appeared to Joseph to tell him what was happening to Mary and that it was going to be alright. The angel quoted the Old Testament and declared, "Behold, a virgin shall be with child, and shall bring forth a son, and they shall call his name Emmanuel, which being interpreted is, God with us" (Matthew 1:23 KJV).

That was the whole point. God wanted to be with us. He still does. The best way to communicate with His creation was to come in the likeness of man and talk face-to-face.

Jesus Christ wants us to know that God the Father wants to be with us – even in our imperfections. Jesus said that those who are well have no need of a physician. He came to be with those who are broken and need help, which is all of us.

During this time, of year stop and spend time with God because God wants to spend time with you – yes , you. Remember that God initiated the conversation. He waits for you.

Merry Christmas.

December 25
The Simplicity of Loving Jesus

We humans can certainly make things complicated.

Because of love, God sent His son into the world, born of a virgin, to restore us to a relationship with God the Father. He demonstrated love and kindness toward fallen humanity, never pointing an accusing finger but showing compassion and forgiveness.

Mankind had so messed up and complicated the pathway to God that no one knew what it was supposed to look like. They took God's program and turned it into a religion with standards of perfection and their view of holiness. Everyone was miserable, creation and Creator.

Jesus came to demonstrate the heart of the Father. He taught His followers that it was all about a love relationship. To love God and to love others.

People have become apathetic toward religion but have a hard time resisting Jesus. Let us give people an opportunity to see kindness, compassion, and love in action all year. As we seek to know Jesus we will become more like Him. Take a few moments to recapture a passionate heart for God. Merry Christmas!

BEING A
FOLLOWER OF JESUS

The fact that you are reading this book now is evidence that you either are a follower of Jesus or that He is calling you to be.

Jesus is God in human form, and He existed with God the Father and the Holy Spirit before the world was ever created. God the Father, Son, and Holy Spirit are perfectly holy. God cannot tolerate sin. He has given every man, woman, boy, and girl a conscience. We know right from wrong because God made us know. Our sinfulness separates us from God. Jesus is sinless perfection but paid the ultimate penalty for our sins by an extremely painful death in our place and was resurrected from the dead so that we, who actually all are guilty, are pronounced guiltless by God because Jesus atoned for us. The Holy Spirit abides in us when we receive God's gift of eternal salvation. All of the above is true. We must confess it and believe it and walk in faith trusting in God to live it out.

Prayer: Father God, I believe in You. I know you are the one and only God. I acknowledge to you that I am a sinner because I know that I've done wrong things in my life. I believe in Your son, Jesus Christ as my Savior and the only one with the power to save me. Forgive me of all my sins, accept me as Your follower, and fill me with the Holy Spirit to guide, strengthen, and encourage me. Father, in the saving name of Jesus Christ, I thank You for your forgiveness and Your mercy and Your love for me. Fill my heart with love for You. Help me to abide in You in Your word and being faithful to You. Teach me how to be just like You. Bring me into fellowship with other Believers so that I can grow, bless, and be blessed. In Jesus name, Amen.

ACKNOWLEDGEMENTS

To Susan, my partner in life. Your graciousness and patience have allowed God to shape me into the man you always knew I could become.

To my children, Amanda, Adam and Melissa. Your unconditional love and belief in your dad have challenged me to be all that I can be. It has been a great joy to be your dad.

To your spouses, Kevin, Nichole and Brian. You have been an answer to prayer and have added infinite value to our family.

To my grandkids, Aleea, Makenna, Madilyn, Abigail, Nathan, Daphne, Alejandra, Elizabeth, Zack, Adeline, Timmy, Everly and Kendall. You have brought a special blessing into our lives. It is my prayer that you will learn to recognize and follow God's breadcrumbs as Jesus leads you into the fullness of your destiny.

To Kathleen Young, my cousin. This book would never have become reality without your vision, passion and dedication. You worked tirelessly on the project and for that I am eternally grateful. Thank you for believing in me and what God is putting together.

To Cody Adams. Your timely entrance into this project has been invaluable and I will be forever grateful for all that you have done. God has raised you up as minister to the nations for such a time as this.

To Aleea Estabrook. The oldest of the grandkids. God has used you and your magnificent brain to add clarity and cohesiveness to this project. Your willingness to take this on late in the game was a God send. Thank you for your love and your compassionate heart. We are proud of who you are becoming.

Most importantly I am forever indebted to my Lord and Savior Jesus Christ. He took a very broken individual, and as only He can, is in the process of bringing me into the fullness of who I was created to be. To God be the glory!

Like us on Facebook. Join the conversation.

Made in the USA
Las Vegas, NV
04 December 2024

13303802R00229